RESEARCH HIGHLIGHTS IN SOCIAL WORK 36

Risk Assessment in Social Care and Social Work

Edited by Phyllida Parsloe

Jessica Kingsley Publishers
London and Philadelphia

Research Highlights in Social Work 36
Editor: Phyllida Parsloe
Secretary: Anne Forbes
Editorial Advisory Committee:

Professor Joyce Lishman	Robert Gordon University, Aberdeen
Ms M. Buist	Independent researcher, Edinburgh
Mr P. Cassidy	Social Work Department, Aberdeen City Council, representing the Association of Directors of Social Work
Ms A. Connor	Independent researcher, Edinburgh
Mr D. Cox	Robert Gordon University, Aberdeen
Mr M. King	Northern College, Aberdeen
Dr F. Paterson	Social Work Services Group, Scottish Office
Dr A. Robertson	University of Edinburgh
Ms C. Smith	Scottish Council for Voluntary Organisations, Edinburgh

Robert Gordon University
School of Applied Social Studies
Kepplestone Annexe, Queen's Road
Aberdeen AB15 4PH

First published in the United Kingdom in 1999
by Jessica Kingsley Publishers
116 Pentonville Road
London N1 9JB, UK
and
400 Market Street, Suite 400
Philadelphia, PA 19106, USA

www.jkp.com

Library of Congress Cataloging in Publication Data
Risk assessment in social care and social work / edited by Phyllida Parsloe.
        p.   cm. -- (Research highlights in social work ; 36)
    Includes bibliographical references and index.
    ISBN 1-85302-689-1 (alk. Paper)
    1. Social service. 2. Risk assessment. 3. Risk management.
    I. Parsloe, Phyllida. II. Series.
    HV40.R57   1999
    368'.0068'1--dc21   99-41624

British Library Cataloguing in Publication Data
A CIP catalogue record for this book is available from the British Library

ISBN 978 1 85302 689 8

Printed and Bound in Great Britain by
Athenaeum Press, Gateshead, Tyne and Wear

Contents

Introduction

Phyllida Parsloe

The topic of this collection, 'the assessment of risk in social work and social care', has many aspects, not all of which has it been possible to address in this volume. This is only partly a matter of space. There have also been difficulties in finding people who had the time and/or the inclination to take on what is, in effect, voluntary work. Thus readers will find that there is no chapter on legal research into risk assessment. Another gap is the assessment of risk with and for people with learning disabilities. Here the untimely death of Philip Seed, whom it had been hoped would write this chapter, is the reason.

What will be clear to readers is the very patchy nature of the existing research about the assessment of risk. In some areas, such as the use of prediction studies and the nature of risk from and to people with mental illness, there has been sufficient work to allow one to talk of a body of research in which one researcher can, to some extent, build upon the work of others, although the results still do not provide firm guidance for practitioners. In other areas, such as the effect of staff training on assessment and the management of risk, there is virtually no research. Thus the chapters which follow of necessity take very different shapes. None the less it is hoped that together they provide an overview of the state of research in this field at the present time.

When I wrote inviting people to write a chapter I purposely did not give them a definition of risk since I was not sure that there was an agreed definition. What the chapters show is that there are several different meanings, particularly about whether risk means only the possibility of harmful outcomes, whether it involves a balancing of possible good and possible harm and whether it includes the idea of positive events. It also seems to be used to cover both situations when possible outcomes are unknown and when positive and negative outcomes can be balanced against each other.

The Oxford English Dictionary defines the noun 'risk' as meaning 'a hazard, a danger, exposure to mischance or peril'. The meanings as a verb are similar: 'to hazard, to endanger, to expose to the chance of injury or loss'. As has been noted, several contributors suggest that to give only negative meanings to risk is wrong and that the term covers satisfactory as well as poor outcomes. This approach may indicate a shift in the meaning of the term or may reflect the fact that, when social welfare staff are assessing risk, they take account of the possibility of positive as well as negative outcomes. Attributing positive outcomes to risk may reflect a confusion between making a general assessment and assessing risk *per se*.

The chapters which follow may be helpful in assisting the reader to think through the meanings of words and phrases which are now in common use in social welfare and social policy: risk itself, risk assessment and the management of risk. We all tend to have our own meanings for everyday words and to assume that for others they have the same meaning. The differences between the authors may give us cause to reconsider such assumptions and check out, with those with whom we work, how we understand the words we are using. This is particularly important in multidisciplinary work, which it is hoped is a feature of risk assessment.

Several authors mention the importance of risk management and suggest that there is little research on this topic. However, it seems possible that what is now being called risk management is part of what social workers and probation officers have always done, although not under that title. Much social and probation work has always consisted of working out with users ways in which they could improve the quality of their life and, in effect, reduce the risk of negative outcomes such as reconviction, ill health, eviction and mental illness, to name only a few. What has always been difficult for workers is to be able to spend sufficient time with users to try to secure these positive outcomes. If risk management means that staff will be able to assist in managing the process towards positive outcomes as well as making assessments, then this is a welcome move, even if the language seems managerial rather than compassionate.

Risk is closely linked to dangerousness, resulting in harm. The issue here is not about defining dangerousness, which it seems to be agreed means harm to self or others, but with the extent of harm which should constitute a risk in various situations and with different kinds of people. Different Acts of Parliament qualify the term 'harm' in different ways. The grounds for a care order under the Children Act 1989 are that the child is suffering 'significant harm'. The Code of Practice for the Mental Health Act 1983 uses the phrase 'existence of a significant risk of mental or physical harm to the patient or others' when stating the evidence required for an emergency admission, while the Data Protection Act refers to 'risk of serious harm' as grounds for refusing someone access to information about him or her self. None of the Acts nor the guidance about them defines these qualifying words and it is difficult to see how they could. What constitutes significant or serious harm will vary according to the age and condition of the person involved and the current norms of society. A shared understanding will only be built up over time through practice and through appeal decisions and probably almost as fast as a consensus is reached changing norms will introduce new uncertainties. This means that social services staff will have to continue to live with uncertainty. Their job will always be to use their professional judgement to decide whether all the facts in a particular case add up to a risk of significant or serious harm within the current context. Professional judgement is about estimating uncertainties. However, professionals would be well advised to note the suggestion of one author, that they should record the reasons for their decision at the time they make it, so as to provide some protection from becoming later victims of the hindsight fallacy.

Included in this volume are chapters about assessment of risk to and from children, old people, those who are mentally ill and those who have been convicted of criminal offences. The collection is intended to draw attention to differences in the nature of risk from and to different groups as well as to differences in the way in which risks are calculated. Social welfare staff usually have to consider three different kinds of risk:

- Risk to service users from other people, usually their own relatives. This is typified by the phrase 'children at risk' but increasingly adults who may be abused are included.

- Risks to users themselves from their own behaviour. At its most severe this may mean suicide but it also covers self-neglect and perhaps some of the self-endangering behaviour of people with dementia.

- Risks to known or unknown others from service users. This category includes 'dangerous parents' but also some offenders and a small number of mentally ill people, especially those who are also substance abusers.

It will be obvious that these categories by no means cover the full range of different types of risk. There are many other risks which are rarely taken into account by social welfare staff, as we shall suggest later.

What factors determine whether a person is assessed as being at risk or constituting a risk to others? This depends upon a number of factors including the person's age, gender and mental capacity. Age determines the extent to which social services have either the legal or the socially approved right to intervene to provide protection or control. Age affects the degree to which an individual is allowed to make his or her decisions about risks to be taken and views about the relevance of age change over time. For example, a hundred years ago the idea of protecting children from their parents and to some of the harms to which society exposes them was only just developing and the idea that children should have a say in their future was yet to come. Now we accept that children are entitled to a range of protection and it is expected that they should be involved, to the extent that their age allows, in decisions made about the care and protection they are to receive. The law backs and reinforces these assumptions. Nevertheless, children have no absolute right to take risks because of their status as minors. They are judged to lack the full capacity of adults.

The idea of mental capacity is important in the assessment of risk and is obviously linked to age. It is also important in decisions about risk taking for and with some people with learning disabilities, with those suffering from some mental disorders and with older people with dementia. The current state of the law is particularly unhelpful in relation to the mental capacity of those with dementia and it is to be hoped that it will soon be clarified.

For such adults assessment may be more appropriately focused upon capacity rather than risk. Provided that no one questions another person's mental capacity, society accepts that that person may engage in behaviour which carries a high risk of injury or serious illness, even when tax payers may have to pick up the financial costs. With adults, protection becomes an issue only in the context of diminished capacity. This is an important difference between the assessment of risk for adults and children. Society now attempts to protect children from their own behaviour, or that of others, which is regarded as risky, because of their status as children who are not fully competent.

It is interesting to note that there is, as yet, little research into the factors which protect most children and most adults, even when they are mentally ill, from potentially dangerous situations. This may be an important area for research and for policy development. It is one to which social welfare staff have much to contribute if they would ask users appropriate questions, listen to what they are told and systematise what they hear. Most parents have strategies for protecting their children from physical and sexual abuse, as do most of those who care for people with dementia. Skilled residential staff have similar knowledge and expertise. Many people who are mentally ill develop their own ways of avoiding the particular dangers they face. Such strategies may be available for the asking but the appropriate questions may not be asked because professionals are concentrating on danger rather than risk management. In so doing they are reflecting the influence of what Parton (1996) quoting Beck, described as the risk society, where the 'axial principle is the distribution not of goods but of bads'.

If we are in fact living in a risk society then, as Parton says, 'the nature of communal concerns and values shifts' (p.109). Much effort in social service agencies is expended on ensuring that procedures are followed so that, in the event of trouble, the agency can show that it acted appropriately and followed the rules, whether these were provided by legislation, by central government or by local agreements. The problem is that professional judgement may be hampered by a rigid application of procedural rules. Some of the authors touch on this but none have mentioned any research which explores the relationship between procedures and judgement in social welfare nor the way in which line management can promote professional judgement within a bureaucratic framework.

It is clear from the chapters that follow that assessment of risk is not a value-free activity although with one exception the authors were not asked to address the ethical and value issues directly. An assessment is a major intrusion into anyone's privacy and it could well be argued that it should require the same kind of informed consent as is necessary in medical interventions. Anyone being assessed is likely to be in a vulnerable position and this vulnerability may be increased if they belong to one of the oppressed groups in society. Social workers may need to pay particular attention to ways of undertaking anti-oppressive assessments. One aspect of such an approach might be a greater emphasis upon user involvement in assessments and, wherever possible, making self-assessment a major part of the process.

There seems to be evidence that at least some mentally ill people and some parents are aware of when they may be becoming a danger to others and this awareness might be a feature of assessment and risk management.

Several of the chapters draw attention to the fact that what is considered as potentially dangerous is socially, and sometimes politically, constructed. The risk of a mentally disordered person injuring others seems to be given more attention than the statistically much greater risk that they will commit suicide. Risks to the identity of offenders and some older people from the regimes to which they are subjected are little discussed; both groups may live in conditions which destroy their capacities. For offenders the arrangements for discharge from prison may precipitate the likelihood of harm to others. We pay more attention to non-accidental injury to children than to accidents, although the latter are more common and arguably more easily prevented. Many features of the environment put us all, but especially children and older people, at risk. Poverty, poor housing and attendant ill health may cause as much significant harm to children as child abuse. Despite all these examples there is no equivalent of the social model of disability to establish the idea that much risk is imposed upon people by social conditions rather than arising from their personal attributes or behaviour. We seem to lack a social model of risk.

A social model of risk obviously includes more than attention to potentially dangerous environmental factors. It involves an assessment of the present and likely future social network of the person who may be in danger or become a danger to others. There is some suggestion, in the chapters which follow, that such an assessment is more likely to be made when a child is involved than with a mentally disordered adult or even with someone suffering from dementia. The reason may be that in the latter cases there is likely to be a medical as well as a social assessment. The power imbalance between doctors and social workers may weaken the social aspects of an assessment.

The authors are in agreement that there are two major types of risk assessment: actuarial and clinical; the one using numerical calculations based on large sample populations, the other using the informed judgements of professional and, occasionally, the views of the people being assessed. In some ways these two approaches parallel the differences between quantitative and qualitative research methods and tend to evoke the same kinds of suspicion by adherents of each method towards the other. However, the two approaches to assessing risk are not quite so distinct as might appear. Clinical judgements are increasingly guided by and, at times, almost completely based upon, checklists of factors to be taken into account. It is not surprising that these factors often bear a close resemblance to the factors used in constructing predictive instruments, although the checklists tend to contain more items.

Ideally these two approaches should complement each other just as qualitative research can be used to add meaning to the statistical information provided by quantitative methods. The most successful predictive instruments achieve only an 80 per cent accuracy which leaves essential space for clinical judgement. But if the two approaches are to be combined much more work is needed on exactly how to put them together.

Within and between actuarial and clinical approaches there are many different underlying theories and political assumptions. We do not know how combinations affect the accuracy of risk assessments. Part of our ignorance stems from the fact that many of those who use either approach are not explicit about the underlying base or have not even thought about it. As several authors say, risk assessment is not a technical matter; it is influenced by the values and unrecognised assumptions of those who undertake the assessment.

Whenever a child dies at the hands of his or her parents or a mentally ill person acts violently and dangerously and social services have been involved, you can be almost certain that the subsequent report will call for better training. Yet we do not know whether training actually makes staff better able to make safer decisions about people who are potentially at risk of harm or of harming others. Nor is it usually spelt out in reports what kind of training is required. It seems possible that some social services staff are much better at assessing risk than are others, but so far as I am aware organisations pay little formal attention to this possibility. To do so could of course mean unpacking the assumptions upon which welfare agencies are based, that all staff give an equal service. The development of clinical governance in the National Health Service is likely to explode this myth, at least so far as surgeons are concerned. Perhaps the equiv-alent of clinical governance may develop in welfare agencies, although this could only occur if there was also a shift away from bureaucracy towards a greater professional accountability. The assessment of risk is thus bound up with organisational philosophies as well as with individual competence.

Just as risk of harm to users depends upon individual, social and environmental factors, so does the quality of professional decision making. Individual staff who have to assess risk need not only good general under-standing of the social sciences relevant to the particular situation; they also need a general understanding of the way they and others perceive risk and the dangers of what the authors here call 'untutored' approaches. But beyond the individual, as another author points out, are organisational and societal factors which influence the optimum use of professional judgement. Some social service staff carry too heavy a burden of very demanding work, some find themselves working in an organisation which does not support them when they have to make hard decisions, and which has not learned to protect staff from the sometimes inappropriate backlash of hindsight. Looking even wider, social service agencies suffer, particularly where children are concerned, from a largely hostile press. It is all too easy for them to become defensive and over controlling of staff.

It is our hope that this volume will help clarify some of the issues surrounding the assessment of risk and provide an impetus for further discussion and more research.

Reference

Parton, N. (1996) *Social Theory, Social Change and Social Work*. London: Routledge.

CHAPTER I

Perceptions of Risk

Kenneth I. Macdonald[1] and Geraldine M. Macdonald[2]

Introduction

The perception of risk is a complex matter. The literature is cross-disciplinary, with assumptions that do not always transfer across disciplines. Our presentation is, therefore, necessarily selective[3] and we concentrate on aspects which are not as commonplace in social work and social care as perhaps they should be, including an attention to positive outcomes, to people as active agents and the dynamic nature of change over time.

Definitions of risk

Before we can handle perceptions of risk we need some specification of what risk is. A powerful, if not watertight, dichotomy was first proposed by Knight (1921): 'If you don't know for sure what will happen, but you know the odds, that is risk' and 'If you don't even know the odds, that is uncertainty.'

The nomenclature (although established in some economic literature) may be confusing since 'uncertainty' has too active a common meaning and 'risk and uncertainty' are often used interchangeably to mean just 'risk'. Therefore, in this chapter we use Ellsberg's (1961) term 'ambiguity' for 'not knowing the odds', and let 'uncertainty' keep its traditional meaning of 'not knowing for sure what will happen' (risk). There are four points to note.

First, this definition of risk concentrates upon the *probabilistic* component in our knowledge, and is agnostic as to whether this involves probabilities of good or bad outcomes. Like the Royal Society 1983 report on risk assessment, which saw risk as 'the probability that a particular *adverse* event occurs', the social services literature has been concerned predominantly with risk assessment to prevent harms. Such indeed is the general focus of this volume, and of both the Kemshall and Pritchard collections (1996, 1997), and of the earlier literature reviewed by Alaszewski and Manthorpe (1991). The sociological literature also is concerned with risk as risk-of-*harms*, and even when considering 'desired risk' reads this as the thrills of exposure to hazard (Machlis and Rosa 1990), or, in Lyng's (1990) phrase, 'edgework'. Within medical sociology Kronenfeld and Glik (1991, p.307) present 'risk perception as reflecting a shift in people's thought processes away from an emphasis on fate, luck, or change, to notions of control', but again focus on harm rather than uncertainty. Notwithstanding the emphases in the literature, the more interesting questions seem to lie in areas where decision making encompasses both good and bad outcomes. Our interpretation of risk is, therefore, closer to Carson (1996, p.29): 'The better view, it is submitted, defines risk taking in terms of comparing and balancing likely benefits with likely harms.' However, as a terminological convenience, we retain the conventional usage of 'risk-taking' and 'risk-assessment' to refer exclusively to adverse outcomes.

Second, Knight's distinction highlights aspects of social welfare intervention which are not apparent if we simply consider 'risk-of-harms'. The perception that 'ambiguity' is involved opens the possibility that reduction of ambiguity may be a powerful motivator: Becker and Brownstone (1964), for example, found that subjects would pay money to avoid making choices in which the probabilities are ambiguous. One of the continuing sociological explanatory embarrassments – of concern to workers in child protection – is the absence of any serious explanation of why people choose to have children. Most of the proffered explanations reduce to redescriptions. Recently Friedman, Hechter and Kanazawa (1994), working within a rational choice sociological framework, have used 'ambiguity reduction' as a postulate to explain human fertility decisions. Whilst having children does not reduce risk of adverse outcomes it may, they argue, reduce ambiguity – having children 'fixes the future'. Further, people in different circumstances may put a different importance upon reducing ambiguity. Griffiths and Waterdog's (1996, p.131) observation that to drug users 'contemplating change can seem more risky than to continue using' could perhaps be rephrased in terms of increased ambiguity. This 'motivational' challenge is familiar to practitioners working in this, and other fields. Similarly, Becker, Landes and Michael (1977) make good use of both risk (knowing the odds) and ambiguity (not knowing the odds) to provide a coherent theory of marital breakdown, starting from the premise that marriage is a subcategory of contract under ambiguity, defeasible by unexpected outcomes (either bad or good). As couples acquire more information, the perception of their anticipated futures shift from ambiguity to risk, where the risks may point to separation as the rational choice. It is also a perspective that informs social learning models of the development of problems in long-term, intimate relationships. So Knight's clarification in the analytic perception of what constitutes 'risk' can have useful explanatory application. In this analysis, effectiveness research does not 'reduce risk', but addresses ambiguity, and this in turn may help practitioners to see how to reduce the probability of harms.

Third, whilst there are problems in measuring risk (more of this under 'reflexive risk' below), we nevertheless hold that there remains a useful distinction between objective odds and subjective perceptions of these odds, despite part of the 1992 Royal Society Report on risk which claimed: 'the view that a separation can be maintained between "objective" risk and "subjective" or perceived risk has come under increasing attack, to the extent that it is no longer a mainstream position' (Pidgeon MD BR *et al.* 1992, pp.89–90). However, Pidgeon *et al.* were more trying to prescribe the 'mainstream' than describe it impartially and much of the appeal of their assertion derives from a concentration upon risk-of-low-probability-catastrophic-outcomes, such as nuclear accidents.

Fourth, we have adopted a simple definition of risk. The definitions others use are more complex, most notably that of Brearley (1982), who was one of the first to write about risk in relation to social work. The opening phases of many subsequent social work articles on risk characteristically refer to Brearley for a *definition* of how risk should be perceived:

> other authors have adequately covered this area in detail (see Brearley 1982…). (Strachan and Tallant 1997, p.16)

> Brearley has developed a useful framework for understanding and assessing risk. (Kemshall 1996, p.139)

Our departure from the mainstream social work literature therefore requires explanation. In brief, we regard Brearley's complexities as obfuscatory, and devote the next section to the task of clearing a path through the undergrowth. This is important because Brearley is much cited, and this might invite the unwary to read and accept a perverse perception of risk which would be unhelpful. Following a critique of Brearley we indicate further ways in which untutored perceptions of risk can mislead, and then suggest some ameliorative strategies.

A criticism of Brearley's perception

Although Brearley places the 'objective of clarifying definitions' (1982, p.156) at the centre of his book not all of his analytic moves are clarificatory.

Some of the definitional haze is illustrated in the following: '"Risk taking" takes place if the actor is conscious of the risk, if the potential loss is irreversible' (Brearley 1982, p.27). Apart from the difficulty of deciding what (other than death) counts as 'irreversible' in human experience, and deciding what constitutes 'consciousness' of the risk, why exclude *reversible* losses? Of course, in one sense all losses are irreversible in that reversal requires resources; for example cars stolen by joyriders have to be repaired, and fractures take time to knit, but, since Brearley distinguishes irreversible losses as a special category this cannot be what is meant.

Again: '"Probability" refers to the relative likelihood of outcomes' (Brearley 1982, p.26). Why *relative* likelihood? A 5 per cent probability of rain is a statement about the likelihood of rain. Again, consider: '"Hazard" refers to any existing factor – an action, event, lack, deficiency or entity – which introduces the possibility or increases the probability of a negative outcome' (Brearley 1982, p.26). Why restrict hazards to existing factors? Are 'actions' not 'events'? What is the difference between a 'lack' and a 'deficiency'? Since a probability can increase from zero, what does 'introduces the possibility' add to the definition?

Brearley's concept of 'danger' is even more perplexing. It is variously a 'feared outcome of a hazard' (p.26) or 'a term concerned more specifically with higher degrees of likelihood in combination with expressions of important value or gravity' (p.104). Such 'slippery' concepts give little help to those struggling to develop a structure for decision-making in complex areas. But least helpful is his central definition of 'risk' itself: '"Risk" refers to the relative variation in possible loss outcomes' (Brearley 1982, p.26).

He illustrates this by an actor aware of three possible outcomes X, Y, Z (Brearley 1982, p.10). Risks, says Brearley, can be represented as the gaps between X and Y and between Y and Z. Overall risk is the gap between X and Z, and presumably, though not stated, the outcomes are ranked on some real or perceived gain/loss continuum. Risk, for Brearley, is thus simply the gap between 'best' and 'worst' outcome, and has nothing to say about the *probability* of outcomes. Hence his subsequent unhelpful disjunction: 'risk and probability are clearly different' (1982, p.11). In social work, as in many other areas of social intervention, decisions pertaining to risk are inextricably tied up with judgements of probability, and the relative likelihood of different patterns or kinds of outcomes. Brearley's attempts at definition divert attention away from these substantive and intellectually challenging issues.

The reader may feel it is ungenerous to cavil at definitions for, at one level, Brearley's heart is in the right place – 'The argument for an organised and systematic approach to the understanding, assessment and management of risk is of central importance in social work' (Brearley 1982, p.156) – but his lack of clarity extends beyond definitions. For example, he cites the case of:

> a young man who developed sadistic fantasies which frightened him. He went to see a professional social worker who did not take him seriously and who thought it ridiculous to think of killing somebody. Subsequently the young man killed a prostitute. (Prins 1975, cited in Brearley 1982, p.107)

Brearley comments:

> The social worker failed to deal with the risk because he was unable to see it as a risk, perhaps through inexperience or lack of knowledge or through inability to believe in the possibility that the man could kill. The likelihood of social workers being unable to perceive risks in reality terms seems to be high. (Brearley 1982, p.107)

Brearley has moved to a probabilistic usage of 'risk' (following common sense, but counter to his own definition), but he makes a basic error in risk assessment:

he seems to regard the outcome as evidence of the prior existence of a risk at a sufficiently high probability to justify intervention. This is a classic example of the hindsight fallacy.

The hindsight fallacy

If a decision involves risk, then even when one can demonstrate that one has chosen the unarguably optimal course of action, some proportion of the time the outcome will be suboptimal. It follows that a bad outcome in and of itself does not constitute evidence that the decision was mistaken. The hindsight fallacy is to assume that it does.

That is obvious, but it is still apparently remarkably difficult to avoid the trap. The Report of the Panel of Inquiry into the death of Jasmine Beckford managed to move from sense to nonsense within one paragraph.

> We are entitled to judge a person's actions by reference to what was and should, reasonably, have been in his or her mind at the relevant time. We are not entitled to blame him or her for not knowing, or foreseeing what a reasonable person would neither have known or foreseen. In assessing whether a reasonable person would have known or foreseen an event, we are entitled to have regard to what actually happened, though, of course, the fact that an event occurred does not mean that a reasonable person would necessarily have known that it would occur or would have foreseen its occurrence. But the fact that it did occur (and was not an Act of God but the result of human action or inaction) gives rise to a presumption – either that there was knowledge that it would occur, or that foresight would have indicated its likely occurrence. (London Borough of Brent 1985, p.32)

The logic of that last sentence can be reviewed in the light of a less emotive subject. Our son is, by common consent (he is small of stature and his heart is elsewhere), exceedingly unlikely to score a try in rugby. Today he returns covered in mud and glory, having scored. The authors of the report would now tell us: 'the fact that the try did occur (and was not an Act of God but the result of human action or inaction) gives rise to a presumption – either that there was *knowledge that it would occur*, or that foresight would have indicated its *likely* occurrence'. Surely not. It happened; but remains unlikely.

The following description (by a professor of philosophy and a professor of social work) of child protection illustrates additional problems:

> Think of her [the social worker] as deciding in which of two categories the child belongs. Category A comprises children so much at risk that they should all be removed to a place of safety; category B comprises those who will be safe, if left at home. The child's death proves that it belonged in category A. Must she not have been incompetent in assigning it to category B? (Hollis and Howe 1987, p.130)

Here confusion is increased by the use of non-exhaustive categories since categories A and B do not, between them, exhaust the possibilities. However, the underlying unclarity is over 'risk': on its own, the child's death does not prove[4] that the prior balance of probabilities and costs entailed removal to a place of safety.

In the psychological literature examples of such over-attention to outcome are often tagged 'hindsight *bias*'. In fact, the 'bias' metaphor may be misleading as it invites us to consider an image of decision making about risk that is broadly 'on course' but tugged slightly awry by over-vivid outcome information. We suggest that what we see here is more accurately described as a *misunderstanding* of risk. One more example, again from a serious, considered source may help to illuminate the argument. Here Blom-Cooper (with colleagues) is considering the events which led to the death of Kimberley Carlisle. They cite, and then comment on, the social worker's perception of the end of one interview:

> *I walked with the family to the door of the building, and watched as they walked across the road to where their old car was parked. I still have a clear mental picture of the way in which they all walked across the road and got into the car, parents holding children by the hand, children leaping around in the car as they got in, laughing, shouting and playing happily with each other. It was almost an archetype for a happy family scene.*

> Far from being reassured, [the social worker] should have been alive to the risk of being manipulated. Plainly he had been deceived ... (London Borough of Greenwich 1987 pp.111–112)

Plainly? Certainly, with hindsight, we know that family was not a 'happy family', but even with hindsight we do not know that 'manipulation' and 'deception' were present in that scene since even dysfunctional families can have happy moments. The implicit criticism is sustainable *only* with the benefit of hindsight; the invited contemporaneous counterfactual is not plausible:

> It was almost an archetype for a happy family scene. So I realised I was being manipulated, and forthwith arranged for the child to be taken into care.

In social work the misreading of the importance of outcome in the hindsight fallacy is often compounded since many risk assessment instruments are evaluated by comparing risk ratings to the consequent decisions of social workers and case conferences, rather than more independent sources of verification or validity (see Millner *et al.* 1998, p.103). In other words, given that risk assessment instruments are often developed on the basis of 'clinical' populations (those families in whose lives social workers have already intervened) it is not surprising that there is a respectable correlation between the proxy 'outcomes' produced by those instruments (judgements of adverse risk) and subsequent decisions. Millner *et al.* note that Johnson (1994) reports no correlation between the clinical predictions of child welfare workers and the recurrence of *actual* abuse.

It should perhaps now be clearer why we have eschewed the 'hindsight *bias*' terminology, and wish to move away from Baron's (1994, p.234) suggestion that what we are seeing is a particular case of the tendency to search for evidence in a biased way. The errors are errors in understanding the logic of decision making under risk, not perceptual biases. Despite appearing censorious, this analysis has constructive implications for the practice of social work. In a world in which 'accountability' is often translated into 'retrospective enquiries into disasters' and the fallibility of juries to the hindsight fallacy is well documented (e.g. Wexler and Schopp 1989) it is unsurprising that some of the literature takes the implication to be a retreat to defensive social work (see, for example, Harris 1987). As Adams astringently observes: 'Excessive prudence is a problem rarely contemplated in the risk and safety literature' (Adams 1995, p.55). But if we are right that the hindsight fallacy follows from misperceiving the nature of decisions, then improving our decision making (and documenting that decision making) may be the better, non-defensive, response. Correctly taken decisions are those for which appropriate information is sought from diverse sources; appropriately weighed against available knowledge of outcomes and probabilities; and whose outcomes are fed back into that knowledge base (both in terms of future organisational practice and, where pertinent, a research base) to inform future practice. This has implications for the content of the administrative requirements we use to constrain our future selves; for example, recording which is task-oriented, and in which opinions are differentiated from fact, and so on. Once again, Carson has got it about right:

> If you have reason to believe that an event is possible, but unlikely, then you should declare and record that likelihood in an explicit form. Unless it can be shown that your estimate was inappropriate it will prove powerful in discouraging any court, or other form of inquiry, from utilising hindsight in order to conclude that the harm, which has now occurred, was more likely than it then seemed. The court has to try to avoid hindsight; why not help it? (Carson 1996, p.10)

Untutored perceptions of risk

Errors of hindsight are only one source of misunderstanding in the way we approach and handle risk, where 'we' covers all the actors in the transaction, not just the social services professionals. A clearer analysis of how actors perceive risk, and how decisions are made under ambiguity, is obviously important for the development of effective social intervention. This section examines some of the problems that arise when individuals (or groups) approach risk without taking active steps to counter key sources of error, in effect 'untutored' approaches to risk. Later we will look in more detail at the problems posed by low-frequency events (in particular, at preventing child homicides), or the *consequences* of 'untutored perceptions of risk'.

Here are some examples of problems. The following scenario was presented to (American) participants by Shafir (1993):

> Imagine that you serve on the jury of an only-child sole-custody case following a relatively messy divorce. The facts of the case are complicated by ambiguous economic, social and emotional considerations, and you decide to base your decision entirely on the following few observations:

> Parent *A*: average income, average health, average working hours, reasonable rapport with child, relatively stable social life

Parent *B*: above-average income, very close relationship with child, extremely active social life, lots of work-related travel, minor health problems.

Half of the participants were asked 'To which parent would you *award* sole custody?'; half were asked 'To which parent would you *deny* sole custody?' Parent *A* is unremarkable whilst Parent *B* has marked positive and negative factors. The majority of the 'award?' group *awarded* custody to Parent *B*. The majority of the 'deny?' group *denied* custody to Parent *B*. Each question addresses the same issue (one parent's award is another's denial) so should elicit the same resolution; but the impact of vivid components in the risk-bundle depends on the question addressed. People are not impartial assessors of the components of risk. The classic example is that in our society we are more exercised by *non*-accidental injury than by accidental injury to children, though the latter damages more children, protective intervention is possible (Roberts, Fanurik and Layfield 1987), and the results are more predictable. As Roberts, Smith and Bryce (1995, p.8) tellingly ask: 'Why do we remove children from "dangerous families" but tolerate "dangerous places"?' The emotional valence of some data, or events, appears to draw our attention at the cost of attending to other, more 'neutral' ones.

When thinking of probabilities it is natural to think in terms of fractions (either 'vulgar fractions' or decimals) which add up to one (if one-quarter of the time our potatoes grow successfully, this entails that they fail three-quarters of the time). And this structure (fractions, summing to one when we enumerate 'all possible events') is in fact the structure assumed by the formal language of probability. But it is easy to lose track of the 'summing to one' constraint, and untutored perceptions of risk also often fail to address minimal formal constraints on the assessment of probability. In an engaging piece of research Robinson and Hastie (1985) asked people to read mystery stories and at a key point in the narrative to indicate the probability that each of the characters was guilty. Most of the participants assigned probabilities that added up to about two. In other words, they lost track of the inherent contradiction in estimating that there is a three-quarters chance that Colonel Mustard is the murderer *and* a four-fifths chance that the murderer is Miss Scarlet.

Again, consider the following question: is Linda, introduced as an active feminist, more likely to be (i) 'a cashier' or (ii) 'a cashier and active in the feminist movement'? The logic of probability entails that the probability of conjoined events ('a cashier *and* active in …') is *always* less than or equal to the probability of any single component event (such as 'a cashier'), but when Tversky and Kahneman (1983, p.297) conducted this experiment, the majority of their respondents chose option (ii). This particular error might be referred to as the 'conjunction fallacy', and we return to it later.

There is an extensive literature concerned to explicate, and make sense of, the rules of thumb under which 'naive' users articulate risk. In terms of developing good practice, narratives which display people as purposive processors working with flawed – but explicable – models, are potentially more useful than those which emphasise the problems introduced to decision making by individual error or inadequacy.

Bayes theorem[5]

Intuitions, not tethered by analysis, map in unpredictable ways to the formal analyses of probability. One of the difficulties faced by students when they first encounter standard statistical tests, such as the chi-squared test for association between two variables, lies in accepting that in these tests *no* account is taken of the prior plausibility of the association, or of previous findings, however well substantiated, about the association. They feel that this is perverse, claiming more ignorance than we possess; the classical statistician would argue it is better to claim ignorance than be trapped into replicating error. But one of the exciting areas of contemporary statistics – so-called Bayesian statistics – aims, in contrast to the classical approach, to incorporate prior knowledge in our assessment of present data about risk. Whilst the underlying intuitions of the Bayesian approach may be more readily appealing than those of classical probability theory, the implications of these intuitions can be unexpected and powerful (for example, Palmer (1998) argues that they may require a rethink of the ways we conduct randomised clinical trials).

The Reverend Thomas Bayes' posthumously published essay 'Towards solving a problem in the doctrine of chances' (1763) contained ideas (largely neglected until 1940) which form the foundation of the 'Bayesian' approach to risk. Roughly, that approach looks at the way our probabilistic *beliefs* about the world (i.e. about risk) should be modified by *information* about the world. The kernel notion depends upon taking some expression of our beliefs about an unknown quantity before the data are available (our 'prior probabilities') and modifying them in the light of that data to arrive at our 'posterior probabilities'. In other words, our judgement of an hypothesis depends on our prior expectations, upon the observed data and upon an estimate of how likely such data might be were the hypothesis true. Though the consequences of this intuition are complex (see, for example, Lee 1997) the central 'Bayes theorem' is straightforward enough, and perhaps best expressed in terms of 'odds'.

We can regard 'odds' as just another way of presenting probabilities. For example, if we estimate the probability of our horse winning as 0.75 (or three-quarters), we imply a losing probability of 0.25 (or one-quarter), so the odds of winning (as against losing) are three to one. In symbols, if p is the *probability*, the odds are given by p divided by $(1-p)$. In some contexts, of which gambling is characteristically one, it is more natural to concentrate on odds (the *ratios* of probabilities) than on the component probabilities, because of the implications for action.

Suppose we intuitively consider that a parent is likely seriously to injure a child. To determine the odds of our hypothesis being true as against not true, given that we have the data and the expectations that we do, we need to invoke two units of information.

1. First, the *prior odds*. This reports the odds of the hypothesis being true as against false, before the data (from detailed observation) are known. Prior odds may be well founded, or (fact of life) our 'best guess' estimate.

2. Second, the *diagnostic ratio*. This is: the probability of the data if the hypothesis were true, against the probability of the observed data arising if the hypothesis were false. You can regard this as some measure of the information[6] provided by the data. If the data are such that they are very probable *if the hypothesis were true* but very unlikely *if the hypothesis were false* then their existence gives much information, and we have good grounds for modifying the prior odds. If the data are equally likely to arise under either

eventuality then their existence gives little information; it should not lead
us to modify our prior belief.

Multiplication of the *prior odds* by the *diagnostic ratio* neatly captures that last
verbal intuition, and is the way in which Bayes theorem calculates the posterior
odds – the 'odds of the hypothesis being true *given* the data'.

One payoff from this mathematical formalisation of our intuitive judgements
is that it enables us to examine the impact of evidence, and there are consistent
experimental findings (e.g. Tversky and Kahneman 1982) showing that
without such formalisation people misperceive the impact of data upon
hypothesis. Further, although the mathematics are uncontroversial, errors can
arise because those using them fail to test the model using all possible
hypotheses. As Klayman and Brown (1993, p.102) rightly observe, there is a
'tendency among hypothesis testers to focus on the relation of the data to the
focal or preferred hypothesis, giving less attention to their relation to alternative
hypotheses'. That error, it can be shown (Macdonald 1994), afflicts even
sophisticated data analysts. It is also a major factor in decision making in social
work, where practitioners fail actively to consider alternative explanations for a
state of affairs, or the consequences of alternative forms of intervention. In the
next section we provide a numeric social work illustration with strong policy
implications.

Low frequency events

Arguably one of the continuing distortions in social service delivery has been an
over-concern with low-probability, high-cost outcomes (such as child deaths
or serious injury) and a systematic lack of attention to high-probability,
low-benefit outcomes (e.g. chiropody services as improving quality of life for
elderly). Within the confines of this chapter we would not venture to settle that
debate. But a Bayesian perspective *does* have something striking to say about the
predictability of low-frequency events within social work and social care, and
that may affect our perceptions of appropriate targets for intervention.

It has been claimed that 'The most crucial issue for the child protection
services is how successful or otherwise they are in their ability to prevent the
deaths of children' (Pritchard 1993, p.645) – and certainly much of the time the
media and the spokespersons for social services appear to act as if this were true.

However if this is the crucial issue it is a difficult one to assess, for we would need to know what deaths there would have been in the absence of the child protection services. This is difficult, not least because as Parton, Thorpe and Wattam (1997, p.50) note: 'We do not even seem to have any agreement on the number of children who die as a result of child abuse', though Creighton (1993) is correct to note *no* decrease in infant homicides – if anything numbers have increased (Noble and Charlton 1994; Macdonald 1995).

The most interesting questions arise around the prediction structure that would be required to underpin an individually interventionist service targeted at the reduction of homicides. Suppose it were possible to develop a test instrument that determines with accuracy whether or not someone is an about-to-be infant murderer. (Accurate means that when presented with an about-to-be infant murderer the test correctly identifies status 90 per cent of the time; of ten potential child murderers, nine are located.) To match this 'false negative' rating, assume that the test has an equivalent 10 per cent 'false positive' score. Now suppose we apply the test to you, and you score positive; what is the likelihood that you are an about-to-be infant murderer?

This is a question firmly in Bayesian territory, which assesses the impact of data on a theory. We could slot the numbers into the Bayesian equations[7], but since an equation is simply a convenience, we follow through the argument in 'longhand'. Let us conservatively concentrate on those with ready access to the infants – say two 'suspects' per birth. There are, in England and Wales, some ten murders of infants (under one year old) *per* 200,000 live births. The test, as imagined, would correctly identify nine of these. But, and this is where the trouble arises, it would also identify as about-to-be infant murderers 10 per cent false positives. In an 'at risk' population of 400,000 there will be some 40,000 'positives'.

Whence, if identified as positive, your probability of being an about-to-be infant murderer is 0.0002 (the chance of being one of the nine 'true' out of the total 40,009 returned positive). Such a low probability can only legitimate benign interventions; and benign interventions – by definition – do not need such legitimation. This low probability is worth emphasising, since mis-perception of the predictive power of such tests is common, even amongst the well trained and educated, as Casscells, Schoenberger and Grayboys (1978) reported in a study of Harvard medical students.

The general point is not novel, and is characteristic of the assessment of any evidence when the underlying events are infrequent; when the *a priori* probabilities are low, true positives are lost in a sea of false positives. It underlies national health service reluctance to apply HIV screening to other than 'high risk' groups; it has been used to query the import of 'genetic fingerprinting' as the sole determinant of guilt. Within social work, Light (1973), Kotelchuck (1983), Dingwall (1989), Browne (1993), Parton *et al.* (1997) have made related points when considering evidence of child abuse in general; but the case is much sharper (because the underlying rates are lower) when we consider homicides. And it may well be that it is this very prospective unpredictability of low-frequency events which leads to their preponderance in our hindsight error examples; since we cannot identify them prospectively we over-weight retrospectively.

'Preventing homicides' is thus not a rational goal, although while intervening to prevent detectable suffering we might incidentally prevent some deaths. But that is very different from aiming to prevent homicides, and being assessed on 'homicides prevented'.

There are emerging strands in the broader literature which support this conclusion. The evidence of what is effective in preventing future occurrences of abuse or neglect in families where this has become a problem is disappointing (Macdonald with Winkley 1998). In the USA, there are growing numbers of academics, practitioners and politicians recognising that it would be more rational to expend resources on strategies that would generally promote 'positive parenting' rather than targeting families already deemed to be neglectful or abusive:

> promoting a positive and responsive parent–child relationship is both a desirable intervention target as well as a viable child maltreatment-prevention strategy. (Wolfe 1993, p.101)

Or, as Parke put it a decade earlier:

> it is clear that successful prediction is very unlikely, and moreover the potentially deleterious consequences of our mistaken predictions may outweigh the

positive benefits of our efforts. It would seem to be more useful to devote
efforts to primary prevention and treatment. (Parke 1983, p.53)

On this analysis, policy aims would not be especially targeted at preventing
abuse and neglect. The hypothesis is that in the course of promoting quality
parenting we have as good a chance of 'preventing' some instances of child
abuse and neglect, and the overall benefits would be worth the shift in
emphasis. In terms of cost-benefit analysis this is not indisputable, and there is
considerable debate as to whether or not 'primary prevention' strategies are
financially viable (see Holtermann 1997). It may well be that in some areas, e.g.
parent training, we would maximise gains by concentrating resources on those
who belong to high adverse-risk groups, e.g. teenage mothers, socially isolated
mothers, parents living in poverty. The verdict regarding these disputes rests, to
some extent, on our ability to identify accurately high adverse-risk groups, and
concomitantly our ability to intervene effectively at earlier, rather than later
points in the aetiology of problems. At present, the evidence is in favour of early
intervention, although the balance is fine, and neither option provides grounds
for complacency (Macdonald with Winkley 1998).

The need to be educated

The discussion has concentrated upon the uncertainty component in 'risk' and
the argument has been that, in the absence of formal guidance on the behaviour
of probability, many intelligent, thoughtful people get the answers wrong.

The basic history of science forms part of general education. Many of us are
aware, for example, that the natural assumption that 'a moving body always
requires a force to keep it moving' had to be replaced by the initially counter-
intuitive Newtonian insight that 'a body would keep moving *unless* affected by a
force'. The history of thought about probability is much less familiar. The
educated citizen can roughly date Newton, but he or she would fare less well
with Arnauld's insight[8] that: 'Fear of harm ought to be proportional not merely
to the gravity of the harm, but also to the probability of the event'. Day by day
in our ordinary lives we make probability decisions without thinking twice
about Bayes or the 'conjunction fallacy'. Indeed some are well satisfied with this
state of affairs. In a 1996 Court of Appeal case, where DNA complicity

conflicted with alibi and identification evidence, and the original case had involved the presentation of Bayes theorem to the jury, the court ruled such presentation inappropriate saying that 'Jurors evaluate evidence and reach a conclusion not by means of a formula, mathematical or otherwise, but by the joint application of their *individual common sense* and *knowledge of the world* to the evidence before them'[9].

But we could become better informed on the history of human understanding of 'risk' (Bernstein 1996, for example, provides an engaging[10] account). The point of looking at the history of 'risk' and 'probability' is to realise that assessing risk is not straightforward; generations got it wrong, and cumulated knowledge was required before progress could be made. Consideration of the fallacies sketched above (and of the counter-intuitive consequences of 'risk compensation' – see below) should lead us to be more sceptical of our intuitive perceptions. Baron, discussing various strategies that people appear to employ when interpreting probabilities (such as averaging – rather than, correctly, multiplying – *prior odds* and the *diagnostic ratio*) observes that people's willingness to make probability judgements despite their lack of training suggests they are using a 'naive theory', like the naive (e.g. pre-Newtonian) theories of physics. This has implications for education in general, and social work education in particular:

> If people thought more thoroughly about what evidence was needed, they would take prior probabilities into account … For most people, however, special instruction, as well as good thinking, is required to learn about probability theory. … When our naive theories can have harmful effects, more systematic instruction may be warranted. Such instruction could include such topics as the relevance of prior probabilities and the dangers of hindsight, availability, and extreme confidence. (Baron 1994, p.238)

It may not take much to remove some of the error. The readers of mysteries whose probabilities summed to two can be reminded of summation conventions. A simple shift of perception may rescue those about to commit the 'conjunction fallacy' over 'Linda': Fiedler (1988) demonstrated that the tendency to choose the wrong answer largely disappears if people are asked for frequencies ('There are 100 people like Linda. How many of them are …?')

rather than the probabilities of events. The 'infrequent events' example, diagnosing rare conditions, may also become more transparent with a shift in perception to frequencies. Casscells *et al.* (1978) reported appropriate responses from less than a fifth of educated medical students. When Cosmides and Tooby reran the same task but with a frequentist final query ('*How many people* who test positive will actually have the disease?') they elicited the appropriate Bayesian answer from 76 per cent of their subjects (see Gigerenzer, Hoffrage and Kleinblting 1991, p.135).

However, some 'errors' may not be resolved by technical means. The Shafir child custody example presented earlier, where the same parent was chosen for both award and denial of custody, is more intractable than the other examples, for whilst it is clear that the participants 'got it wrong' (by displaying inconsistency) the mere avoidance of inconsistency would be a very weak mark of a proper adjudication. However, understanding why participants 'got it wrong' may help. One source of error is the impact of what psychologists refer to as 'vividness' (Nisbett and Ross 1980). Vivid data are concrete and often carry high emotional valance, hence the salience of Parent *B* in the choice. Alone, however, it does not account for the asymmetry in people's choices. Unsurprisingly, we again prefer accounts stressing the role of individuals as active explainers. For example, Pennington and Hastie have argued that evaluation in complex assessment decisions is explanation based (Pennington and Hastie 1988, p.521). If this is so, it may account for the outcomes in Shafir's data: invited to tell a story, respondents found it easier in each case to tell a story about Parent *B*. Although analyses which emphasise the processes of decision making do not in themselves identify 'correct' decisions, they do make us more alert to causes of error, and strategies for managing them, including the management of perceptual bias.

There is, however, one radical analysis of the substantive issue of risk and ambiguity in child custody decisions which has clear decision implications. Elster (1989) argues persuasively that above threshold values of minimum parenting competence, ambiguity is so high (we just do not know the odds of long-term happiness associated with any factors we might assess), and the cost of delaying in an attempt to reduce ambiguity is so damaging to children (their lives will not stand still whilst information is gathered), that random allocation (of custody to parents) may be the rational strategy. Analytically separating risk and ambiguity helps us realise that ambiguity is here so ineluctably high that any considered evaluation of risk is just pretence. Intuition says: agonise, weigh the factors, do risk assessment. Reflection says: toss a coin.

So we are not arguing for *extensive* education in mathematical statistics, nor claiming that all problems have simple technical solutions. But we do need to know *something* about the literature on risk perception and *something* about the formal structure of probabilities to provide workers with the capacity to formulate and record defensible assessments of risk. This would also reduce their vulnerability to erroneous 'hindsight' evaluations. In the closing years of the twentieth century, such instruction is not characteristically part of social work education.

Users likewise

It is not just social workers who face risk and ambiguity. Clients/customers/ users themselves take risky decisions and face problems of perception of risk. The bulk of the professional social services literature, as we have noted, centres on protection of others from adverse risk.

Intervening in the lives of others, to affect the negative risks they encounter, is a fraught balancing act that it is easy to get wrong. Strachan and Tallant (1997) provide a simplifying summary of the work of Kahneman and Tversky in terms of 'framing', observing that when people consider themselves to be in the 'zone of gains' (doing well) they are risk averse, when they view themselves to be in the 'zone of losses' (doing badly) they are more likely to adopt risk-seeking behaviour, and suggest that 'The crux of framing's relevance to risk-assessment is to move people into the zone of gains where their decision-making will be less risk-seeking' (Strachan and Tallant 1997, p.19).

Even accepting the analysis does not entail that judgement, and the judgement is a strong intrusion on the life of another. Such intrusions are tempting throughout the social services. As Littlechild and Blakeney (1996) note, anomalies exist; many groups in society are free to engage in risk taking and decide the level of danger to which they expose themselves; but older people are often subjected to over-protectiveness (see also Norman 1980). Perhaps the classic example is the very disparate qualifications required of natural and of foster parents. In reaction, some workers have tried to give risk back to the people. That too can generate its impositions. As one parent of a disabled child, quoted by Russell (1996, p.47), tartly observed of her social worker: 'It's all very well talking about "dignity of risk" when you are not the parent.' To surrender the assessment of risk may not be wise.

> An essential element of assessing and managing risk is enabling the voice of the child to be heard. Our judgements must be informed by what children have to say, individually and collectively, about how they perceive the risks to them. (van Meeuwen 1996, p.41)

Listening to children is important (their present values matter), but social workers have to deal with risks (both positive and negative) not just perceived risks; indeed since much of the concern must be with the probabilities of future occurrences, children may, unfortunately, be peculiarly ill placed to help with these judgements (they lack experience, and information on what maturation does to perceptions and goals).

A possible way of addressing the balancing task is to connect the 'risk' discussion to that other currently fashionable topic, 'empowerment':

> Empowerment can be considered as a central feature of citizenship and social care service delivery (Stevenson 1994). It can be understood as the entitlement to take risks and exercise choice, but also as an entitlement to protection from undesirable risks. (Kemshall and Pritchard 1997, p.13)

We are not persuaded that the introduction of empowerment in these terms is helpful. Consideration of the observed definitional diversity of the term and the extent to which the interpretation of 'empowerment' is determined by prior political ideology leads Parsloe (1995, p.1) to suggest that 'power sharing might be a more honest, albeit more difficult, aim for social work'. We share her concerns and see the merit of her resolution, but have argued (Macdonald and Macdonald 1999) that while some 'empowerment' is straightforwardly about intraorganisational power, some of what might be called 'deep' empowerment where empowerment is seen as defining of the self, can only be achieved by the acquisition of skill and knowledge. To set out to make another free is arrogant and dangerous. To set out to provide another with knowledge and skills is a more modest, although not easy task which may make them free. Thus an emphasis on providing knowledge of the structure of risk to client, consumer and user, as well as practitioner, becomes important. Of course there remain awkward decisions that must be taken on risk management, perhaps particularly in the spheres of child protection, mental health and criminal justice. But the dominant intervention may be to provide clients with the skills to handle risk and ambiguity in decision making. This may also be 'empowering', properly understood. Further, it involves no condescension, since it is sharing an education we ourselves require.

Further research is needed

Much of the preceding argument has been that some apparent puzzles in the perception of risk are perhaps better understood than untutored perception might assume. However, some issues in the perception of risk remain more unsettled and intractable than the bulk of the literature assumes. Confronting the literature with the real concerns of daily decision making may help to augment the practical relevance of theory (the connections between theory and practice are not unidirectional). So in this section we wish to indicate some specific 'fillings-in' of the map of 'risk' which would assist the practical concerns of social work. Though the gaps considered are interconnected, they are presented discretely. However, whilst not presented in any particular order there is, connecting our discussion of these gaps, a central theoretical dissatisfaction with static models of risk; we advocate an emphasis on the dynamic and interacting characteristics of decisions – affecting both good and bad outcomes over time.

Complex risk

Risk may be more complex than the dominant models in the literature assume. Although, as we have indicated, the literature on risk and decision is rich, there are three characteristic and significant omissions.

First, as Lopes observes in a stimulating and influential article:

> Most research on risk has concentrated on gambles in which there are only two outcomes. ... Real world risks, on the other hand, hardly ever have just two outcomes. More often they range continuously over the outcome variable. (Lopes 1997, p.690)

Lopes proposes getting some leverage on this by presenting subjects with a variety of distributional outcomes, and attempting to locate pertinent (attended-to) summary aspects of these distributions. This intuition was present in Douglas (1986, p.37):

> A theory of decision-making that takes the mean of distribution probabilities disregards the very thing that risk-taking is all about, the distribution itself

although, as Adams (1995, p.55) notes, Douglas only considered simple aspects of the distribution. Social work deals – even at the adverse-risk level – with complex outcomes. When we opt for an 'all outcomes' definition of risk the complexity escalates. Though Lopes' work is probably closest, there is not yet a theory of risk which adequately handles such outcome assessment. More work is needed.

Second, quoting Lopes (1997, p.710) again:

> Psychologists who study risky choice don't talk about a surprisingly large number of factors that are psychologically relevant to choosing among risks … Here are some words that are not found in the theoretical vocabulary: fear, hope, safety, danger, fun, plan, conflict, time, duty, custom.

To understand the real choices of clients and users analysis needs to incorporate (or demonstrate the redundancy of) such variables. The list of required enrichments can be extended:

> for example, when comparing two sources that have statistically similar probabilities, as well as comparable outcomes, but are not comparable in terms of whether they are voluntarily undertaken or not. (Pidgeon *et al.* 1992, p.121)

There are good research grounds for in general opting for a minimalist theoretical vocabulary, but for fruitful social-work application some inter-translation is required.

Third, the risky choice literature is characteristically concerned with adverse risks-to-the-risk-taker, and whilst some of what social workers do can be recast in this mould (as you act you risk *your* career, or *your* standing with your colleagues, or …) the translation is awkward, and social workers are more concerned with the risk environment of others – so the layered evaluations of risk become more complex (we have the workers' perceptions of the clients' perceptions of the actual risk) and the perceptual effects are layered in their distortions. Again, we need to know more.

Risk over time

Besides being complex, risk exists in time and changes over time. We need a more interactive and temporally aware set of models. This lack is perhaps sharpest in the area of adverse risk, where the quantitative risk assessment literature is dominated by simple additive risk and does not attend to inter-temporal change.

For example, the extensive probation risk modelling (for a good summary see Kemshall 1996) has tended to downplay interactions (Macdonald 1977). Again, at-risk assessment of children has tended towards the static; as Millner *et al.* remark:

> Although demographic or case variables may statistically predict [at-]risk status, many variables (e.g. gender, severity of past incident, SES, caretaker's childhood history of abuse) are not responsive to intervention and therefore are useless for treatment planning. (Millner *et al.* 1998, p.102)

We must also retain sight of actors reacting to their changing environment. The authors of a challenging work on childhood accidents observe:

> [Researchers] seem far less interested in how people keep children safe than in the relatively few occasions on which safe-keeping strategies fail. As a consequence, little is known about the ways in which a desire to maintain child safety is incorporated into the routine behaviours which structure daily life. (Roberts *et al.* 1995, p.13)

Their research reveals actors making complex adjustments well informed by the structure of local risks (compatible with our scepticism on the untutored handling of probabilities). Perhaps the overall message is the need for adequate models of process; as Rutter observes:

> Most of the literature on the testing of causal hypotheses in relation to psychopathology has tended to focus on risk factors or variables of some sort. As a result, a great deal is known about indices of risk ... [but] ... it is absolutely crucial in the testing of causal hypotheses to go beyond the variable indexing risk to some postulated mechanism by which it might operate. Unless this is

> done, there is a serious danger of drawing wrong conclusions and there is a tempting pressure to adopt the 'football score' approach to any review of research findings. Thus if seven studies show an effect and three do not, the causal hypothesis 'wins'. That however makes no sense. Unless the negative findings are a consequence of differing methodologies or different qualities of data (and each may be the case), the negative findings must carry a message. (Rutter 1994, p.933)

The optimum research tools needed to resolve these issues remain in dispute. Rutter (1993a) provides a robust and stimulating overview of the utilities of longitudinal data in assessing causality, though, as Carr-Hill and Macdonald (1973) noted, part of the impediment remains a lack of articulated theoretical frameworks embodying 'sequence', and, we would now add, risk and ambiguity. But certainly longitudinal data unsettles simple assumptions as to static determinations of risk. This is an important issue because (as Rutter, Quinton and Liddle 1983, note) the strength of risks often looks different when viewed prospectively than when assessed retrospectively – echoes of the hindsight fallacy. A further advantage of longitudinal data lies in its provision of greater leverage on the assessment of the frequency with which children escape from adverse risk, and the routes that encourage them or enable them to escape (Rutter 1993a, 1993b). Frequency of 'escape from adverse risk' matters; longitudinal studies have been crucial in showing that, even with very extreme conditions of environmental adversity, there can be a surprising degree of recovery when children experience a radical environmental change (Skuse 1984). Although interpretation and assessment of 'resilience' remains complex (Apfel and Seitz 1997), such findings affect our perception of the nature of adverse risk. In brief, there is a need for, and possibility of, more complex models of risk explicitly incorporating interaction and time.

Reflexive risk

Perception of risk is not static; we may modify our behaviour in line with perceived risk, which in turn leads to shifts of perception. A shorthand for this might be 'reflexive risk'. Reflexivity can lead to counter-intuitive risk behaviour. Adams (1995) provides a persuasive[11] theoretical account of one particular category of apparently perverse effects, which he calls 'risk compensation'. For example, when playgrounds are made safer by providing rubber matting, accidents may not decrease, because children take more risks. When drivers wear seat belts they may feel more secure, drive faster, and cause pedestrian injuries. If humans are, to varying extents, risk-taking animals we might expect them to adjust their risk taking upwards as the environment becomes safer.

> The potential safety benefit of most improvements to roads or vehicles is, it seems, consumed as a performance benefit; as a result of safety improvements it is now possible to travel further and faster for approximately the same risk of being killed. (Adams 1995, p.144)

So, interventions to reduce adverse risk may have the opposite or no effect. Some social work may aim to reduce adverse risk, and clients are themselves actors, not passive, so there might be opportunity for 'risk compensation'. Although we have at present no documented plausible examples, Adams' work suggests that we should at least evaluate the possibility that some social work support may be translated into extended activity, maintaining the level of adverse risk.

Perhaps more immediately pertinent to social work is another interesting and possibly paradoxical component of Adams' discussion: his rejection of near misses as good measures of risk (Adams 1995, p.89). He notes that near misses increase vigilance and hence decrease the probability of accidents: that is they form part of the risk-compensation loop and so cannot be taken as independent measures. This may have implications in social work settings. For example the uncontrolled anger which leads someone to hit and injure their child may, by shocking them into realising they might have done even more serious damage, reduce rather than increase the likelihood of serious injury. Parton *et al.* make a similar substantive point (though without reference to Adams) in discussing a case presented by Pecora and Martin (1989).

> Might it also be possible to say that if the mother did over-discipline her child one day that would put the child at less risk because the mother would appreciate the seriousness of her actions? (Parton *et al.* 1997, p.88)

If apparent predictors can sometimes be inhibitors, this has obvious interconnections with our earlier discussion on the predictability of homicide.

These translations of 'reflexivity' to the social work setting have, the reader will have noted, been hedged around with 'may' and 'might'. We simply do not know whether the phenomena discussed by Adams are prevalent in social care and social work. But Adams' insights have provided a clearer perception of risk in those areas (characteristically accident prevention) to which he has applied them. The social care and social work parallels are worth exploring[12].

Moral evaluation

Many of our moral actions involve decisions in a context of risk and ambiguity. Shifts in our perception and understanding of risk should therefore entail shifts in our moral understanding. For example, once we realise that the prediction of homicide is technically inappropriate as a goal this affects our perception of what we 'ought to do about it'. Again, reflection on the preventable risks of childhood accidental injury may affect our perception of their moral status. But the impact on understanding can run both ways, and stubborn moral intuitions may affect our perception of risk. For example, on any straightforward calculus of probability and outcome we habitually over-weight low-risk extreme outcomes (as in fear of flying, or fear of nuclear plant failure, or – arguably – child deaths). One analysis might reject the worries as consequently irrational, or tied to 'culture' (Douglas and Wildavsky 1982; Douglas 1992). More interestingly, we might explore for underlying rationality, with consequent implications for the perception of risk:

> The importance of having safe fallback positions in real life may account for the fact that the perceived riskiness of technological hazards ... reflects dread of outcomes that are perceived to be uncontrollable, catastrophic, not easily reversed. (Lopes 1997, p.715)

If the psychology of the 'irreversible' holds up, this maps to social theory concerns about 'trapdoor functions' in policy making, concerns which arise from a consideration of the logic of moral evaluation within a temporal ordered frame (Macdonald 1980).

The preceding paragraph settles no issues. All we are here concerned to do is illustrate that there may be fruitful mileage in critically revisiting the moral assertions made around 'risk' in the light of a theoretical understanding of decision making under risk and ambiguity and the empirical constraints imposed by imperfect information and temporality.

Outcome assessment

Finally, underlying all of the above, and following from our emphasis on 'risk' as a consideration of *all* outcomes and their payoffs, we need detailed and precise information on the efficacy of social work interventions if we are to reduce 'ambiguity' and aid informed, rational decision making. This need is not just practical but ethical (see Macdonald and Macdonald 1995). Decisions require not simply risk assessment, but detailed information on the probability of success and the efficacy of different interventions. We need to know probabilities of costs and probabilities of payoffs for a portfolio of potential interventions before we can move forward.

> The most vociferous arguments here take place between those who espouse positivist approaches as the most persuasive and the ideal to be pursued, at least as a long term goal (e.g. Macdonald and Sheldon 1992; Thyer 1993) and those who believe that positivist designs may have a significant place in social work research but also have many important limitations connected with their scope, their responsiveness to social work practice as it is, and their feasibility (e.g. Cheetham *et al.* 1992; Smith 1987). (Cheetham 1994, p.93)

One underlying argument of this chapter has been that our untutored, intuitive perceptions of risk are likely to be systematically misleading. The same point applies to outcome research, which might well be seen as a continual battle against the bewitchment of our understanding by immediate experience. Of course, formal experimental designs are hard work (and the complexities sketched above are real); but we need them precisely because without that work we run too much (documented) danger of wishful thinking. As has been suggested elsewhere (Macdonald 1997a), critics over-emphasise the intractability of randomised controlled trials, and under-perceive the limitations of other approaches. So, whilst the 'vociferous arguments' do indeed continue, and this chapter lacks the space to elaborate further (but see Macdonald 1996, 1997b, 1998), an astringent, scientific approach would be best placed to aid 'tutored' perceptions of risk and may, in fact, alter probabilities: an effective intervention for anger management may reduce the probability of adverse outcomes, and change decisions. But there is much to be done. As periodic reviews of a decade's-worth of findings (Fischer 1973; Reid and Hanrahan 1980; Macdonald and Sheldon 1992) have suggested, we still *know* relatively little about 'what works' with what problems in what circumstances – which is not to hold that knowledge is unattainable, pace the following Department of Health review 'Research can never produce an exact answer about the degree of risk of a particular placement for an individual child because the interplay of the factors which determine success or failure will be unique in each case' (Department of Health 1991, p.65).

If this is simply to remind us that the error component will remain large, there is no dispute. If it means what it says ('the interplay ... will be unique in each case') it is either a misunderstanding of the logic of modelling, or a comprehensive (but unsubstantiated) rejection, which we do not share, of the possibility of social knowledge.

Conclusion

We have tried to give some indication of the complexities in perceiving and assessing risk. For some of these there are available formal tools which can reduce confusion. Some require further research and understanding (for example, to fill in the gaps about prevalence). Some will remain ineluctably morally evaluative although, as always, more knowledge will impact on the evaluation. Professional judgement will always play a part. We have suggested possible strategies for developing 'appropriate' decisions, and pointed to areas where thought and research may be productive. But risk evaluation in the field of human agency is a daunting task. We need all the help we can get, and those for whom we are held accountable, and to whom we owe a duty of care, deserve our attention to formal tools – perhaps particularly when they lead to apparently counter-intuitive perceptions. Minimally if we have, in this chapter, contributed a little to our collective humility we shall be content.

Notes

1. Kenneth.Macdonald@nuf.ox.ac.uk

2. Geraldine.Macdonald@bris.ac.uk

3. The best *general* guide to the diverse literatures on risk and decision making is undoubtedly Baron (1994): though structured around his own resolution of the issues, he provides sufficient detail to enable critical reading. Pidgeon *et al.* (1992) organise the literature on the perception of risk of adverse outcomes, and Adams (1995) provides some radical and critical perceptions. Gibbs' (1991) text on scientific reasoning for social workers, subtitled 'bridging the gap between research and practice' and Gibbs and Gambrill's (1996) workbook on 'critical thinking' provide much intelligent guidance on the translation between such 'thinking about thinking' and the daily activities of social care and social work.

4. For a fuller discussion see Macdonald (1990).

5. The present-day form of the theorem which bears Bayes' name is actually due to Laplace's work in 1812 – see e.g. Sivia, 1996, p.7.

6. Though we here describe the diagnostic ratio as derived from probabilities, in some situations we may be more confident in estimating the diagnostic ratio than in estimating the component probabilities.

7. Gibbs, 1991, p.227, Gibbs and Gambrill 1996, p.124, though Gibbs mistypes 'sensitivity' in place of 'specificity' in his presentation of the formula.

8. Dated 1662 – see e.g. Hacking, 1975, p.77.

9. Reported in the *Times Higher Education Supplement*, 24 October 1997, p.23. For a related discussion, with further unsettling citation, see Smith (1996, pp.370–373).

10. Though Bernstein is better on contextual detail than on the central logic of the ideas, for example, he dodges the task of explaining what Bayes is about (Bernstein 1996, p.133).

11. When reading Adams it may be worth noting that his analysis is hindered by his desire to incorporate the views of 'cultural theory' on a bounded set of 'viable ways of life' (Schwarz and Thomson 1990). As Bellaby (1990) notes even in its own terms that theory needs to be modified to incorporate more explicit recognition of the dynamic aspects of social life. We would see its lack of a narrative of change-over-time as being a disqualification, particularly in the context of Adams' own interactive view of risk perception. The bottom line is that Adams' insights do not require acceptance of 'cultural theory'.

12. Research in this field might incidentally extend the theory of risk – it is, for example, not obvious that all 'near-miss' behaviour falls under 'risk compensation'.

References

Adams, J. (1995) *Risk*. London: University College London Press.

Alaszewski, A. and Manthorpe, J. (1991) 'Literature review: Measuring and managing risk in social welfare.' *British Journal of Social Work 21*, 277–90.

Apfel, N. and Seitz, V. (1997) 'The firstborn sons of African American teenage mothers: Perspectives on risk and resilience.' In S. S. Luthar, J.A. Burack, D. Cicchetti and J.R. Weisz (eds) *Developmental Psychopathology: Perspectives on Adjustment, Risk and Disorder.* Cambridge: Cambridge University Press.

Baron, J. (1994) *Thinking and Deciding.* (2nd edition). Cambridge: Cambridge University Press.

Becker, G.S., Landes, E.M. and Michael, R.T. (1977) 'An economic analysis of marital instability.' *Journal of Political Economy 85*, 1141–87.

Becker, J.W. and Brownson, F.O. (1964) 'What price ambiguity? Or the role of ambiguity in decision making.' *Journal of Political Economics 72,* 62–73.

Bellaby, P. (1990) 'To risk or not to risk? Uses and limitations of Mary Douglas on risk acceptability for understanding health and safety at work and road accidents. *Sociological Review 38*, 465–83.

Bernstein, P.L. (1996) *Against the Odds: The Remarkable Story of Risk.* New York: Wiley.

Brearley, C.P. (1982) *Risks and Social Work: Hazards and Helping.* London: Routledge and Kegan Paul.

Browne, K. (1993) 'Home visitation and child abuse: The British experience.' *American Professional Society on the Abuse of Children 6*, 4, 11–13.

Carr-Hill, R.A. and Macdonald, K.I. (1973) 'Problems in the analysis of life-histories.' *Sociological Review Monograph 19*, 57–95.

Carson, D. (1996) 'Risking legal repercussions.' In H. Kemshall and J. Pritchard (eds) *Good Practice in Risk Assessment and Risk Management 1*. London: Jessica Kingsley Publishers.

Casscells, W., Schoenberger, A. and Grayboys, T. (1978) 'Interpretation by physicians of clinical laboratory results.' *New England Journal of Medicine 299*, 999–1000.

Cheetham, J. (1994) 'The Social Work Research Centre at the University of Stirling: A profile.' *Research on Social Work Practice 4*, 89–114.

Cheetham, J., Fuller, R., McIvor, G. and Petch, A. (1992) *Evaluating Social Work Effectiveness.* Buckingham: Open University Press.

Creighton, S.J. (1993) 'Children's homicide: An exchange.' *British Journal of Social Work 23*, 643–4.

Davis, M. (ed) (1991) *The Sociology of Social Work.* London: Routledge.

Department of Health (1991) *Patterns and Outcomes in Child Placement.* London: HMSO.

Dingwall, R. (1989) 'Some problems about predicting child abuse and neglect.' In O. Stevenson (ed) *Child Abuse: Professional Practice and Public Policy.* London: Harvester Wheatsheaf.

Douglas, M. (1986) *Risk Acceptability According to the Social Sciences.* London: Routledge.

Douglas, M. (1992) *Risk and Blame.* London: Routledge.

Douglas, M. and Wildavsky, A. (1982) *Risk and Culture: An Essay on the Selection of Technical and Environmental Dangers.* Berkeley, California: University of California Press.

Ellsberg, D. (1961) 'Risk, ambiguity and the Savage axioms.' *Quarterly Journal of Economics 75*, 643–99.

Elster, J. (1989) *Solomnic Judgements.* Cambridge: Cambridge University Press.

Fiedler, K. (1988) 'The dependence of the conjunction fallacy on subtle linguistic factors.' *Psychological Research 50*, 123–9.

Fischer, J. (1973) 'Is casework effective?: A review.' *Social Work 17*, 1–5.

Friedman, D., Hechter, M., Kanazawa, S. (1994) 'A theory of the value of children.' *Demography 31*, 375–401.

Gibbs, L.E. (1991) *Scientific Reasoning for Social Workers: Bridging the Gap Between Research and Practice.* New York: Merrill.

Gibbs, L.E. and Gambrill, E. (1996) *Critical Thinking for Social Workers: A Workbook.* California: Pine Forge Press.

Gigerenzer, G., Hoffrage, U., Kleinbölting, H. (1991) 'Probabilistic mental models: A Brunswikian theory of confidence.' *Psychological Review 98*, 506–28.

Griffiths, R. and Waterson, J. (1996) 'Facts, fantasies and confusion: Risks and substance abuse.' In H. Kemshall and J. Pritchard (eds) *Good Practice in Risk Assessment and Risk Management 1.* London: Jessica Kingsley Publishers.

Hacking, I. (1975) *The Emergence of Probability: A Philosophical Study of Early Ideas about Probability, Induction and Statistical Inference.* London: Cambridge University Press.

Harris, N. (1987) 'Defensive social work.' *British Journal of Social Work 17*, 61–9.

Hollis, M. and Howe, D. (1987) 'Moral risks in social work.' *Journal of Applied Philosophy 4*, 123–33.

Holterman, S. (1997) 'The benefits and costs of preventive work with families' a report for the Joseph Rowntree Seminar, 25 November 1997.

Johnson, W. (1994) 'Maltreatment reference as a criterion for evaluating risk assessment.' In T. Tatara (ed) *Seventh National Roundtable on CPS Risk Assessment.* Washington, DC: American Public Welfare Association.

Kemshall, H. (1996) 'Offender risk and probation practice.' In H. Kemshall and J. Pritchard (eds) *Good Practice in Risk Assessment and Risk Management 1.* London: Jessica Kingsley Publishers.

Kemshall, H. and Pritchard, J. (eds) (1996) *Good Practice in Risk Assessment and Risk Management 1.* London: Jessica Kingsley Publishers.

Kemshall, H. and Pritchard, J. (eds) (1997) *Good Practice in Risk Assessment and Risk Management 2: Protection, Rights and Responsibilities.* London: Jessica Kingsley Publishers.

Klayman, J. and Brown, K. (1993) 'Debias the environment instead of the judge: An alternative approach to reducing error in diagnostic judgement.' In P.N. Johnson-Laird and E. Shjafir *Reasoning and Decision Making.* Amsterdam: Elsevier.

Knight, F.H. (1921) *Risk, Uncertainty and Profit.* New York: Harper and Row.

Kotelchuck, M. (1983) 'Child abuse and neglect: Prediction and misclassification.' In R.H. Starr (ed) *Child Abuse Prediction: Policy Implications.* Cambridge, MA: Harper and Row.

Kronenfeld, J.J., Glik, D.C. (1991) 'Perceptions of risk: Its applicability in medical sociological research.' *Research in the Sociology of Health Care 9*, 307–34.

Lee, P.M. (1997) *Bayesian Statistics: An Introduction.* 2nd edition. London: Arnold.

Light, R. (1973) 'Abused and neglected children in America: A study of alternative policies.' *Harvard Educational Review 43*, 556–98.

Littlechild, R. and Blakeney, J. (1996) 'Risk and older people.' In H. Kemshall and J. Pritchard (eds) *Good Practice in Risk Assessment and Risk Management 1.* London: Jessica Kingsley Publishers.

London Borough of Brent (1985) *A Child in Trust: The Report of the Panel of Inquiry into the Circumstances Surrounding the Death of Jasmine Beckford.* London: London Borough of Brent.

London Borough of Greenwich (1987) *A Child in Mind: The Report of the Commission of Inquiry into the Circumstances Surrounding the Death of Kimberley Carlisle.* London: London Borough of Greenwich.

Lopes, L.L. (1997) 'Between hope and fear: The psychology of risk.' In W.M. Goldstein and R.M. Hogarth (eds) *Research on Judgement and Decision Making: Currents, Connections and Controversies.* Cambridge: Cambridge University Press, reprinted from L. Berkowitz (ed) (1987) Advances in Experimental Social Psychology, Volume 20. San Diego: Academic Press.

Lyng, -S. (1990) 'Edgework: A social psychological analysis of voluntary risk taking.' *American Journal of Sociology 95*, 851–86.

Macdonald, G. (1990) 'Allocating blame in Social Work.' *British Journal of Social Work 20*, 525–46.

Macdonald, G. (1996) 'Evaluating the effectiveness of social interventions.' In A. Oakley and H. Roberts (eds) *Evaluating Social Interventions.* Ilford: Barnardos.

Macdonald, G. (1997a) 'Social work: Beyond control?' In A. Maynard and I. Chalmers (eds) *Non-Random Reflections on Health Services Research.* London: BMJ Publishing Group.

Macdonald, G. (1997b) 'Social work research: The state we're in.' *Journal of Interprofessional Care 11*, 57–65.

Macdonald, G. (1998) 'Promoting evidence-based practice in child protection.' *Clinical Child Psychology and Psychiatry 3*, 71–85.

Macdonald, G. and Macdonald, K.I. (1995) 'Ethical issues in social work research.' In R. Hugman and D. Smith (eds) *Ethical Issues in Social Work.* London: Routledge.

Macdonald, G. and Sheldon, B. (1992) 'Contemporary studies of the effectiveness of social work.' *British Journal of Social Work 22*, 6, 615–43.

Macdonald, G. with Winkley, A. (1998) *What Works in Child Protection.* Ilford: Barnardos.

Macdonald, K.I. (1977) 'Path analysis.' In C. O'Muircheartaigh and C. Payne (eds) *Model Fitting.* New York: Wiley.

Macdonald, K.I. (1980) 'Time and information in political theory.' In M. Freeman and D. Roberston (eds) *The Frontiers of Political Theory.* Brighton: Harvester Press.

Macdonald, K.I. (1994) 'What data can say: The case of denominational switching.' *Social Science Research 23*, 197–218.

Macdonald, K.I. (1995) 'Comparative homicide and the proper aims of social work: A sceptical note.' *British Journal of Social Work 25*, 489–97.

Macdonald, K.I. and Macdonald, G.M. (1999) 'Empowerment: A critical view.' In W. Shera and L.M. Wells (eds.) *Empowerment Practice in Social Work: Developing Richer Conceptual Foundations.* Toronto: Canadian Scholar's Press.

Machlis, G.E. and Rosa, E.A. (1990) 'Desired risk: Broadening the social amplification of risk framework.' *Risk Analysis 10,* 161–8.

Millner, J.S., Murphy, W.D., Valle, L.A. and Tolliver, R.M. (1998) 'Assessment issues in child abuse evaluations.' In J.R. Lutzker (ed) *Handbook of Child Abuse Research and Treatment.* New York: Plenum Press.

Nisbett, R. and Ross, L. (1980) *Human Inference: Strategies and Shortcomings of Social Judgement.* Englewood Cliffs, New Jersey: Prentice-Hall.

Noble, B. and Charlton, J. (1994) 'Homicides in England and Wales.' *Population Trends 75,* 26–29.

Norman, A. (1980) *Rights and Risks.* London: Centre for Policy on Ageing.

Palmer, C. (1998) 'Trial with too much error.' *Times Higher Educational Supplement,* April 17, 20.

Parke, R.D. (1983) 'Theoretical models of child abuse: their implications for prediction, prevention and modification.' In R.H. Starr (ed) *Child Abuse Prediction: Policy Implications.* Cambridge, MA: Harper and Row.

Parsloe, P. (1995) 'The concept of empowerment in social work practice.' *Hong Kong Journal of Social Work 29,* 1–11.

Parton, N., Thorpe, D. and Wattam, C. (1997) *Child Protection: Risk and the Moral Order.* London: Macmillan.

Pecora, P.J. and Martin, M.B. (1989) 'Risk factors associated with child sexual abuse: A selected summary of empirical research.' In P. Schene and K. Bond (eds) *Research Issues in Risk Assessment for Child Protection.* Denver: American Association for Protecting Children.

Pennington, N. and Hastie, R. (1988) 'Explanation-based decision making: Effects of memory structure on judgement.' *Journal of Experimental Psychology: Learning Memory and Cognition 14,* 521–33.

Pidgeon, N., Hood, C., Jones, D., Turner, B. and Gibson, R. (1992) 'Risk perception.' In *Risk: Analysis, Perception and Management. Report of a Royal Society Study Group.* London: The Royal Society.

Prins, H. (1975) 'A danger to themselves and to others.' *British Journal of Social Work 5,* 298–309.

Pritchard, C. (1993) 'Re-analysing children's homicide and undetermined death rates as an indication of improved child protection: A reply to Creighton.' *British Journal of Social Work 25*, 645–52.

Reid, W.J. and Hanrahan, P. (1980) 'The effectiveness of social work: Recent evidence.' In E. Goldberg and N. Connolly (eds) *Evaluative Research in Social Care*. London: Heinemann.

Roberts, M.C., Fanurik, D. and Layfield, D.A. (1987) 'Behavioral approaches to prevention of childhood injuries.' *Journal of Social Issues 43*, 105–118.

Roberts, H., Smith, S.J. and Bryce, C. (1995) *Children at Risk? Safety as a Social Value*. Buckingham: Open University Press.

Robinson, L.B. and Hastie, R. (1985) Revision of beliefs when a hypothesis is eliminated from consideration. *Journal of Experimental Psychology: Human Perception and Performance 11*, 443–56.

Russell, P. (1996) 'Children with disabilities.' In H. Kemshall and J. Pritchard (eds) (1996) *Good Practice in Risk Assessment and Risk Management 1*. London: Jessica Kingsley Publishers.

Rutter, M. (1993a) 'Cause and course of psychopathology; some lessons from longitudinal data.' *Paediatric and Perinatal Epidemiology 7*, 105–20.

Rutter, M. (1993b) 'Resilience: Some conceptual considerations.' *Journal of Adolescent Health 14*, 626–31.

Rutter, M. (1994) 'Beyond longitudinal data: Causes, consequences, changes and continuity.' *Journal of Consulting and Clinical Psychology 62*, 928–40.

Rutter, M., Quinton, F. and Liddle, C. (1983) 'Parenting in two generations: Looking backwards and looking forwards.' In N. Madge (ed) *Families at Risk*. London: Heineman.

Schwarz, M. and Thomson, M. (1990) *Divided We Stand: Redefining Politics, Technology and Social Choice*. Hemel Hempstead: Harvester Wheatsheaf.

Shafir, E. (1993) 'Choosing versus rejecting: Why some options are both better and worse than others.' *Memory and Cognition 21*, 546–56.

Sivia, D.S. (1996) *Data Analysis: A Bayesian Tutorial*. Oxford: Clarendon Press.

Skuse, D. (1984) 'Extreme deprivation in early childhood: Theoretical issues and a comparative review.' *Journal of Child Psychology and Psychiatry 25*, 543–72.

Smith, A.F. (1996) 'Mad cows and ecstasy: Chance and choice in an evidence-based society.' Journal of the Royal Statistical Society, Series A, 159, 367–83.

Smith, D. (1987) 'The limits of positivism in social work research.' *British Journal of Social Work 17*, 401–416.

Stevenson, O. (1994) 'Social work in the 1990s: Empowerment – fact or fiction?' In R. Page and J. Baldock (eds) *Social Policy Review 6*. Canterbury: Social Policy Association.

Strachan, R. and Tallant, C. (1997) 'Improving judgement and appreciating biases within the risk assessment process.' In H. Kemshall and J. Pritchard (eds) *Good Practice in Risk Assessment and Risk Management 2: Protection, Rights and Responsibil ities*. London: Jessica Kingsley Publishers.

Thyer, B.A. (1993) 'Social work theory and practice research: The approach of logical positivism.' *Social Work and Social Services Review 4*, 5–26.

Tversky, A. and Kahneman, D. (1982) 'Evidential impact of base rates.' In D. Kahneman, P. Slovic and A. Tversky (eds) *Judgement Under Uncertainty; Heuristics and Biases*. Cambridge: Cambridge University Press.

Tversky, A. and Kahneman, D. (1983) 'Extensional versus intuitive reasoning: The conjunction fallacy in probability judgement.' *Psychological Review 90*, 293–315.

van Meeuwen, A. (1997) 'Making family placements: working with risks and building on strengths.' In H. Kemshall and J. Pritchard (eds) *Good Practice in Risk Assessment and Risk Management 2: Protection, Rights and Responsibilities*. London: Jessica Kingsley Publishers.

Wexler, D.B. and Schopp, R.F. (1989) 'How and when to correct for juror hindsight bias in mental health malpractice litigation: Some preliminary observations.' *Behavioural Sciences and the Law 7*, 485–504.

Wolfe, D.A. (1993) 'Prevention of child neglect: Emerging issues.' *Criminal Justice and Behavior 20*, 90–111.

CHAPTER 2

Rehabilitation and the Distribution of Risk

Brian Caddick and David Watson

Examining ideas linked to risk

The idea of risk does not go out alone at night, nor during the day. It is conceptually connected to a range of other ideas it will serve us to identify, and in particular it is useful to notice its links with the ideas of harm and interests.

To talk of 'risk' is to talk of probability. However, to be more specific, when we talk of risk, the probability is of *harm*. We do not always describe gambling as risky, though it deals in probabilities; it is usually only described as 'a flutter' – at least until it is discovered that the stake is next month's rent or that the betting is compulsive. In short, identification of an activity as introducing risk also rests upon value judgements in which prospective consequences are ranked as more or less harmful. And to what? To interests.

In the example above, appropriately as we shall see, the interests under threat are in secure shelter, which is a precondition of an expanded *autonomy*: the opportunity to engage in a readily identifiable range of valued activities not available if you are 'of no fixed abode'; and, where compulsive behaviour is concerned, the interest is in autonomy itself: the capacity to choose one's activities as opposed to being driven to behave in a particular manner by psychological, genetic or other such causes. And, quite differently but probably more frequently important for autonomy, we should remember contexts in which the capacity to choose one's activities is restricted or denied because we are compelled by others. We shall return to consideration of the criminal justice system as a setting for this second kind of compulsion.

In the context of social policy risk assessment carries these references to judgements of harm to interests. But it carries more, too.

There is first a presumption that behaviour which is risky is activity which might be deterred, reformed or otherwise *changed*. That is, there is a presumption that those who put interests at risk have some *choice* in the matter, and that others whose interests are put at risk have some choice about appropriate intervention, as individuals or collectively.

Second, in the setting of social policy, this presumption requires us to develop an account of interests, a ranking of harms as more or less serious, and a rationale for the distribution of autonomy and for the distribution of the authority to restrict autonomy.

In what follows we hope to fulfil two aims. First, to outline a conceptual and evaluative framework in which risk may be identified, because interests are identified and harms ranked. This will allow us a clear picture of what may be put at risk in social life, and the seriousness of that risk. It is also a framework in which individual and social responses to risk may be judged as justified or unjustified. Not surprisingly, in the history of ideas more than one such framework has been developed, but here we focus on that derived from *individualist* thinking.

Individualism is arguably the dominant ideology of our times, and certainly features in justifications for social policy reform, including those developments in criminal justice to which we shall return later in our discussion.

In textbooks on social theory, individualism is presented sometimes as a *description* of things: an account of what people and social life, as a matter of fact, are like. At other times it is presented as a *social ideal*: an account of our potential, of what people could be like given the right social circumstances – which are then described, or we are offered an account of what social life ought to be like to allow our potential to be realised (see for example Hayek 1960; Lukes 1973; Nozick 1974; George and Wilding 1976).

In our view, individualism as a description of any present people or society is false. Here we are more interested in individualism as a social ideal, for the simple reason that an account of what people could be like, and of how social life therefore should be organised if this possibility is to be realised, is a powerful source for a critical review of ourselves, of the organisation of our society, and of our management of the distribution of risk. It is easier to think critically about how things are when conscious of how different things might be. We are not, then, endorsing individualism as a social ideal but deploying it to facilitate our second, more specific aim in the present discussion: we wish to challenge current trends in thinking about the treatment of offenders evidenced in recent policy documents.

In general terms, the trend has been to assert, but not to argue, that in the context of the criminal justice system, risk to the public is a paramount consideration in the treatment of offenders and to be avoided whenever possible, while risk to offenders is of little or no significance. This may state the position too starkly, but our hope is to unsettle an easy consensus by reminding readers of the conceptual and evaluative framework out of which much of the present concern for public safety has grown. We contend that a position is being taken in respect of the proper distribution of risk which deserves closer scrutiny.

The framework, then, is individualism. We shall reach the particular context in which policy and practice are analysed in the light of individualist thinking in Section III. But before this we need to give more attention to the relevant details of the individualist ideology.

Individualism recognises interests which may be put at risk, and it allows us to discriminate serious from less serious threats. But it has other features neglected in current debate. More important, within limits we shall examine, it denies that risks to the legitimate interests of *any* individual can be set aside in social policy. To put the same point differently: it denies extreme privilege in the distribution of risk, since this would ultimately be to deny autonomy. In the context of a system of criminal justice it may be argued that some offenders, by their offences, forfeit the right to autonomy. But individualism sets a principled limit.

Individualism presents a social ideal in which human interests have at their centre the interest in autonomy. If that is set at nought, then we deny the humanity of the offender and deny their actual or possible future membership of our community: rehabilitation. We sentence them to internal exile, as we once sentenced them to external exile, or at the extreme, we sentence them to death. The individualist commitment to autonomy is incompatible with a distribution of risk which, at the extreme, denies the possibility of rehabilitation to the liberties of members of society.

Individualism also provides an account of the proper distribution of authority over risk taking. Its defence of autonomy is a defence of individual authority over risk, and individual responsibility for use of that authority in respect of risk to one's own interests and risk to the interests of others.

Use of that authority is not beyond censure or sanction, and individualism provides a principled position on the proper limits of its use. The individual has no right to impose unwanted serious risk on others, but at the same time has the right first, to place his or her own interests at risk, and second to be held responsible for his or her conduct.

In assessing risk, and talking about 'serious risk', we should distinguish between when we might call the mathematics and the morals. Talk of 'serious risk' can refer to questions of probability, with no comment on whether what is very probable is also very harmful. On the other hand, it can also reflect judgements as to what is very harmful, with no comment on whether what is held to be very harmful is also very probable.

When it comes to discussions of intervention, it may prove useful to distinguish four cases which are presented here in ascending order of justifiable intervention, from the individualist standpoint. First, cases in which there is low probability that a minor harm will occur; second, cases in which there is a high probability that a minor harm will occur; third, cases in which there is a low probability that a major harm will occur; fourth, cases in which there is a high probability that major harm will occur.

As probability rises, and as the prospective harm to the interest of others becomes more severe, the justification for restrictions on autonomy grows. And where harm is actually done to the interests of others, any subsequent punishment might arguably include forfeit of the rights mentioned, but not irrevocably; otherwise, from the individualist standpoint, we deny offenders' humanity by denying the prospect of autonomy.

Further, just as individualism opposes the state placing any person permanently where they can pose no risk either to themselves or to others, so it also opposes the state securing some people permanently beyond risk from others. This is simply the other side of the same principled coin.

Individuals have a right to protection from unwanted risk to their interests, but not to the extent of complete and permanent security, even if it were achievable. This would be a world in which trust was unnecessary because autonomy would be extinct.

The public, or some members of it, may call for such total protection, but in the individualist social ideal the desire is improper, denying some fellow citizens the prospect of a form of rehabilitation which respects their capacity to live, in due course, as autonomous human beings, whatever their offence.

Rehabilitation, from this perspective, involves an individual carrying responsibility for his or her own conduct, and in particular in relation to the interests of themselves and others. It is not necessarily a matter of the individual behaving responsibly. Rather, an individual recovers the opportunity to behave responsibly in respect of these interests, but, by the same token, rehabilitation restores the opportunity to do harm.

The standpoint outlined here in respect of the criminal justice system might be developed in respect of other social policy settings; care for the elderly or for people with disabilities being the more obvious ones in which individualists might raise fears of 'over-protection'.

However, having introduced the general direction of the analysis called for by the individualist standpoint, it is time to put more flesh on the bones. After that, we can turn to our more particular discussion of the implication for policy in the criminal justice system.

Individualism as self-determination

Individualism has been introduced as constructed around a central commitment to autonomy. In some discussions the same commitment is introduced as a commitment to *self-determination*. Behind this idea is a conception of each person having the potential at least to be independent of others, rational and the best judge of their own interests.

It is not generally denied that we sometimes misjudge our own interests, but individualists keep to the fore the point that we generally learn from our mistakes, adding that we certainly will not learn much if we are protected from making mistakes, or entirely protected from their consequences.

Nor is it generally denied that we are sometimes irrational. What is claimed, rather, is that we have the natural capacity to formulate plans and purposes of our own, reflecting our judgement of what is in our interests. This capacity is presented as what makes individuals worthy of respect; it is the basis for the individualist account of human dignity: dignity for human beings is said to lie in life in a society which respects this capacity for autonomy by structuring opportunities so that it can be realised.

And along with this capacity to formulate plans and purposes of our own goes the capacity to develop an understanding of the way nature and the social world work, to a point good enough to permit us to calculate how to get what we want. We are capable of an instrumental rationality in pursuit of our goals.

Nor is it claimed that in judging what is in our best interests, or in formulating purposes of our own, we are by nature self-interested, nor are we recommended to be self-interested. The capacity in question need not be exercised in our own private interests. We can choose to set those interests aside, with difficulty or with ease: we may be indifferent to our interests. And of course our own interests may be shared by others and pursued collaboratively.

Naturally, there is room for discussion as to whether all human beings possess even the capacity for autonomy, mental or physical. The history of the advance of individualist ideas into policy is one in which classes of human being previously denied autonomy on the grounds that they lacked the capacity entirely, or lacked the capacity to any significant degree, are shown to be limited largely by social constraints. Thus racist and sexist generalisations were exposed.

Individualists do not have to claim that all human beings, whatever their history and circumstances, are capable of autonomy, but they demand that the burden of proof be reversed, requiring that those who would limit social support for development of the capacity for autonomy justify such apparent neglect of fellow human beings. Some of us may be beyond all hope of autonomy, but social history has shown us often premature in that judgement (see Weale 1978; Mendus 1989).

The talk of our capacity for independence is a way of asserting that each one of us, so far as possible, should be free to pursue a life of his or her own: a life in which each one determines his or her own purposes and routes by which to achieve them. The life may be selfish, or selfless. In the individualist social ideal, society is to be structured so as to extend this possibility so far as possible. Individualism is misunderstood if it is thought to tolerate inequalities of opportunity, where these constrain autonomy, except where they are brought upon oneself in the exercise of autonomy, and even then opportunities to recover autonomy should be fostered.

Individuals with a life of their own, in a society making the usually substantial adjustments to sustain the possibility, in access to resources needed to make this possible, and then to sustain the possibility, *do* form one kind of community. It is one in which collaboration for mutual purposes may occur, and in which it might be the purpose of one person to support realisation of the purpose of another. But above all it is a community in which autonomy is respected.

And thus it includes a distinction between public and private life. To explain: in one form or another at different moments in the history of individualism, a distinction is drawn between what are sometimes called other-regarding actions (public) and what then are called self-regarding actions (private). For our purposes, this distinction is, respectively, between actions which risk harm to the interests of others and actions which risk harm to the interests of oneself.

Perhaps any action might, in strange enough circumstances, risk harm to the interests of others. This, at least, has been a point raised in objection to the important division between what is private and what is public. But for our purposes we can leave this debate aside. Even if the proper scope of privacy and autonomy is never beyond question, we can proceed with our project: to review the implications of an individualist framework – in which autonomy is of paramount importance and the foundation of an account of human dignity and of human rights – for our present thinking in respect of the distribution of authority over risk taking and over-intervention in the use of that authority.

Individualism is a social ideal in which authority over risk taking is distributed as widely as possible. Intervention may be justified only when one person's exercise of autonomy threatens that of another. The right to intervene is itself founded in the right of all others to autonomy. The structures through which the autonomy of others is protected or restored should themselves not threaten autonomy. The state, perhaps more than other individuals, can be dangerous for our autonomy.

Private life is sacrosanct in this perspective, but public life is *defined* as that part of our social life in which the interests of at least one individual might be harmed by another individual in pursuit of his or her own plans. On such occasions, intervention might be justified, but otherwise not. And in saying intervention might be justified, this should not be understood as saying it *is* justified, but rather says only that the possibility must be reviewed.

It cannot be known in advance that in making present or future choices I will value the autonomy of others. Equally, and more significantly for the present discussion, nor can it be presumed that I will *not* value that autonomy. Otherwise even the possibility of a private life would be lost, as my actions were constantly monitored, keeping watch for suspicious behaviour indicating a threat to the interests of others. A commitment to autonomy is a commitment to risk through a commitment to trust.

Trust, of course, may not be rewarded, and then, within the individualist ideal, intervention may be warranted and punishment supported. But again, because the commitment to autonomy is fundamental, we are restricted to forms of treatment or punishment which promote the responsible use of authority over autonomy, responsible self-regulation: we must not extinguish the prospect of rehabilitation to autonomy and trust.

Of course, professionals in the criminal justice system are often themselves held accountable for clients' breaches of trust, when autonomy is exercised to harm the interests of others. At this point the individualist framework can help us to resist the temptation for others to place all the responsibility in such cases upon professionals, and the temptation of the professionals themselves to take it.

Professionals are assigned responsibility for their own judgements and actions, but an autonomous client breaking trust is responsible himself or herself for that act. Experienced professionals will notice that this last remark reminds us that life may not be so simple, and so individualism, in its account of an achievable autonomy, may be simplistic. Even so, we have from it a conceptual and evaluative framework which identifies risk as risk of harm to interests, and which also promotes self-regulation in risk taking; we have a framework where intervention is warranted by irresponsible risk taking, threatening the interests of others, especially interests closest to the core interest in autonomy; but all the while we are recommended to intervene only in forms which promote responsible self-regulation. If that is achieved, the offender is rehabilitated to trust and of course regains the opportunity to do harm in regaining the opportunity to do good.

Individualism and the criminal justice system

In this third section our aim is to connect the individualist social ideal with certain aspects of policy and practice in the criminal justice area as a means of developing critical commentary. In restricting our attention to activities of the probation service we take cognisance of Kenshall's observation that it is 'the agency now primarily responsible for the identification and regulation of risky offenders ... [and] ... must acknowledge and respond to public fears, implement penal policy, and deal with individual offenders' (1997, p.251). We will have cause to return to the phrase 'respond to public fears' later but must first make plain how the service is expected to deal with individual offenders, which itself requires reference to important policy intentions associated with the 1991 Criminal Justice Act.

These intentions were made explicit in the White Paper which preceded the 1991 Act (*Crime, Justice and Protecting the Public* (Home Office 1990)). The government of the time sought, among other things, to control the size of the prison population by enacting legislation which would lead sentencers to have more confidence in, and make greater use of, some form of community supervision as a disposal. A feature of the 1991 Criminal Justice Act, then, was its redefinition of community orders as community *sentences,* its incorporation of a new – purportedly 'tougher' – penalty (the combination order) and its explicit reference to the restriction of liberty associated with community sentences (Section 6(2)(b) of the Act). It was anticipated that the probation service would find itself having to deal with more serious and difficult offenders than it had up to that point.

Whether this has in fact been the outcome will not occupy us here. What is important for our discussion is that the statutory purpose for community supervision was also reformulated to take this intention into account. As presented in the *National Standards for the Supervision of Offenders in the Community* (Home Office 1995) that purpose was seen as:

- securing the rehabilitation of the offender

- protecting the public from harm from the offender, or

- preventing the offender from committing further offences.

This formulation has continued unamended since the 1991 Act.

Two things can now be said. First, this statutory purpose is not – in *prima facie* terms at least – incompatible with an individualist perspective for it appears to require commitments both to the interests of the offender (assuming a particular interpretation of the term 'rehabilitation') and to the interests of the public. Second, and again from the same perspective, the purpose appears to give an important mediating role to the service itself. That is, in the process of working to re-establish the autonomy of the offender the interests of individual members of the public should not be ignored. But neither, in seeking to protect the interests of the public, should the interests of the offender be put aside as irrelevant.

Of course, mediation of this kind does not stand apart from risk assessment. Indeed, it provides something of a reason for it since a certain weighing of respective interests and threats to those interests is implicit in the task. So if policy and practice were to be guided by individualist thinking we might reasonably expect that risk assessment and risk management would play a part in supervision and that the interests of the public and of the offender would each be given their due measure of attention.

But reference to the *National Standards* reveals something quite different. Certainly risk assessment in relation to the interests of public is a significant and recurring theme. In preparing presentence reports for the courts, during supervision of community sentences and in connection with prisoners supervised after release from custody, it is clearly stated that the risk posed by the offender to the public is to be assessed. Nor is this to be limited to individuals charged with dangerous offences (for example, those who have committed violent or sexual offences); all offenders are to be subject to assessment which, additionally, is required to be ongoing over the period of supervision. Meanwhile, the need for an assessment of risk to the offender is acknowledged only in connection with the risk of suicide or self-harm. Yet these are acts not generally associated with community sentences; and we might also note that assessment thus focused is of distinctly limited scope insofar as the restoration of autonomy is concerned, even if it deals with the precondition of being alive.

Risk management with the *National Standards* appears to be similarly skewed. Should circumstances change during supervision so as to increase the risk of harm to the public then application can be made to the court to amend an order, or to revoke it and resentence or, in the case of supervision after release from custody, to prompt the possibility of a recall to prison. If, on the other hand, there is judged to be a reduction in the risk of harm to the public, then for probation orders an early termination may be applied for. But risk management in relation to the interests of the offender receives no comment. The critical measure is the probability of harm to the public. Accordingly, the offender is to be confronted about offending behaviour, challenged to accept responsibility for the crime and its consequences, made to be aware of the impact of the crimes committed and motivated towards a greater sense of personal responsibility and discipline.

There is a direction in all of this which the individualist framework makes transparent. Most obvious is the privileged distribution of risk established by a concern for the interests of the public and an apparent indifference to those of the person whose liberty has, to some extent, been curtailed. Further, the absence of a definition of what is a reasonable level of risk, taken together with this privileged distribution, makes more likely a drift towards 'false positive' assessments; that is, judgements which interpret the crime risks as higher than they are in fact ('just to be on the safe side') and which may result in a ratcheting upwards of the control exerted over the offender. Third, the requirement for ongoing or regular assessments of risk to public interests inevitably means more surveillance of the offender. And finally, much of the emphasis in intervention is to be in the nature of an injunction directed at the offender who, it is clear, should be left in no doubt about what others expect.

For the offender, all this stands in sharp contrast to earlier parts of the process by which it was determined that supervision would be the outcome. As

Garland has said, and except where individual control of conduct is deemed formally to have broken down, 'modern courts will insist that individuals generally direct their own actions, have choice, will, intention, rationality, freedom and so on and … will usually proceed to treat the offender in these terms' (1990, p.268). But in the later part of the process responsibility in relation to future behaviour has been converted into personal deficit in all supervisees, a presumed inability to exercise self-control which must be addressed by compelled participation in programmes of admonishment, heightened surveillance and possible additional constraint.

There is an inconsistency here which is stark. But for now we do no more than acknowledge it before reminding ourselves that the risk of harm to the public has not always been the principal focus of the probation service. The 'new penology', as Kemshall (1997) has described it, represents a shift away from what was a predominant concern with certain risks to the offender – as seen in the 'risk of custody' scale described by Bale (1987) – to a preoccupation with risk to the public from the offender. From an individualist point of view, such a shift resembles nothing quite so much as a swing of a pendulum from one pole to the other. Kemshall suggests that a number of factors may have contributed to this shift – the dramatisation of crime and the enhanced coverage of real events by the media; the commercialisation of crime control (following Christie 1993) with its marketing emphasis on security; political discourses which rule certain perspectives into the policy debate and certain perspectives out – and she expresses a concern that the probation service has been pushed into assessing risks to the public in ways which may be seriously flawed. But such a concern, while valid, implies an acceptance of the shift rather than a challenge to it. This easy consensus should be disturbed.

We can start by noting an influential ambiguity in phrases like 'respond to public fears'. This can mean efforts to develop policy and practice on the assumption that public fears are widespread and well founded; it can also mean testing out that assumption and developing policies and practices accordingly, which might include educating the public to be less fearful or encouraging individuals or communities to take reasonable crime prevention measures. Of course, the debate as to whether public fears in relation to crime are exaggerated is complex and may not be open to objective resolution (Harris 1992; Hough

1995). Thus to proceed on the assumption that public fears *are* well founded has advantages for those whose terms of office may depend on the significant electoral constituency (around a quarter of the public according to Hough's findings) who claim to be 'very worried' about crime. But responsible professionals, however narrowly channelled by the policies of their political masters, might strive to remember that 'respond to public fears' is still open to a less calculated and more thoughtful interpretation.

And so it is, too, with 'securing the rehabilitation of the offender'. The *National Standards* make brief reference to actions 'to remedy practical obstacles preventing rehabilitation' (mentioning as examples of such obstacles, homelessness, drug and alcohol misuse, illiteracy, absence of skills) but conspicuously fails to follow through with an account of these activities as steps towards the enhancement of autonomy, which they undoubtedly are. Instead they are placed within a set of objectives whose more detailed specification implies that rehabilitation is essentially about learning to behave responsibly. Of course, it is not a part of our criticism that learning to behave responsibly is undesirable. But securing the rehabilitation of the offender is more than this. It should include a principled concern for that person's needs and rights and not just the structured inculcation of his or her responsibilities. And individualism provides a means by which those needs and rights might be identified, by reference to their serving autonomy.

This analysis of skewed interpretations can be further extended to considerations linked with 'harm to the public'. In the so-called new penology the relationship between offender and the public is largely construed in terms of the offences which the former might visit upon individual members of the public and from which they must be protected. But there is a wider relationship in which these (possible) acts are set and that is the social contract of trust and respect which was damaged when the actual offences were first committed. For as long as this social contract remains damaged, the public continues to be harmed, even if this is only experienced by some as a vague and somewhat diffuse anxiety. We should note, however, that that harm is not made good simply by controlling the offender.

Michael Howard was right, in a highly restricted sense, to claim that 'prison works' because, of course, the incarcerated offender is no longer able to commit crimes in the community. This, to the victims, is understandably important. But the public is not made fundamentally more secure as an ever-growing proportion of it is incarcerated. What is needed is for the social contract to be restored. This requires recognition of the centrality of trust and that, as we have argued earlier, implies a commitment to risk. Trust which is demonstrated only in the absence of risk is not in fact demonstrated, and is a poor and misconceived objective for criminal justice policy and practice.

When the demand is made that offenders should be dealt with in such a way that in due course they come to 'behave responsibly', we must be careful too to note the ambiguity in the description of this objective.

It may be a matter of coming to behave in ways widely regarded as responsible simply because of the fear of sanctions, because the offender has been made very aware of the suffering which will follow further offences; or it may be a matter of the offender accepting social norms concerning responsible behaviour, just because they are the prevailing, widely held view.

From the individualist point of view, neither outcome deserves support, and neither is likely to prove effective in providing protection for the public. The objective of responsible behaviour, understood in these ways, promotes *obedience* and *conformity*, not autonomy. For individualists, responsible behaviour is behaviour chosen because it is believed to be right, and it is not made right nor is any reason to believe it is right provided by sanctions feared or by the popularity of a belief.

Individualism exposes the drift in present policy away from a commitment to autonomy, and also the drift towards an implausible psychology which pretends that rehabilitation to trustworthy membership of our community can be achieved by close control. We do not say that control has no part to play, but if it is not over time reduced, it yields alienation and brutalisation which harms offenders and, on their release, increases risk to the public rather than the reverse, since the relationship between the parties as autonomous members of the community, trusted to behave responsibly, has been greatly weakened, if not destroyed.

Only by reducing control can we foster autonomy, and only by the same means can we show trust and demonstrate it to be deserved. And at the same time we inescapably introduce risk: to be free to act well is to be free to act badly.

If we as a society wish to avoid such risks, we must privilege the autonomy of some over others: we must skew the distribution of risk, abandoning commitment to the rehabilitation of offenders through the restoration of autonomy. Probation officers, apparently, have not yet taken that path (see Kemshall 1996), and they should not be led up it by the drift in policy and interpretation identified here.

Note

Philosophical research in this field is sporadic since it is minimally funded. Here we apply a conceptual framework evolved over many years into a respectable body of discussion, though inevitably challenged. It will surface from time to time in journals such as *Philosophy and Public Affairs* (Princeton University Press) and the *Journal of Applied Philosophy* (Carfax). More recent uses of individualist thinking to consider the extent of social obligations include Richard Lindley, *Autonomy* (Macmillan 1986); Will Kymlicka, *Liberalism, Community and Culture* (Clarendon 1989); John Gray *et al.*, *The Moral Foundations of Markets* (Institute of Economic Affairs 1992); Stephan Mulhall and Adam Swift, *Liberals and Communitarians* (Blackwell 1992); and Preston King (ed), *Socialism and the Common Good* (Frank Cass 1996).

References

Bale, D. (1987) 'Using a "risk of custody" scale.' *Probation Journal 34*, 4, 127–31.

Christie, N. (1993) *Crime Control as Industry*. London: Routledge.

Garland, D. (1990) *Punishment and Modern Society: A Study in Social Theory*. Oxford: Clarendon Press.

George, V. and Wilding, P. (1976) *Ideology and Social Welfare*. London: Routledge.

Harris, R. (1992) *Crime, Justice and the Probation Service*. London: Routledge.

Hayek, F. (1960) *The Constitution of Liberty*. London: Routledge.

Home Office (1990) *Crime, Justice and Protecting the Public*. Cm.965. London: HMSO.

Home Office (1995) *National Standards for the Supervision of Offenders in the Community*. London: Home Office.

Hough, M. (1995) *Anxiety About Crime: Findings from the 1994 British Crime Survey*. Home Office Research Study 147. London: Home Office.

Kemshall, H. (1996) 'Risk assessment: Fuzzy thinking or "decisions in action"?' *Probation Journal 43*, 1, 2–7.

Kemshall, H. (1997) 'Sleep safely: Crime risks may be smaller than you think.'
   Social Policy and Administration 31, 3, 247–59.

Lukes, S. (1973) *Individualism.* Oxford: Blackwell.

Mendus, S. (1989) *Toleration and the Limits of Liberalism.* London: Humanities Press.

Nozick, R. (1974) *Anarchy, State and Utopia.* Oxford: Blackwell.

Weale, A. (1978) 'Paternalism and social policy.' *Journal of Social Policy 7,* 155–72.

CHAPTER 3

Risk Assessment and Prediction Research

Bill Beaumont

As social work is pressed into focusing on risk (Kemshall *et al.* 1997), one key issue emerges – can we handle worrying situations by accurately predicting risks of adverse outcomes? Objectively, this is clearly a preposterous question – risk and uncertainty are deeply intertwined, and where calculable certainty exists notions of risk are irrelevant. Nevertheless, social work agencies are expected (and are coming to expect themselves) to assess risk amidst intolerance of the inevitability of imprecision. How accurate can risk assessments become?

The literature distinguishes two broad approaches to risk assessment – actuarial (or statistical) and clinical (or expert) prediction. The research verdict on clinical prediction has been damning. Gottfredson and Gottfredson (1985), for instance, conclude that 'statistical prediction devices can be developed that are both more reliable and more valid than unguided or intuitive clinical predictions' (p.55). This conclusion, from criminology, echoes mental health research (Monahan 1981) and indeed draws largely on the same studies (for example Meehl 1954; Sawyer 1966; Mosteller 1977). It is not surprising that Milner and Campbell (1995) advise clinicians whenever possible to use 'statistical procedures to increase the accuracy of clinical prediction' (p.21). This poses two further questions – how widely available are well-tested statistical devices and how good are the best? Social work faces an unfortunate choice between relying on clinical prediction (claiming expertise where psychiatry has proved inexpert) or venturing wide-eyed into the unknown world of statistical prediction. The probation service, for instance, is being pressed by the Home

Office to use reconviction predictors routinely and by criminological entrepreneurs to rely instead on patented risk/needs assessments.

Other areas of social work may face similar pressures as increased reliance on statistical prediction is promoted. Some research effort has already been devoted to the statistical prediction of child abuse (see Corby 1993 and Milner 1995 for summaries of this research). In the field of mental health, work has been done on the prediction of both violence and self-harm (see Chapter 6). Little work has been done on statistical prediction in other areas of community care social work. Alaszewski, Harrison and Manthorpe (1998) accord it scant attention in their overview of risk issues in relation to health and welfare concerns, although clearly it could have some relevance (for instance, in relation to elder abuse or the prospects for successful independent living). The claimed superiority of statistical approaches to risk prediction (and its introduction in some areas of social work) suggest that all social workers need to be able to understand, and evaluate the strengths (and weaknesses) of the relevant research.

This chapter reviews the state of such research in relation mainly to offending, where statistical prediction has been most extensively studied. It draws on earlier reviews to identify some general features of prediction studies. Risk prediction has been attempted in many areas of criminal justice practice (for example sentencing, Gottfredson, Wilkins and Hoffman 1978; institutional allocation, Mannheim and Wilkins 1955; and escapes from custody, Thornton and Speirs 1985) but here we will focus on the three main areas of research – predicting delinquency, predicting reconviction and predicting 'dangerousness'. The chapter ends by assessing the merits of this research and identifying some messages for other fields of social work.

Messages from earlier reviews

Criminological prediction studies have a long history – Simon (1971) reviewed some early research and two major reviews from the 1980s summarised the considerable body of evidence accumulated (Farrington and Tarling 1985a; Gottfredson and Tonry 1987). They highlight some general features helpful in understanding prediction research.

Remember, in a generally technical discourse, that prediction studies raise important *ethical issues*. Partly for this reason, interest in criminological prediction has waxed and waned, becoming unfashionable in the 1960s when the difficulties seemed overwhelming. Three major concerns were: the stigmatising effects of predicting high risk; injustices resulting from (inevitable) cases of false prediction; and, since some American studies found 'race' predictive of reconviction, researchers had to choose whether to ignore it or, by including it, compound the effects of racism (Farrington and Tarling 1985b). Interest in reconviction predictors picked up again as the 'nothing works' message (Martinson 1974) combined with a new punitiveness to produce policies of 'selective incapacitation' in many US jurisdictions. These (predictably) contributed to a huge increase in the US prison population as preventive sentences were widely used. Ethical doubts were marginalised by an over-riding focus on public protection. Some contributors to the reviews of the 1980s were still defensive on ethical issues (see Wilkins 1985; Tonry 1987). However, Farrington and Tarling (1985b) concluded robustly that, since informal predictions are made by decision makers (police, sentencers, parole boards and probation officers), they could see no ethical objection to more formal devices – while it will 'never be possible to predict offending with 100 per cent accuracy ... in the interests of justice, those predictions should be made as accurately as possible' (p.26). Nevertheless, researchers (and practitioners) still need to be actively concerned about potential abuses of such work.

'Prediction studies' suffer a misnomer since almost all are *retrospective*. Most adopt a similar approach. Once follow-up data on an outcome is available, information from the sample's records is analysed to identify factors correlated to that outcome. The factors most strongly associated are then treated as 'predictors' and combined into the 'prediction device' which best fits the known outcomes in this 'construction' sample. That device is then usually tested against a 'validation' sample (normally the second half of a randomly divided original sample). The emphasis is purely on *statistical association*, not causal links (though factors are sometimes analysed because of causal hypotheses).

A range of *predictor variables* have been used in criminological studies (see Table 3.1 for some examples). Because most studies are retrospective the choice of variables tested is determined mainly by what is readily available in case records, usually simple demographic and criminal history factors (Hill 1985 summarises studies based instead on institutional experiences). Many problems result – information may be incomplete or unreliable, records are shaped by administrative (not research) priorities and interesting factors remain unexplored because they are not systematically recorded.

Table 3.1 Predictor variables used in parole studies			
Predictor Variables	*Parole Study*		
	Nutall *et al.* 1977	Willbanks 1985 *(factors tested)*	Copas *et al.* 1996
Personal			
Age	✓	✓	✓
Sex			✓
Ethnicity			✓
Class			✓
Marital status	✓		✓
IQ		✓	
Social history			
Marital failures		✓	
Education		✓	✓
Employment history	✓ (2)	✓	✓ (2)
Living arrangements at time of offence			
Narcotics use		✓	✓
Gambling or substance abuse			✓
Criminal history			
Offence	✓	✓	✓
Co-defendants	✓	✓	✓
Value of Property Stolen	✓		

Predictor Variables	Parole Study		
	Nutall *et al.*	Willbanks	Copas *et al.*
	1977	1985	1996
		(factors tested)	
Previous Convictions	✓	✓ (2)	✓
Previous Sex Offences		✓	✓
Previous Narcotics Offences		✓	
Previous Property Offences			✓
Previous Violence			✓
Prison Sentences	✓	✓	✓
Custody as juvenile	✓		
Sentence length		✓	✓
Age at first conviction	✓	✓	✓
Juvenile supervision orders			✓
Previous probation orders	✓	✓	✓
Probation/parole violations		✓	
Time 'at risk' prior to offence	✓		
Institutional history			
Prison escapes	✓		
Prison punishments		✓	✓
Prison merit score (local system)		✓	
Academic achievement in custody		✓	
Type of prison discipline offences			✓
Social prospects			
Living arrangements on release	✓		✓
Employment position on release	✓		✓

Table 3.1 continued

Note: (2) indicates two different indicators used in relation to that variable.

Outcome criteria also pose problems. Although some criminological studies have used other criteria (such as re-arrest or licence failure) most have focused on reconviction. For social workers interested in risks such as child abuse, reconviction may seem an encouragingly clear outcome. However, even by 1985 Farrington and Tarling expressed reservations about this deceptively simple measure (for example, the loose connection between reoffending and reconviction, problems relating to the follow-up periods and cut-off points used, and the significance of features of reoffending such as seriousness and frequency) which have since been more rigorously examined (Lloyd, Mair and Hough 1994).

One major research focus has been the technical question of how to *combine predictors* to maximise accuracy (see Farrington and Tarling 1985a for a full discussion). Early point-scoring approaches (Burgess 1928; Glueck and Glueck 1950) were criticised for lack of statistical sophistication. More complex techniques were tried but comparative studies using different methods on the same data (for example, Simon 1971; Gottfredson and Gottfredson 1985) found the simpler approaches more robust. Sophisticated methods generally fitted the construction sample better but did less well on validation. Prediction devices always do less well on a second sample (even where validation is on the second half of the same original sample), a phenomenon known as *shrinkage* in the prediction trade. Even more 'shrinkage' (or increased inaccuracy to those not in the trade!) is experienced when a device is used on fresh samples.

Farrington and Tarling (1985b) outline the complexities involved in specifying *accuracy*. Overall accuracy (the percentage of cases where the outcome is correctly predicted) conceals two types of error with different consequences – false positives (here, those predicted to be reconvicted who are not) and false negatives (those predicted to avoid reconviction who do not). Overall accuracy has to be considered in relation to frequency – rare events are difficult to predict and overall accuracy can be misleading. In an extreme example, researchers (Wenk, Robinson and Smith 1972, cited by Farrington and Tarling 1985b) found only 2.5 per cent of their sample were reconvicted for violence. A hypothetical prediction device which said none would be reconvicted could claim overall accuracy of 97.5 per cent (much better than real devices), no false positives and only 2.5 per cent false negatives. Despite these impressive indicators, it would of course have failed to predict all occurrences of violence! To judge a prediction device's usefulness you need to know overall accuracy, rates of false positives and negatives, and percentages of actual reconvictions and non-reconvictions predicted.

Random allocation of offenders into reconvicted and non-reconvicted groups would get some 'predictions' right by *chance*. If reconviction within two years following any particular penalty occurs in about half of all cases (roughly true in England and Wales according to Lloyd *et al.* 1994) chance would get about half these 'predictions' right. Therefore a prediction device in this field has to do considerably better than 50 per cent overall accuracy to be of any use at all. It must also be shown to improve significantly on *expert prediction*. It is inherently *difficult to predict rare events* statistically – this limits the potential of statistical prediction in relation to many issues vexatious to social work agencies and policy makers.

Statistical prediction devices have been used for a range of criminal justice purposes: in research (for instance, comparing outcomes from different interventions), administratively (for instance, reviewing cases refused parole) and to aid criminal justice decision making (for instance, parole decisions). The importance of ethical issues clearly increases the more closely prediction devices influence (or even potentially substitute for) human decision making.

An illustration of the 1980s 'state of the art' is provided by Willbanks 1985. In his Texas parole study one-third were 'successes' and two-thirds 'failures' (split evenly between reconvictions and other parole 'violations'). The sample (854) was divided randomly and one half used to construct five prediction scales applying different combination approaches to the same 20 variables (see Table 3.1). Multiple regression and predictive attribute analysis best matched the construction sample but the simpler Burgess and Glueck methods were more accurate on validation. So how good was Willbanks' best device? It produced 23 per cent errors, evenly split between false positives and false negatives (his worst device produced 28 per cent errors). Thus 'state of the art' prediction (circa 1985) produced just under 80 per cent *overall accuracy*, with about one in ten prisoners wrongly predicted to fail on parole and one in ten predicted to 'succeed' when they were reconvicted or otherwise violated parole. Although this study combined reconviction and parole violation as 'failures', studies focused on reconviction alone produced similar results. Statistical prediction devices could perform better than chance but still fell substantially short of the level of certainty required for use as a main basis for criminal justice decision making. Farrington and Tarling (1985b) suggest prediction devices are more accurate at the extremes than in the middle ranges.

Farrington and Tarling (1985c) identified eight targets for further research:

1. Choice of predictors, outcome criteria and combination methods should be based on theory not convenience.

2. Greater certainty over the accuracy of predictor and outcome information, preferably confirming information from a range of sources.

3. Use of multiple outcome measures.

4. More work on mathematical models of selecting and combining predictors.

5. Agreement on how to specify accuracy.

6. More work on generalisability over time and place.

7. Using instruments at different stages of the criminal justice process.

8. Using them to build computer models for evaluating penal policy changes and criminological theories.

It is worth reflecting to what extent those priorities have been pursued.

Predicting delinquency

There have been few attempts to predict offending amongst the general population. Glueck and Glueck (1950) compared 500 institutionalised delinquents with a matched sample of unconvicted boys. They developed a prediction table using five factors – paternal discipline, maternal supervision, father/son affection, mother/son affection and family cohesiveness – which compare oddly with more recent predictors (see Table 3.1). They suggested their table could be used to identify potential delinquents starting school, so remedial measures could be applied. Their research was fiercely criticised for methodological flaws – use of two extreme groups, possible bias in rating 'predictors', assuming parent/adolescent relationships had pertained since childhood, and absence of any validation. Farrington and Tarling (1985b) claim that, despite these flaws, 'a number of validation studies ... showed that the Glueck Social Prediction Table did have some predictive power' (p.8).

The Cambridge Study in Delinquent Development (West 1982) was a thorough prospective study following up 411 London boys from 1961 to 1980, its duration alone emphasising one reason prospective studies are rare. Information was gathered from the boys, their parents and teachers, and criminal record searches were supplemented using self-reported delinquency questionnaires. Fascinatingly, for an area of research dominated by reliance on official convictions, only half the self-reported delinquents were also convicted offenders! Using this data, Farrington (1985) later constructed prediction scales using five combination approaches but concluded 'it was difficult to identify a group with much more than a 50 per cent chance of delinquency and, conversely, to identify more than 50 per cent of the delinquents' (p.150). He was pessimistic that prediction methods could be improved enough to be useful in identifying future delinquents in the general population but thought it might be feasible to predict the most persistent offenders after their first conviction. The Cambridge sample included 23 chronic offenders who accounted for about half of all convictions and over a quarter of self-reported offences. Fifteen were amongst the highest scorers on one prediction device – other high scorers were 22 convicted young men and 18 without convictions. Farrington (1985) claims 'these results suggest that, to a considerable extent, the chronic offenders can be predicted at age 10' (p.170). However, for each chronic offender his device picked out, between two and three others would have been targeted. The number of completely false positives (unconvicted by age 25) outnumbered the chronic offenders successfully identified and one-third of the chronic offenders escaped his trawl. Given this level of imprecision, Farrington's conclusion seems over-optimistic.

Apart from replication studies using the Glueck Social Prediction Tables, Farrington and Tarling (1985b) identified only two other studies attempting to predict delinquency in the general population (Feldhusen, Aversano and Thurston 1976; Wadsworth 1978) and I have not uncovered any later studies in researching this chapter. Further thorough research in this area is clearly desirable to test out criminological theories but there is little indication that practically useful prediction instruments can be developed.

Predicting reconviction

Much prediction research instead tries to predict reconviction amongst populations of known offenders, with parole the major focus (probation research is discussed in Chapter 5). Space precludes discussion of American systems (for which see Gottfredson, Wilkins and Hoffman 1978; Gottfredson and Tonry 1987), so this review focuses on parole in England and Wales. The Reconviction Prediction Score (RPS) was developed by the Home Office Research Unit (Nuttall 1977) to support the introduction of parole in 1967. Primarily intended for research, it was also used administratively. It was constructed from the records of 2276 men released in 1965 from sentences over 18 months (the original parole eligibility threshold) of whom 54 per cent were reconvicted within two years. Sixteen variables (see Table 3.1), which were consistently correlated with reconviction, were weighted plus or minus one for each 5 per cent deviation from that rate. There was a high level of association between score-band and proportion reconvicted;

> About a quarter of the men in each sample score +15 and above (the reconviction rate for this group is 80%) and about a fifth of each sample score -11 or below (the reconviction rate for this group is under 20%). (Nuttall *et al.* 1977, p.18)

So its predictive accuracy was in line with other contemporary devices – well above chance, best at the extremes but still producing a substantial number of false positives and negatives. A RPS was then calculated, as a percentage probability of reconviction, for all men considered for parole.

Although satisfied with RPS as a working aid, Nuttall *et al.* (1977) identified several weaknesses – like other prediction devices, RPS was based on previous experience and therefore necessarily outdated; it could not take account of changes in the criminal justice system or parolee responses; the scale needed periodic revalidation and was only an aid to judgement. Its major administrative use was to compare local parole refusals and refer low-risk cases to the parole board for reconsideration. As a research instrument, it was used to compare predicted and actual reconvictions for groups of paroled and non-paroled prisoners. Nuttall *et al.* (1977) reluctantly concluded 'there was no evidence that parole reduced the number ... reconvicted over a two-year period' (p.74), though there was a reduction in expected reconviction rate over the first six months (then the average parole period). The history of RPS illustrates neatly one major problem surrounding prediction scales. Revalidation studies are cumbersome, so even in this ideal case (a national device, developed by government, with a rich data base to hand, and used in the sensitive area of parole) revalidation was accorded low priority. Ward (1987) finally reported on a revalidation study conducted after 1983.

Using a sample of 3554 men released from sentences over one year between 1977 and 1979, Ward found the rate of reconviction (44 per cent) lower than the average RPS estimate (52 per cent). By the late 1970s, therefore, RPS was erring on the side of safety. He concluded there was a case for changing some weightings and including three additional variables (sentence length, employment plans on release and custody type). However, such updating required new work on more recent releases providing both construction and validation samples and he recommended against this on economic and practical grounds. RPS had never covered women but Ward (1987) recommended against addressing that omission, arguing the numbers of long-sentence women would not support construction of a valid separate scale. His study highlights another hazard in making prediction instruments valid long term – the parole system had been repeatedly changed over the intervening years in response to a varying political agenda. Thus, for instance, RPS had never been applicable to the many shorter sentence prisoners paroled following the Criminal Justice Act 1982.

Ward (1987) confirmed that the main direct use of RPS was in reviewing local parole refusals and reported that the parole board released a fifth to a third of these low-risk cases referred annually. Given this main use, Ward's recommendations against further research may have been acceptable but what if RPS had played a larger part in parole decision making? An 8 per cent average over estimate of risk could have led to many prisoners experiencing parole refusal or delay, on the basis of an outdated prediction scale. Of course, this revalidation study could be read as a triumph by supporters of prediction devices – given the 'shrinkage' experienced when devices are first validated, the 'shrinkage' found in applying RPS to a new sample drawn over 12 years later was a pretty good result. The civil libertarian (should there be any left in the criminal justice system) is more likely to be worried that the significant proportion of false positives found originally (20 per cent of reconviction predictions wrong in the highest risk group) had indeed been amplified over time.

Political pressures rolled on and RPS was never comprehensively over-hauled before time caught up with the parole system itself. The Criminal Justice Act 1991 replaced parole with a new system of automatic conditional release for sentences under four years and discretionary conditional release (DCR) for longer sentence prisoners. The parole board was retained to operate DCR and the Home Office commissioned a replacement for RPS. The Carlisle Report (1988) urged the parole board to consider the risk of reoffending and particularly of serious offences during DCR – for the first time the parole board was specifically directed by the Home Secretary to consider statistical risk predictions (Copas, Marshall and Tarling 1996). The new Risk of Reconviction (ROR) score was constructed using a sample discharged from prison in 1987, so once again a device was based on dated information.

Copas *et al.* (1996) used records on most men released from sentences of four years and over in 1987 and all long-sentence women released in 1986 and 1987; difficulties in tracing records produced final samples of 1191 men and 56 women. The initial analysis examined 12 personal and 14 criminal history variables (see Table 3.1) against six follow-up criteria (reconviction, reconviction dates, offence dates, time till first offence, type of offence and sentence on reconviction). Ethnicity was included for the first time in a British prediction study. This study departed methodologically from earlier research, employing the technique of statistical modelling to construct the prediction device. Copas *et al.* (1996) say this method aims 'to formulate an accurate mathematical description of the way in which each factor influences reoffending' (p.9) and claim three advantages for it: the resulting score is usually based on fewer factors; account is taken of intercorrelations between factors; and it produces a concise description of what has been observed in the data, capable of independent verification. Unfortunately the method's details cannot be followed without considerable statistical knowledge, so criminal justice personnel will mostly have to accept the outcome on face value! The study also calculated the probability distribution of time to first reoffending by a process analogous to actuarial survival analysis. Under ministerial direction a distinction was made between 'any reconviction' and 'serious reconviction'.

The 26 initial predictor variables were whittled down to the twelve most strongly associated with reconviction – age at conviction, sex, employment status at time of offence, time in last job, marital status on release, type of offence, age at first conviction, previous convictions, previous property offences, youth custody sentences, prison sentences and juvenile supervision orders. Lower rates of association were found for three other factors (previous probation, years in full-time education and prison disciplinary offences) but they did not add usefully to prediction once the top 12 were used. A further analysis on the men reduced the prediction device to only five factors. Women were less likely to have been reconvicted than this device predicted so a sixth factor is used in applying ROR to women. The ROR calculation is shown in Table 3.2.

ROR scores were used to develop a survival model for reoffending over time and when this was checked against actual data for three subsamples (low, medium and high risk) it fitted well.

Copas *et al.* (1996) provide two ready reckoner tables from which their calculated probability of reconviction and serious reconviction, over any given period, can be read off. A hypothetical prisoner (ROR score 110) is said to have a 40 per cent probability of reconviction within nine months, rising to 59 per cent if allowed 18 months DCR and (with a higher serious offending ROR score of 114) posing a 31 per cent risk (over 18 months) that reconviction would be for a serious offence. This new device generates very detailed predictions from a small range of variables and use of a computer programme to generate printouts adds to the impression of great precision. The printout is included in the dossier given to parole board members and a copy goes to the prisoner. It assures the prisoner: 'The Parole Board of course takes account of much other information in assessing the risk of re-offending by an individual prisoner' (Copas *et al.* 1996, p.37).

Table 3.2 Calculating risk of recorrection scores		
	Weights (start from 100)	
Variable	Risk (any offending)	Risk (serious offending)
Age at conviction	- (1 × age)	- (1 × age)
Youth custody sentences	+ (3 × no.)	+ (4 × no.)
Adult custody sentences	+ (2 × no.)	+ (3 × no.)
Previous convictions	+ no. up to max. 25	+ no. up to max. 25
Offence type:		
Violence	-1	+1
Sexual	+1	+8
Drugs	-8	-11
Burglary	+4	+3
Theft	+8	+9
Other	-4	-10
If female	-13	-1

Source: Derived from Copas *et al.* 1996.

Our hypothetical prisoner would be informed that 48 per cent of prisoners like him had been reconvicted within 12 months, half of them for serious offences (no definition of 'serious' is offered on the printout). Prisoners may feel their efforts to earn DCR were wasted and that the factors used in the prediction amount to a mathematical version of the old adage 'once a wrong 'un, always a wrong 'un'.

Several features are worrying about this study despite its methodological sophistication. It is again entirely retrospective and predictor variables were still determined by availability – it is not clear whether the final decision to use only five predictors (six for women) was based entirely on statistical significance or influenced by convenience. The published study omits mention of ethnicity – we are left to assume it was not amongst the 15 best predictors, but the lack of any comment is surprising given the significance of that issue in American research. The study confusingly shifts terminology between reoffending and reconviction but remains essentially a reconviction predictor. It did tackle one problem in relation to reconviction as an outcome measure by tracing offence dates (an average delay of six months to conviction was found) but other problems went unexplored. Ministerial imperatives are apparent in the study's definition of a 'serious' offence as any 'which resulted in the imposition of a new custodial sentence' (Copas *et al.* 1996, p.5). This excessively broad definition verges on the unbelievable and leaves this device, unfortunately, with little connection to predicting what most people would consider 'serious' offences. It is nevertheless interesting that even such a broad definition cuts predicted reconviction rates roughly in half. The published study does not make it clear what level of accuracy is being claimed for this prediction scale and there appears to have been no attempt to apply it to a validation sample. Copas *et al.* merely comment that it needs to be revalidated on a sample of prisoners actually released on DCR. These researchers have made little effort to spell out their device's limitations, which is particularly serious since it is clearly intended to directly influence parole board decisions. ROR is an advance in terms of technical sophistication and complexity, but it is unclear how accurate it will prove and its creators have been much less careful regarding ethical issues than their more cautious predecessors.

Predicting 'dangerousness'

It is not a surprise that there has been particular concern over achieving accurate predictions in relation to the most serious offences. Murray (1989) argues that 'no clear and convincing consensus has emerged on what constitutes ... a dangerous individual' (p.2). However, public concern focuses on offences involving serious bodily harm to others, including rape and most other sexual offences (where the major harm may often be psychological rather than physical). Some other offences (such as arson or supplying drugs) which risk, rather than necessarily cause, bodily harm are also commonly classed as 'serious'. Recent legislation on stalking indicates that the concept of 'danger-ousness' is generally broadening to include both physical and psychological harm. As already shown, much predictive research has demonstrated a surprising failure to distinguish between all offending and such serious offending. This discussion will consider in turn prediction research on violent offenders, sex offenders and 'mentally disordered offenders'.

Compared with predicting reconviction amongst known offenders, trying to predict serious offending (even amongst known serious offenders) is the researcher's equivalent of hunting a needle in a haystack. This enterprise has been dogged by the statistical problems of predicting low frequency events. Although we live in a culture which feels itself menaced by increasing criminal violence, such events are still gratifyingly uncommon. With a low base rate, both clinical and statistical approaches produce particular problems of over-prediction, identifying many more people as potentially dangerous than are subsequently proved to be so. Livermore, Malmquist and Meehl (1968) tellingly illustrate the difficulty:

> Assume that one person out of a thousand will kill. Assume also that an exceptionally accurate test is developed which differentiates with 95 per cent effectiveness those who will kill from those who will not. If 100,000 were tested, out of the 100 who would kill, 95 would be isolated. Unfortunately out of the 99,900 who would not kill, 4995 people would also be isolated as potential killers. In these circumstances, it is clear that we could not justify incarcerating all 5090 people. (Cited in Monahan 1981, p.84)

Monahan (1981) though was particularly severe on the reliability of clinical judgement:

> Psychiatrists and psychologists are accurate in no more than one out of three predictions of violent behaviour over a several-year period among institution-alised populations that have both committed violence in the past (and thus had high base rates for it) and who were diagnosed as mentally ill. (p.48)

He supported the use of statistical devices to aid clinical judgement. In a British review, Floud and Young (1981) agreed but were concerned that American research had failed to produce false positive rates lower than 50 per cent. In a Home Office research review, Murray (1989) comprehensively outlined the difficulties experienced in predicting 'dangerousness', concluding that: 'we have not yet succeeded in producing criteria which can ensure that a prediction of future violence would be right more often that it would be wrong' (Bluglass 1988, cited in Murray 1989, p.31).

Despite these difficulties, and because clinical predictions were none the less still having to be made in the psychiatric and criminal justice fields, researchers (Steadman 1982; Monahan 1988) wanted to press on to second-generation prediction studies which overcame the methodological limitations of earlier work, which Monahan and Steadman (1994) identified as follows.

1. *Impoverished predictor variables* – studies had used a narrow range of predictors, mostly poorly associated with theories of violent behaviour. There was too much reliance on static variables, which neither the offender nor others could change, and too little attention paid to situational and environmental variables.

2. *Weak criterion variables* – studies had used differing criteria for failure (reconvictions, rearrest, rehospitalisation) over different follow-up periods; reconviction is likely to under-estimate even serious reoffending; there had been a tendency to binary prediction (dangerous/not dangerous) rather than probability of reconviction over time (as in criminological studies); and a failure to distinguish seriousness and type of violence risk (for example, against family members or the public).

3. *Constricted validation samples* – action taken in response to risk (such as increased medication, delayed release, better aftercare) may succeed in reducing reoffending and then look like over-prediction. Some studies using small samples focus only on the highest risk cases in order to find enough reoffending to permit statistical analysis but this leaves the resulting predictive instrument less applicable to more typical populations.

4. *Non-comparability of studies* – lack of consistency makes it difficult to aggregate results or draw conclusions even from a substantial body of research.

These problems, of course, strongly resemble the difficulties identified by Farrington and Tarling (1985b) in relation to reconviction prediction studies generally.

Monahan and Steadman (1994) have since claimed a 'Rejuvenation of Risk Assessment Research'. The MacArthur Violence Risk Assessment Study (Steadman *et al.* 1994) has followed up a thousand patients admitted to three American hospitals (including augmented subsamples of women, black and Hispanic patients) for one year after discharge. Incidence of violence was tracked through official records (rearrest, reconviction and rehospitalisation) supplemented by self-report information and interviews with a 'collateral informant' named by the research subject. This impressively thorough and prospective study involved fieldwork from 1992–96, illustrating again the substantial effort required to mount quality prediction research. The study aims to identify 'robust markers of violence risk' and, rather apocalyptically, the collaborators say if this is not achieved it 'will stand as testimony to the intractable difficulties clinicians face in assessing the likelihood of a behaviour as complex and multi-determined as violence in a population as diverse and poorly understood as the mentally disordered' (Steadman *et al.* 1994, p.316). The outcome is awaited eagerly.

Work with violent offenders has remained a very specialist corner of British social work. Here, the literature has focused on clinical assessment rather than statistical prediction. A leading British contributor, Prins (1986), dealt with the question, 'Can dangerous behaviour be predicted?' in two pages of a 248-page book and concluded: 'there are no reliable actuarial and statistical devices as yet that can predict with any degree of certainty the likelihood of dangerous behaviour' (p.87).

Murray (1989) recorded low overall rates of reconviction for serious offenders released from prison or secure psychiatric care in Britain – only six per cent of restricted patients released between 1977 and 1980 had been convicted of 'grave' offences within five years. Although in some ways counter-intuitive (we expect serious offenders to remain 'dangerous'), lower than average reconviction rates are found across the full spectrum of serious offences and in studies across time and different jurisdictions (Pritchard 1979). Studies of serious offenders have often used long follow-up periods – Soothill and Gibbens (1978) followed up a group of 174 sex offenders for 22 years – but reconviction rates remain significantly below the average for all offenders. Of course, interpreting this reconviction data is fraught with complexity – for example, serious offenders are older by the time they are released and have mostly spent long periods in prison or hospital; attention paid to the risk they pose (during detention and following release) may help prevent reoffending; and the fact they have been released at all (in the case of indeterminate sentences or hospitalisation) means they have been judged (by parole boards or clinicians) to be the better bets.

Campbell (1995), in an edited collection, provides a useful review of progress on the prediction of interpersonal violence in relation to sex offenders, child abusers and domestic violence. Limandri and Sheridan (1995) contribute an informative summary of clinical approaches to prediction in America – these have clearly become somewhat defensive, under threats of legal action from victims should predictions prove wrong. Although Milner and Campbell (1995) advise clinicians to use statistical predictions in their practice, they also point out the lack of thoroughly validated predictors. They present some evidence on the use of the Index of Spouse Abuse scale (Hudson and McIntosh 1981) but conclude there was insufficient evidence of its stability in use over time and different populations. A revised version, the Partner Abuse Scales (Hudson 1990), has now been marketed with claims of good reliability but (as yet) little supporting research evidence. A growing commercial interest in the production of patented scales seems to be a barrier to thorough independent validity testing. So, even in relation to the most prevalent offence covered in Campbell's review, work on statistical prediction devices has not yet produced reliable instruments for routine use by practitioners.

Moving on to consider prediction and sexual offending, it must be noted that in this area there is currently particular confusion about prevalence and the relationship between offending and conviction. Abel *et al.'s* (1987) study, which reported startlingly high rates of undetected offences admitted by convicted sex offenders, has led practitioners in this field to adopt a pessimistic view. Barker and Morgan (1993) and Fisher (1994) have both warned that those dramatic findings may be unrepresentative and other studies have reported much lower rates of undetected offending (see for example Beckett *et al.* 1994). When a calmer climate allows more careful comparisons with other types of offending, there may prove to be less difference in the ratio of undetected to detected offending than Abel *et al.'s* (1987) study indicated. Reconviction rates may command as much (or rather equally little) credence in this field as in others. Since sex offenders (like other serious offenders) have low rates of reconviction prediction attempts again face the difficulties of low base rates.

In relation to sex offending, clinical predictions of 'dangerousness' have predominated – Marshall and Barbaree (1989) provide a full account of assessment processes in their Canadian treatment programmes and Beckett *et al.* (1994) describe clinical assessment processes used in Britain. Less work has been done on statistical prediction. Fisher (1994) reports that Abel *et al.* (1988) claimed 86 per cent success in predicting outcome over a one year follow-up using five factors. Quinsey *et al.* (1995) have more recently produced a prediction device using a sample of 178 male rapists and child molesters, 28 per cent of whom were reconvicted for sexual offences over an average 50 months' 'opportunity to offend'. Many factors were found to be associated with sexual reconvictions including prior convictions, never having married, previous incarcerations, some victim characteristics, psychopathy ratings and a deviance score (based on phallometric testing). Using a method similar to RPS, the scale constructed correctly 'predicted' outcome in 77 per cent of cases, a level of accuracy strikingly similar to other criminological prediction devices. Quinsey *et al.* (1995) suggest their scale is good enough to be used not as one factor amongst others, but 'to anchor clinical judgement by having the clinician start with an actuarial estimate of risk and then to alter it by examining dynamic variables such as treatment outcome and intensity and quality of supervision' (p.132).

However, they warn it could not be applied to dissimilar offender populations. It should also be noted that its 'success' was on its construction sample and 'shrinkage' might have been considerable in a validation sample. It was also constructed on a much smaller sample than other researchers have considered adequate for the valid application of statistical procedures. Clearly much work remains to be done if a statistical reconviction predictor is to be developed for use with sex offenders.

To conclude this review of prediction studies on 'dangerousness' we turn specifically to 'mentally disordered offenders'. Serious crimes committed by the mentally ill have been a particular focus of media concern in Britain in recent years. Formal inquiries have been made mandatory whenever a homicide has been committed by a person with a history of contact with mental health services and this has produced a series of inquiry reports (see Reith 1997 for some examples) reminiscent of the child protection inquiries which have so influenced social work practice. The link between violence and mental disorder has been controversial for many years. Monahan and Steadman (1983), in a review of over 200 studies, concluded that once other factors were taken into account there was little association between violence and mental disorder. However, Monahan (1993) has since retracted this conclusion and now argues that 'mental disorder may be a robust and significant risk factor for the occurrence of violence' (p.299). However, he continues to suggest its contribution is modest in comparison with other factors and therefore mental health status 'makes at best a trivial contribution to the overall level of violence in society' (p.300). The emerging research consensus therefore supports a conclusion likely to be drawn from practice – that only a small minority of mentally ill people pose any significant risk of violence but a significant minority of incidents of serious violence involve people whose characteristics include some mental health problems.

Whether someone convicted of serious violence is classified as a 'mentally disordered offender' depends on many chance factors and Murray (1989) suggests there is no clear distinction between such offenders held in prisons and offender-patients sent instead to special hospitals. He identified 12 British follow-up studies of mentally disordered offenders, most of which did not attempt to construct prediction scales. However, Payne and others (1974) did construct a scale from data on 334 restricted patients discharged from NHS hospitals (during 1963/64) within one year of admission. The factors predictive of reoffending included previous convictions, admission for dishonesty offences and psychopathic diagnosis. Soothill, Way and Gibbens (1980) used this scale on a sample of 220 male restricted patients, followed up for between five and nine years after release, and found it showed quite good discrimination between those reconvicted and those not. Copas and Whiteley (1976) devised a prediction model from a study of 100 male 'psychopaths' discharged from Henderson Hospital and found it applied well to a second sample of discharged patients. They found marriage, good education and a good employment record diminished the incidence of reconviction. Black and Spinks (1985) sought to construct prediction devices using data from earlier research in which they followed up (for five years) all 128 men released from Broadmoor directly into the community between 1960 and 1965. Nearly half had been convicted of homicide but only 10 per cent committed further serious assaults (none had committed a homicide in the follow-up period, though two did subsequently). They found several factors predictive of reconviction – previous convictions, property or assault offences, age, less time in Broadmoor, psychopathic diagnosis, serving a fixed sentence, strangers as victims, emotional disturbance, impulsiveness and extroversion. The scale they devised to 'predict' further assaults proved unsuccessful – it predicted 'success' well but picked out less than half those who committed further assaults.

Murray's (1989) Home Office review did not identify a usable prediction device in relation to mentally disordered offenders and was pessimistic about the prospects for progress. He advocated more research on 'models based on the logical manipulation of expert knowledge (supplemented by actuarial data) in a rule based model such as is used in modern expert systems' (p.45).

More work has been done on reconviction predictors in America, much of it focused on mentally disordered offenders and resulting in the do or die MacArthur Study (Steadman *et al.* 1994) whose outcome may or may not provide a spur to the use of statistical prediction in this difficult field.

Criminological prediction research evaluated

What then are the strengths and weaknesses of this body of research? Some of the researchers' own reservations have already been noted and some have identified weaknesses requiring further research (see the lists from Farrington and Tarling 1985c and Monahan and Steadman 1994 cited earlier), much of which remains to be done. Here, I will focus specifically on how immediately useful this research is to social work agencies. Only two areas stand out as having been extensively researched – prediction of reconviction amongst known offenders and prediction of serious violence by mentally disordered offenders. In all other areas relevant to social work it would be fair to conclude that research evidence on statistical risk prediction is as yet skimpy or non-existent, and much work remains to be done to establish a usable knowledge base.

Prediction of reconviction amongst known offenders provides the strongest body of research evidence, backed by long-term experience of making some use of prediction scores in parole decision making in this country and the USA. The strengths of this research can be summarised briefly:

- a broad measure of agreement has been established

- a variety of predictor variables have been tested; it would not be difficult to extract from the literature, for a particular purpose, a list of factors likely to be strongly associated with reconviction

- some studies have used large samples, allowing fairly high degrees of statistical reliability to be achieved

- studies have tested different techniques for combining predictors on the same data sets and agreed that simple techniques produce more generalisable prediction instruments (it remains to be seen how the statistical modelling technique used by Copas *et al.* 1996 fares in such tests)

- a number of devices have already been produced which can predict reconviction amongst known offenders significantly more accurately than chance

- devices can achieve overall accuracy rates between 70 and 80 per cent but there then appears to be a barrier to more accurate prediction not yet overcome by research.

From a practice perspective there remain crucial weaknesses in the research evidence, even in this best-researched area. Amongst them are the following:

1. A prediction device offering 80 per cent accuracy is usable to underpin expert judgement or for evaluative research but is not ethically acceptable as a main or sole ingredient of decision making. Prediction devices cannot yet, and probably never will, take the uncertainty out of risk assessment.

2. Most research has focused on reconviction rather than reoffending. It is surprising that criminologists, who should have known better, have relied on such a weak outcome measure for so long – a charge of professional laziness seems appropriate. Amongst the main problems identified with

reconviction rates (Lloyd *et al.* 1994) are that only about 3 per cent of offences result in the cautioning or conviction of an identified offender; self-report research emphasises that both known offenders and (as yet) unconvicted people admit lots of undetected offences; delays between offence commission and conviction complicate any follow-up period used; most studies have treated reconviction as a binary phenomena ignoring seriousness, frequency and time at risk, and also the fact that many offences may be dealt with at one court appearance for sentencing (usually used as a proxy for reconviction). Other confounding factors may also be significant – not all reconvictions are just; known offenders may experience discriminatory policing; and offenders who learn to become better criminals (or police informers) will be under-represented amongst reconvictions. Credible studies now need to follow the example of more recent work (Steadman *et al.* 1994, Dobash *et al.* 1996) by trying to draw reoffending information from self-report studies and other sources (family, friends and/or victims) as well as official records.

3. Existing research suffers from another sort of professional laziness – 'predictive studies' are almost all retrospective. Here researchers share responsibility with the funders and users of research; unwillingness to pay for more careful prospective studies and impatience for results (however flawed) reinforce the researcher's preference for quick and easy studies. There is now a need for well-designed prospective studies and the patience to await their findings.

4. Although the research has included a range of variables, prediction devices have ended up using a very limited range of demographic and criminal history factors. These have been called 'static predictors' (Monahan and Steadman 1994) – there is nothing the offender or others can do to change the predicted level of risk. Prediction devices therefore lend themselves to a pessimistic air of inevitability and do not help with either risk reduction or risk management. They lend credence to penal notions such as selective incapacitation and can perpetuate past disadvantage and discrimination. Insufficient criminological research has been done on risk

factors which can be worked upon positively and it is encouraging to see this being taken seriously elsewhere (Steadman *et al.* 1994).

5. Since prediction devices can lend an air of scientific respectability to pessimistic prejudices ('give a dog a bad name'), there is a particular ethical duty on researchers to ensure they carry a robust 'health warning' to policy makers, who are only too likely to abuse them. While many researchers have done this in the past, there now seems a trend either to give policy makers what they want for immediate use (Copas *et al.* 1996) or sacrifice ethical principles to commercial interests in order to 'sell' a device as the best on the market.

6. As in many areas of research, studies have been uncoordinated and patchy, with a lack of replication and validation studies. A more coordinated research effort could, by now, have produced 'best practice' reconviction predictors for various purposes.

7. As in many other areas of criminological research, inadequate attention has been given to women offenders. Most research concerns only male offenders (though this is not always specified).

8. The way 'race' should be handled in reconviction predictors also remains unresolved. The spectre of selective incapacitation on grounds of 'race' still haunts the American research (see Petersilia and Turner 1987) and needs to be faced by British researchers.

9. The latest developments (for example, Copas *et al.* 1996) have started to move beyond mere occurrence of reconviction to pay attention to its seriousness. Looking back, it seems incredible that so little attention has been paid to distinguishing serious reconvictions from the majority of offences. Attention is also now being paid to survival times and the rate of reoffending. Future studies need to take these issues into account but must use a more satisfactory definition of 'serious' reconviction than the one adopted by Copas *et al.* (1996).

10. Researchers associated with prediction studies seem fixated on numerical end products (lending support to the feminist observation 'boys like

numbers'). Given the degree of imprecision in all scales devised so far, and the fact that probabilities apply to groups of offenders not individuals, more realistic end products would use a few broad categories (such as high, medium or low risk) rather than attaching misleadingly precise percentage risks to individual offenders. Unfortunately the latest British scheme (Copas *et al.* 1996) seems to be heading in the opposite direction.

11. Researchers have shown surprisingly little interest in the people who confound their prediction scores – they have been treated merely as 'errors' and surely deserve better. Those who 'succeed' despite a gloomy reconviction score are the group most interesting to probation and youth justice services. Are they really 'successes' who have not reoffended or merely 'successes' in avoiding detection? If they have not reoffended, why not? What worked for them? Are there any lessons to be learnt which can apply to others? The groups who 'fail' where success was predicted also merit further investigation – what happened to them? It seems indicative of the rather narrow focus of some researchers that so little effort has been devoted to such intriguing questions.

12. Finally, the fascination with statistical prediction has deflected attention from other research interests. For instance, few recent studies have bothered to compare statistical prediction with expert judgement. Clearly risk prediction instruments are only of value if they are significantly more accurate than unaided staff judgement. There are some intriguing hints in the research that the expert judgement of probation officers is rather good in relation to some issues (see for instance Bale 1989; Roberts 1989; Wilkinson 1994). Prospective studies should test expert judgements against prediction devices and more research is needed on the factors which affect such judgements.

It would clearly be possible from the weaknesses listed to construct a lengthy agenda for further research on reconviction predictors. If they are to be used directly as an aid to decision making by probation officers, courts, prison staff or parole boards then there is clearly an urgent obligation to rectify the most obvious deficiencies. A safer conclusion would be that even 'state of the art' devices are too error prone to offer a sound basis for decision making. Research should therefore focus on making them sufficiently reliable and generalisable for three uses:

- researching the relative impact of different measures
- monitoring expert decision making in ways which provide extra safeguards
- as one underpinning for expert judgement.

In the current state of knowledge, routine use of a general reconviction predictor by staff at any stage in the criminal justice process may place too much reliance on its accuracy and encourage an unhelpfully pessimistic, defensive practice with offenders.

One of the ironies in reconviction prediction seems to be that where accuracy matters most (where public safety from serious physical and psychological harm is at risk) the technology of statistical risk assessment is at its weakest. The over-riding difficulties of predicting rare events have not yet been overcome despite a considerable research effort. The best devices yet constructed still have high error rates and, if relied upon, would put at risk both public safety (by failing to predict some offenders as still dangerous) and civil liberties (by attributing dangerousness to many more people than will eventually prove to be so). The MacArthur Study (Steadman *et al.* 1994) is an impressive attempt to improve our knowledge in predicting violence amongst mentally disordered offenders. It remains to be seen whether it will achieve its objective to allow more accurate risk assessment. If it does so, then an instrument devised in the USA would need to be revalidated for use here. It focused on hospitalised offender-patients and a comparable exercise would clearly be justified in relation to imprisoned offenders. It is easier to mount such studies in the USA where size ensures that even rare events are numerous enough to allow use of large samples. In Britain, studies of similar size would need to use whole populations of offenders imprisoned or hospitalised for serious offences. However, the human costs of failures surely justify expenditure on large-scale, high-quality research. It might also indicate that government was really interested in improving public protection rather than allocating blame. Whatever the quality of research, it seems unlikely that the prediction of serious offending will ever reach the level of precision necessary to form the main element in criminal justice or psychiatric decision making. A more realistic aim may be that proposed by Quinsey *et al.* (1995) – a prediction device good enough to act as an anchor for clinical or expert judgement.

Messages for social work

Similar limitations have been encountered in applying statistical prediction devices to other areas of social work interest, though research has been less extensive. Their use in the mental health field, to estimate risks of violence, reoffending and self-harm, has already been reviewed here or elsewhere in this volume (see Chapter 6). The other field in which a substantial body of knowledge already exists is the prediction of physical child abuse.

Corby (1996) argues that child abuse risk assessments take place at three stages – attempts at preventive screening amongst general populations; initial assessments once parents have been reported and are under investigation; and assessments of the risk of further abuse when subsequent decisions are being made to return children home or remove them from the register (assessments might also be appropriate, of course, in relation to the risk of abuse while a child is in public care). He cites three research studies dealing with preventive screening (Kempe and Kempe 1978, Lealman *et al.* 1983, Browne and Saqi 1988) but concludes: 'Although it is possible to predict many parents who turn out to abuse their children physically (between two-thirds and three-quarters), in the process a large number of non-abusing parents are included in the prediction' (Corby 1996, p.18). In Browne and Saqi's (1988) study, for instance, only 6 per cent of the parents identified as high risk proved to be abusers in a two-year follow-up. These findings, of course, echo those of criminology in relation to predicting low-incidence events.

In a recent European study, Agathanos-Georgopolou and Browne (1997) compared the characteristics of 197 physically abused children and their families with those of 163 non-abused children. The 118 variables studied yielded 15 predictive factors which were grouped as:

- *high* (child hygiene poor on referral, parent's mental health, poor relationship between parents, adverse life experiences in parents, mother strictly disciplined as a child)

- *medium* (adverse recent life events for the parents, child not with both natural parents, mother relies on nobody when in crisis, father unemployed or in unsteady employment, mother under 21 at child's birth)
- *low* (child's delayed psychomotor development, child had other illnesses prior to referral for abuse, child not breast fed, parents expect immediate obedience, parental absence prior to referral).

These factors were combined into a predictive device using a simple point scoring approach (as in the Burgess tradition within criminological research). This 'predictor' correctly placed over 90 per cent of children in both the abused and non-abused groups.

Although claiming a higher degree of discrimination than earlier studies, Agathanos-Georgopolou and Browne pointed out that if their device was used to screen all children born in Greece (where they estimated about 60 of the 100,000 children born in any one year would later be identified as having been abused): '52 potential abusing families would be identified as High Risk and eight would be missed. However, 3998 non-abusing families would be incorrectly identified as High Risk ...' (p.730).

Thus only about 1 per cent of the cases identified as high risk would turn out to be abusing families, while 13 per cent of abuse cases would be missed by the screening process. Agathanos-Georgopolou and Browne argue that this would at least leave the protective services searching for their needle in a smaller haystack. Again these results have striking similarities to the criminological research. The study also illustrates that researchers in other fields are failing to learn from what would now be seen as weaknesses in the early criminological research. Like the Gluecks (1950), Agathanos-Georgopolous and Browne used equal-sized experimental and control groups while studying a low-incidence event, used criteria which involved researcher interpretation in a situation where the researchers knew which families belonged to which group, and made no attempt to test out their predictor on a validation sample. The prediction device was developed using smaller samples than would have been considered appropriate for statistical analysis in the criminological research. As with prediction of offending in the general population, screening devices for physical child abuse seem likely to remain very imprecise tools for social work.

Milner (1995) instead recommends using statistical prediction in Corby's (1996) second stage – during investigations of those parents reported for suspected abuse. He points out that American research indicates abuse is considered present in between 35 and 50 per cent of such referrals, so screening at this stage avoids the problems associated with predicting low incidence events and can take place in near-ideal conditions. He reports that standard pschological testing has produced mixed results in predicting abuse in such cases and therefore favours the development of specific prediction devices. He identifies only two devices which offer adequate reliability and validity data – the Michigan Screening Profile of Parenting (Helfer, Hofmeister and Schneider 1978) and his own device, the Child Abuse Potential Inventory (Milner 1986, 1990), which he proceeds to describe in detail. He cites a range of studies which have found his device to yield correct classifications of between 70 and 90 per cent. His claims for this device (which is of course patented and commercially available) are similar to the claims made currently for devices used to predict reoffending amongst known offenders. Milner (1995) argues for the use of such statistical prediction devices alongside other assessment methods in child abuse cases (such as structured clinical interviewing, third party interviews and direct observation), rather than as a replacement for them.

There seems to have been less research interest so far in Corby's (1996) third stage of risk assessment – risk of further abuse in cases of established abuse – where clinical (or expert) assessment seems as yet unchallenged. Overall, Corby (1996) concludes that although some practical use has been made of statistical prediction devices in America (Wald and Woolverton 1990; English and Pecora 1994; Milner 1995), in Britain more reliance has so far been placed on clinical judgement aided by instruments such as Greenland's (1987) checklist or the Department of Health's 167-question guide (1988).

So what conclusions might social work practitioners draw from all this? The most obvious is that prediction research raises complex issues and does not offer a 'quick fix' to intractable problems in risk assessment. It is also clear that, even in the best-researched areas, many problems remain to be overcome. However, the body of knowledge already available about offenders provides a base on which other research can build – there is no need to reinvent this particular wheel (a lesson which as we have seen some studies have ignored)! Statistical prediction is more likely to be useful in relation to common risks rather than the rare events (such as child abuse deaths) which cause social workers and their agencies most difficulty. To be at all useful prediction devices need to do substantially better than both chance and expert prediction – it may well be advisable to start by checking how accurate your 'experts' already are! If they are predicting outcomes (in relation to 50/50 risks) correctly in more than 75 per cent of cases then the evidence suggests you will struggle to arrive at a statistical prediction device which does much better.

Beware hawkers! Statistical prediction devices need to be thoroughly researched. Expect to be able to check very carefully accuracy claims. Don't be bamboozled by statistician's gobbledygook – if they can't express accuracy in simple terms, they are probably hiding something. Expect to see evidence that a device has been used at least on a validation sample without losing much predictive accuracy – preferably expect evidence it has been used on new samples and proved generalisable. Don't expect to buy a device off the peg – unless recently validated on a population very similar to yours, expect to have to test it on a reasonably large sample of your own cases before deciding whether it has validity in your situation. Be alert to commercial exploitation – there now seem to be academic and social work entrepreneurs willing to profit from human misery by developing patented devices. Such devices may need particularly careful evaluation since accuracy claims may be tainted by commercial interest. Faced with such a sales pitch, it may be worth exploring the relevant literature since similar devices may well be on offer free!

Finally, be realistic about why you want to use a statistical risk predictor and what you might gain. They can usefully strengthen your evaluative research and therefore help develop good practice. They may be useful for monitoring practice and providing checks on expert decision making (for instance, are your case conferences routinely keeping on child protection registers children statistically rated low risk?). If introduced carefully, they may provide social workers with a useful starting point in making risk judgements. But they will not take the uncertainty out of risky situations.

References

Abel, G., Becker, J., Cunningham-Rathner, J. and Rouleau, J. (1987) 'Self-reported sex crimes of 561 non-incarcerated paraphiliacs.' *Journal of Interpersonal Violence* 2, 6, 3–25.

Abel, G., Mittelman, M., Becker, J., Rathner, J. and Rouleau, J. (1988) 'Predicting child molesters' response to treatment.' *Annals of the New York Academy of Sciences* 528, 223–34.

Agathanos-Georgopolou, H. and Browne, K. (1997) 'The prediction of child maltreatment in Greek families.' *Child Abuse and Neglect 21,* 8, 721–35.

Alaszewski, A., Harrison, L. and Manthorpe, J. (eds) (1998) *Risk, Health and Welfare.* Buckingham: Open University Press.

Bale, D. (1989) 'The Cambridgeshire risk of custody scale.' In G. Mair (ed) *Risk Prediction and Probation.* London: Home Office.

Barker, M. and Morgan, R. (1993) *Sex Offenders: A Framework for the Evaluation of Community Based Treatment.* London: Home Office.

Beckett, R., Beech, A., Fisher, D. and Fordham, A. (1994) *Community-based Treatment for Sex Offenders.* London: Home Office.

Black, T. and Spinks, P. (1985) 'Predicting outcomes of mentally disordered and dangerous offenders.' In D. Farrington and R. Tarling (eds) *Prediction in Criminology.* Albany, New York: State University of New York Press.

Bluglass, R. (1988) 'Psychiatric approaches to aggression and violence.' *Issues in Criminology and Legal Psychology 12,* 24–33.

Browne, K. and Saqi, S. (1988) 'Approaches to screening for child abuse and neglect.' In K. Browne, C. Davies and P. Stratton (eds) *Early Prediction and Prevention of Child Abuse.* Chichester: Wiley.

Burgess, E. (1928) 'Factors determining success or failure on parole.' In A. Bruce, A. Harno, E. Burgess and J. Landesco (eds) *The Workings of the Indeterminate-Sentence Law and the Parole System in Illinois.* Springfield, Illinois: Illinois State Board of Parole.

Campbell, J. (ed) (1995) *Assessing Dangerousness: Violence by Sexual Offenders, Batterers and Child Abusers.* London: Sage.

Carlisle Report (1988) *The Parole System in England and Wales: Report of the Review Committee.* London: HMSO.

Copas, J., Marshall, P. and Tarling, R. (1996) *Predicting Reoffending for Discretionary Conditional Release.* London: Home Office.

Copas, J. and Whiteley, J. (1976) 'Predicting success in the treatment of psychopaths.' *British Journal of Psychiatry 129,* 388–92.

Corby, B. (1993) *Child Abuse: Towards a Knowledge Base.* Buckingham: Open University Press.

Corby, B. (1996) 'Risk assessment in child protection work.' In H. Kemshall and J. Pritchard (eds) *Good Practice in Risk Assessment and Risk Management 1.* London: Jessica Kingsley Publishers.

Department of Health (1988) *Protecting Children: A Guide for Social Workers Undertaking a Comprehensive Assessment.* London: HMSO.

Dobash, R., Dobash, R., Cavanagh, K. and Lewis, R. (1996) *Research Evaluation of Programmes for Violent Men.* Edinburgh: Scottish Office.

English, D. and Pecora, P. (1994) 'Risk assessment as a practice in child protection services.' *Child Welfare 53,* 451–73.

Farrington, D. (1985) 'Predicting self-reported and official delinquency.' In D. Farrington and R. Tarling (eds) *Prediction in Criminology.* Albany, New York: State University of New York Press.

Farrington, D. and Tarling, R. (eds) (1985a) *Prediction in Criminology.* Albany, New York: State University of New York Press.

Farrington, D. and Tarling, R. (1985b) 'Criminological prediction: An introduction.' In D. Farrington and R. Tarling (eds) *Prediction in Criminology.* Albany, New York: State University of New York Press.

Farrington, D. and Tarling, R. (1985c) 'Criminological prediction: The way forward.' In D. Farrington and R. Tarling (eds) *Prediction in Criminology.* Albany, New York: State University of New York Press.

Fisher, D. (1994) 'Adult sex offenders: Who are they? Why and how do they do it?' In T. Morrison, M. Erooga and R. Beckett (eds) *Sexual Offending Against Children: Assessment and Treatment of Male Abusers.* London: Routledge.

Floud, J. and Young, W. (1981) *Dangerousness and Criminal Justice.* London: Heinemann.

Glueck, S. and Glueck, E. (1950) *Unraveling Juvenile Delinquency.* Cambridge, Massachusetts: Harvard University Press.

Gottfredson, S. and Gottfredson, D. (1985) 'Screening for risk among parolees: Policy, practice and method.' In D. Farrington and R. Tarling (eds) *Prediction in Criminology.* Albany, New York: State University of New York Press.

Gottfredson, D. and Tonry, M. (eds) (1987) *Prediction and Classification: Criminal Justice Decision Making.* Chicago, Illinois: University of Chicago Press.

Gottfredson, D., Wilkins, L. and Hoffman, P. (1978) *Guidelines for Parole and Sentencing.* Lexington: Heath.

Greenland, C. (1987) *Preventing CAN Deaths: An International Study of Deaths Due to Child Abuse and Neglect.* London: Tavistock.

Helfer, R., Hoffmeister, J. and Schneider, C. (1978) *MSPP: A Manual for the Use of the Michigan Screening Profile of Parenting.* Boulder, Colorado: Test Analysis and Development Corporation.

Hill, G. (1985) 'Predicting recidivism using institutional measures.' In D. Farrington and R. Tarling (eds) *Prediction in Criminology.* Albany, New York: State University of New York Press.

Hudson, W. (1990) *Partner Abuse Scales.* Tempe: Walmyr.

Hudson, W. and McIntosh, S. (1981) 'The assessment of spouse abuse: Two quantifiable dimensions.' *Journal of Marriage and the Family 43,* 873–85.

Kempe, R. and Kempe, C. (1978) *Child Abuse.* London: Fontana.

Kemshall, H., Parton, N., Walsh, M. and Waterson, J. (1997) 'Concepts of risk in relation to organizational structure and functioning within the personal social services and probation.' *Social Policy and Administration 31,* 3, 213–32.

Lealman, G., Haigh, D., Philips, J., Stone, J. and Ord-Smith, C. (1983) 'Prediction and prevention of child abuse – an empty hope?' *Lancet,* 1423–4.

Limandri, B. and Sheridan, D. (1995) 'Prediction of intentional interpersonal violence: An introduction.' In J. Campbell (ed) *Assessing Dangerousness: Violence by Sexual Offenders, Batterers and Child Abusers.* London: Sage.

Livermore, J., Malmquist, C. and Meehl, P. (1968) 'On the justifications for civil commitment.' *University of Pennysylvania Law Review 117,* 75–96.

Lloyd, C., Mair, G. and Hough, M. (1994) *Explaining Reconviction Rates: A Critical Analysis.* London: HMSO.

Mannheim, H. and Wilkins, L. (1955) *Prediction Methods in Relation to Borstal Training.* London: HMSO.

Marshall, W. and Barbaree, H. (1989) 'Sexual violence.' In K. Howells and C. Hollin (eds) *Clinical Approaches to Violence.* Chichester: Wiley.

Martinson, R. (1974) 'What works? Questions and answers about penal reform.' *The Public Interest 35,* 22–54.

Meehl, P. (1954) *Clinical versus Statistical Prediction.* Minneapolis, Minnesota: University of Minnesota Press.

Milner, J. (1986) *The Child Abuse Potential Inventory: Manual.* (2nd edition) Webster: Psytec.

Milner, J. (1990) *An Interpretive Manual for the Child Abuse Potential Inventory.* Webster: Psytec.

Milner, J. (1995) 'Physical child abuse assessment: Perpetrator assessment.' In J. Campbell (ed) *Assessing Dangerousness: Violence by Sexual Offenders, Batterers and Child Abusers.* London: Sage.

Milner, J. and Campbell, J. (1995) 'Prediction issues for practitioners.' In J. Campbell (ed) *Assessing Dangerousness: Violence by Sexual Offenders, Batterers and Child Abusers.* London: Sage.

Monahan, J. (1981) *Predicting Violent Behaviour: An Assessment of Clinical Techniques.* Beverley Hills, CA: Sage.

Monahan, J. (1988) 'Risk assessment of violence among the mentally disordered: Generalising useful knowledge.' *International Journal of Law and Psychiatry 11,* 249–57.

Monahan, J. (1993) 'Mental disorder and violence: Another look.' In S. Hodgins (ed) *Mental Disorder and Crime.* London: Sage.

Monahan, J. and Steadman, H. (1983) 'Crime and mental disorder: An epidemiological approach.' In N. Morris and M. Tonry (eds) *Crime and Justice: An Annual Review of Research.* Chicago, IL: University of Chicago Press.

Monahan, J. and Steadman, H. (1994) 'Towards a rejuvenation of risk assessment research.' In J. Monahan and H. Steadman (eds) *Violence and Mental Disorder: Developments in Risk Assessment.* Chicago, Illinois: University of Chicago.

Mosteller, F. (1977) 'Assessing unknown numbers.' In W. Fairley and F. Mosteller (eds) *Statistics and Public Policy.* Reading: Addison-Wesley.

Murray, D. (1989) *Review of Research on Re-offending of Mentally Disordered Offenders.* London: Home Office.

Nuttall, C. *et al.* (1977) *Parole in England and Wales.* London: HMSO.

Payne, C., McCabe, S. and Walker, N. (1974) 'Predicting offender-patients' reconvictions.' *British Journal of Psychiatry 125,* 60–4.

Petersilia, J. and Turner, S. (1987) 'Guideline-based justice: Prediction and racial minorities.' In D. Gottfredson and M. Tonry (eds) *Prediction and Classification: Criminal Justice Decision Making.* Chicago, Illinois: University of Chicago Press.

Prins, H. (1986) *Dangerous Behaviour, the Law and Mental Disorder.* London: Tavistock.

Pritchard, D. (1979) 'Stable predictors of recidivism.' *Criminology 17,* 15–21.

Quinsey, V., Lalumiere, M., Rice, M. and Harris, G. (1995) 'Predicting sexual offences.' In J. Campbell (ed) *Assessing Dangerousness: Violence by Sexual Offenders, Batterers and Child Abusers.* London: Sage.

Reith, M. (1997) 'Mental health inquiries: Implications for probation practice.' *Probation Journal 44,* 2, 66–70.

Roberts, C. (1989) 'The potential of predictive instruments to aid clinical judgement: The case of probation officers and their Social Enquiry Reports.' In G. Mair (ed) *Risk Prediction and Probation.* London: Home Office.

Sawyer, J. (1966) 'Measurement and prediction, clinical and statistical.' *Psychological Bulletin 66,* 178–200.

Simon, F. (1971) *Prediction Methods in Criminology.* London: HMSO.

Soothill, K. and Gibbens, T. (1978) 'Recidivism of sexual offenders – A reappraisal.' *British Journal of Criminology 18,* 267–76.

Soothill, K., Way, C. and Gibbens, T. (1980) 'Subsequent dangerousness among compulsory hospital patients.' *British Journal of Criminology 20,* 289–95.

Steadman, H. (1982) 'A situational approach to violence.' *International Journal of Law and Psychiatry 5,* 171–86.

Steadman, H., Monahan, J., Appelbaum, P., Grisso, T., Mulvey, E., Roth, L., Robbins, P. and Klassen, D. (1994) 'Designing a new generation of risk assessment research.' In J. Monahan and H. Steadman (eds) *Violence and Mental Disorder: Developments in Risk Assessment.* Chicago, Illinois: University of Chicago.

Thornton, D. and Speirs, S. (1985) 'Predicting absconding from young offender institutions.' In D. Farrington and R. Tarling (eds) *Prediction in Criminology.* Albany, New York: State University of New York Press.

Tonry, M. (1987) 'Prediction and classification; Legal and ethical issues.' In D. Gottfredson and M. Tonry (eds) *Prediction and Classification: Criminal Justice Decision Making.* Chicago, Illinois: University of Chicago Press.

Wadsworth, M. (1978) 'Delinquency prediction and its uses.' *International Journal of Mental Health 7,* 43–62.

Wald, M. and Woolverton, M. (1990) 'Risk assessment: The Emperor's new clothes.' *Child Welfare 69,* 483–511.

Ward, D. (1987) *The Validity of the Reconviction Score.* London: HMSO.

West, D. (1982) *Delinquency: Its Roots, Careers and Prospects.* London: Heinemann.

Wilkins, L. (1985) 'The politics of prediction.' In D. Farrington and R. Tarling (eds) *Prediction in Criminology.* Albany, New York: State University of New York Press.

Wilkinson, J. (1994) 'Using a reconviction predictor to make sense of reconviction rates in the probation service.' *British Journal of Social Work 24,* 4, 461–73.

Willbanks, W. (1985) 'Predicting failure on parole.' In D. Farrington and R. Tarling (eds) *Prediction in Criminology.* Albany, New York: State University of New York Press.

CHAPTER 4

Social Services Staff
Risks They Face and Their Dangerousness to Others

Peter Burke

There have been an apparently increasing number of enquiries into tragedies involving people for whom the social services were providing help. Some were children subject to abuse, others people with mental health problems, and yet others lived in residential homes. These events lead to a questioning of the professional responsibility of the social service staff and whether, in some ways, social workers are a danger to their clients.

There are a number of ways in which social workers may endanger their clients. Those which receive the most public attention are acts of physical or sexual abuse perpetrated by staff who have a responsibility to provide care to the people they abuse. The victims have been both children and adults living either in residential homes or foster placements. These events have shocked both the public and the profession and have led to various procedures to try to ensure that people who have any history of abusive behaviour cannot obtain positions as social service carers. There are, however, less obvious forms of danger which arise from what may be errors of professional judgement. It is with this type of danger that this chapter is concerned although, as will become clear, there is little research on which to draw.

I shall start by clarifying the meaning of the concepts 'risk' and 'dangerousness' in relation to professional practice in social services before considering issues internal to the profession. I shall complement illustrations from the literature by reference to my own research (Burke 1990) which illustrates the dual responsibility of social workers; they have to make assessments within the context of agency requirements and at the same time provide support for the dangerous individual when they may have made an active intervention such as removing a child from what they assess to be a dangerous parent.

Ideas about risk and dangerousness are not new. The assessment of risk to and by users is well documented (see for example Kemshall and Pritchard 1997; Manthorpe *et al.* 1997); equally the concept of dangerousness has been discussed at some length by Dale *et al.* (1986) in relation to families but is also found in more diverse areas ranging from a mid-nineteenth-century study of 'the dangerous classes' of juveniles in prisons (Carpenter 1851) to problems with system dynamics (Land and Smart 1994). However, the fact that social services staff, in their daily activities, not only face risks from users but may themselves be a danger to users, changes the focus from the user to the professional as a potential source of danger. The social work profession may be a danger to the public. It is part of the professional responsibility of the social worker to make assessments of risk for users. Sometimes these assessments will be based on poor judgements and lead to inappropriate action. The risk of such behaviour may be exacerbated by the fact that the situations about which judgements have to be made are often very stressful for workers as well as for users. Part of the stress is caused by the fact that some assessments may result in actions which have extremely serious consequences for the people whom they are intended to help.

The potential for mistakes is compounded by poor professional training, excessive and conflicting pressures at work and indecision and delays in making decisions. Some of these difficulties may arise from a lack of clarity about who is responsible and from inadequate support and line management for front-line staff. It has also been suggested by Thomas (1994) commenting on an argument advanced by Valentine (1994) that the constant, usually hostile media scrutiny of social work practice creates a situation in which social services feel under threat and respond by introducing more control and more regulations which may at times hamper professional judgement.

The concepts of risk and dangerousness require a more detailed examination before we can identify a model for locating them in social work practice.

Risk

The Oxford English Dictionary defines 'risk' as: 'To hazard, endanger; to expose to the chance of injury or loss'. Alaszewski *et al.* (1997) refer to their own earlier definition, which catches the essence of the dictionary definition: 'The possibility that a given course of action will not achieve its desired outcome but instead some undesirable situation will develop' (Alaszewski and Manthorpe 1991, p.277).

Day-to-day experiences inevitably involve some degree of risk, be they climbing the stairs, crossing the road or driving a car. Definitions of risk in professional practice differ little from the everyday sense. They reflect a degree of uncertainty about the outcome of some course of action. Assessing risk is concerned not just with what may happen following some intervention, but also about what might happen were no action to be taken. It should be recognised that once the outcome of previous risky decisions are known they can provide more certainty for the future (Manthorpe *et al.* 1997; Tindall 1997). Such learning from outcomes of risk taking minimises future risks for the user.

Dangerousness

The concept of dangerousness is illustrated by Dale *et al.* (1986) with reference to its use in psychiatric hospitals where a history of violent behaviour is used as an indicator of potential future violent behaviour. This illustrates the saying that the best predictor of future behaviour is past behaviour, but does not seem to allow for the possibility of change. In this example dangerousness means harming others and the harm may be intended or accidental. An example of unintentional dangerousness might be a parent who shakes a baby. He or she might explain that they did not know of the harmful consequences. Nevertheless the child is at risk of injury and the parent was a danger to the child. Professional workers may also be dangerous because they are ignorant. They may fail to take action or do so inappropriately because of a lack of professional knowledge.

A comment on dangerousness

When making an assessment social workers may sometimes have to balance a need for protection against the right of an individual to autonomy. For example, to arrange for the removal from home of a child apparently the subject of abuse affects the freedom of choice of both the parents and the child. Should either party object it will be seen by them as an infringement of their rights and perhaps of their liberty. Should the matter come to court, the social worker will be obliged to justify the removal on the grounds that it was in the 'best interests of the child'. This is itself an anything but clear test. There may be disagreement about what will be best for the child between all or any of the parties involved – the court, the parents, the child and the social worker. This potential for disagreement is fundamental to understanding the difficulties faced by social services workers when they try to find the best way to minimise the risks for a child. The social services need a way to identify risks in potentially dangerous situations so that a strong coherent case can be made in the face of possible disagreements.

When an action taken by a social service agency is seen as risky this implies that the desired outcome may not be achieved. Such a situation is not limited to child abuse cases; as the literature shows it may apply to those with learning difficulties and other user groups. Alaszewski and Manthorpe (1991) refer to Bentman and Barwood's (1990) work about people with learning difficulties and the risk analysis described by Brearley (1980) was about the admission of anyone to residential care.

Indicators of risk and danger

The identification of risk by inadequately tested predictive indicators is one way in which false positives are created. Parton (1986) illustrated this tendency when discussing the case of Jasmine Beckford, the four-year-old child who died after being physically abused by her stepfather. He referred to the work of Greenland (who identified 'high-risk' families as those with a number of factors including, for example, a mother under 24 years old, living with only one biological parent etc) to show that identifying risk through the presence of these factors was unsafe since they were developed from families where a child had been abused but it remained unknown how many non-abusing families may share the same factors. Nevertheless, social services staff were criticised for not identifying these so-called indicators of abuse in Jasmine Beckford's case and thus, it was said, under-reacting to the danger faced by the child. While it is a fact that 80 per cent of children killed by their parents have been abused previously, as Parton points out this indicator has not been tested on control groups and fails to follow basic sampling techniques. Thus a 'dangerous family' can only be recognised as dangerous after a violent act. The dangerousness can only serve as a predictor of dangerousness after it has already occurred.

As the Macdonalds argue in Chapter 1, a rare event like child murder is likely to be subject to the statistical fallacy of a false positive (see page 31). Some social workers may fail to recognise this phenomenon and may be putting their faith in invalid indicators. False positives in child abuse cases could lead to children coming in to care because too much reliance had been placed upon Greenland-type indicators. An example was the excessive and exclusive reliance on anal dilation as an indicator of sexual abuse in the Cleveland cases. It was criticised in the Butler Sloss Report (1988) because it was not sufficiently reliable evidence on which to instigate a Place of Safety Order and as a result of an over- reaction by health and social service staff a number of children were taken from their homes.

When an adult or child is said to be at risk the social services agency is under pressure to act quickly. This may make it impossible to undertake a full assessment if the person concerned would remain at risk during the assessment period. Were he or she to come to any harm the agency would face severe criticism for not having acted as soon as they were aware of the risk.

When public agencies take risks this should mean that the chances of a poor or unexpected outcome have been assessed as being lower than the chances of a favourable outcome. The chances can be measured in various ways. For example, a surgical procedure may have been found to have a success rate of say 95 per cent. Should it result in improved functioning this might be an acceptable level of risk. Were the level of success only 10 per cent the risk might well be unacceptable to both the surgeon and the patient. However if the alternative to operating were not just decreased functioning but a rapid death a 10 per cent chance might be considered by the patient to be worth taking. It should be noted that in this example the risks will be discussed with the person who is subject to them and in fact the operation will not take place without the patient's consent. In this example the possible consequences of the action were known.

Assessment: a case illustration

The case of Jason Mitchell illustrates the risk involved in making a professional assessment. Mr Mitchell was a restricted patient in Easton House at St. Clement's Hospital, Ipswich. He asked to leave the house one evening after a period of good behaviour and this was agreed to. He was expected back the same evening. He returned to the family home, killed a newly retired couple and then some days later killed his father. An inquiry, led by Louis Blom-Cooper (1996) reported that the killings were not considered preventable but had the case been managed differently the outcome might also have been different.

Clearly Mr Mitchell was dangerous, but the level of his dangerousness had not been correctly assessed. The inquiry suggested that a more precise assessment might have identified more of Mr Mitchell's difficulties, particularly if the various professionals involved had shared their views.

It seems likely that more precise assessments might be achieved if they are based on the views of all the professionals concerned. Vital signs might be spotted which could prevent harm to the public and the risk of professional negligence through omission reduced. Multiprofessional assessment may mean that different professionals have different opinions about risks of danger. This may present difficulties but it may mean that a wider range of issues are considered and the responsibility for the decision shared. Clearly it is preferable that agreement is reached rather than one profession exercising their legal authority. One way to reach agreement is to develop a model on which to base decisions. The 'locus of control model' offers such a possibility.

Identifying the locus of control

A central idea in social learning theory is that people explain their experiences in terms of what happens to them. What can happen to social service staff does not differ greatly from what happens to other people who, because, perhaps, of excessive stress in their lives, take a hasty decision based on poor information and with little understanding of the consequences. There is an assumption in social learning theory that abnormal behaviour (in this example due to stress) is no different from normal behaviour, both are based on the same factors and both can be modified (Brown and Christie 1981). Cognitive behaviour therapy contributes the recognition that the behaviour of one human being is influenced by and influences the behaviour of another. The cognitive behavioural therapist can point out the interactions which have negative outcomes and thus reinforce the desired change.

The idea of a locus of control suggests that control is viewed as either internal or external. Individuals who take responsibility for their own actions and see rewards as a consequence of their efforts are said to have an internal locus of control. Those who see situations and outcomes as outside their influence and who believe their lives are subject to the control of others have an external locus of control.

This idea of the locus of control can be applied to the assessment of dangerousness by social service staff. Clients who are considered to be dangerous are seen as having an internal control which has developed abnormally and is exhibited as violence towards others. The professional worker may try to replace this distorted locus of control by his or her authority – that is by substituting an external locus of control. Alternatively they may decide to remove any person who is assessed as being at risk from the dangerous individual. These decisions need to be based on a full assessment involving other professionals. This helps to guard against the risk of a dangerous client meeting a dangerous professional.

The dual responsibility of social workers

When dealing with dangerous situations or individuals social workers are in a difficult position because of their dual responsibility to assess the level of danger and also provide support for the person whom they have assessed as dangerous. Social workers have been trained in the belief that they should usually attempt to help their clients to remain in the community. They expect to follow the theories of normalisation and the ideology of care in the community. However, when they deal with what could be a dangerous situation or individual they may be torn between a wish to help the individual move towards a normal life, and a desire to 'play safe'. The problem is that risk to the worker and risk to the agency may mean different things. My own research illustrates the day-to-day situations faced by social workers.

My research

This was designed to explore risk in social work by looking at the nature of social work responses to the problems presented by clients. I analysed all the referrals to two area teams, in different parts of the country, over a two-year period. I developed three categories: service delivery, responses to risk and advisory. All referrals for residential accommodation, including reception of a child into care and placements in hostels or the provision of day care, were categorised as service delivery. All referrals of children or adults considered to be at risk were categorised as responses to risk. Requests for support of various kinds were categorised as advisory work.

The cases which were categorised as responses to risk did not fit either of the other categories. They were distinguished by an element of danger for either the client or the social worker. The two other categories comprised the basic response level required of social services. For the purposes of my study the original category was maintained to the end point at which an outcome decision was agreed, despite the fact that dangers might have become apparent during the course of the work. I did not always find it easy to decide on the categorisation but a close examination of the data helped. The social workers were asked to complete a questionnaire which included questions about the social worker and their involvement with the user as well as the recorded outcome at the time of closure. See Burke (1997) for details.

Outcome

Of all the cases, 312 were examined after they had been closed. A considerable number had either no resolution or only a partial resolution. In some cases there was disagreement between worker and supervisor as to whether the case should be closed and there the management decision prevailed. The results were analysed to find out whether there were differences between qualified and unqualified workers in relation to the status at closure. The findings are shown in Table 4.1.

Table 4.1 Outcomes of case closure decisions		
A. Worker Status	*Qualified workers*	*Unqualified workers*
Per cent of cases fully resolved	40%	31%
Per cent of cases partially resolved	36%	58%
B. Type of Care	*Service cases*	*Risk cases* *Advisory cases*
Per cent of cases not resolved	21%	30% 27%

The figures suggest that in a majority of cases there were some unresolved issues despite the fact that the case was closed. Such uncertainty represents some risk to the user (or possibly to others) since the worker ends his or her professional relationship thinking that more could, perhaps should, have been done and perhaps leaving the user feeling dissatisfied. This could compound any risk elements in the case and increase the risk of dangerousness to self or others.

The apparent finding that unqualified workers were less decisive in resolving cases is not statistically significant. Any explanation can be only speculative. Unqualified workers may not want to make what seem like premature decisions to end cases, or they may be allocated unresolvable cases, although this would not square with a policy of allocating more difficult cases to qualified workers. Alternatively it is possible that qualified workers were more focused in their interventions with users and able to reach outcome decisions. Unqualified staff may be more tentative in reaching firm closure decisions and may wait to be guided by their team leaders.

It also seemed that higher levels of supervision were associated with cases which had a less satisfactory outcome and thus also with risk cases. It is possible that increased supervision in risk cases was to ensure that no situations arose which could reflect adversely on the agency.

Conclusion

Risk could be defined as 'an agency measure of concern' and would thus indicate a responsibility and a duty towards the user. Risk cases seem to be complex and require considerable social work commitment and time to reach a satisfactory resolution. It may be necessary to separate risk work from crisis work. The nature of risk work uncovered in my research seems different from that which Beresford and Croft (1986) define as crisis. This was work which required a 'quick response'. My research suggested that an agency view of risk indicated a need for continuing worker involvement. It seems that risk and crisis are not identical; risk may require investigation and crisis a particular method of intervention. However risk work is associated with crisis and more research is required to tease out the connections and the differences.

In dealing with prediction and risk what is needed are indicators which identify when a situation is dangerous and which help to show how it might be avoided or prevented. A simple example is the child who unwittingly shakes a baby. If taught that such action is dangerous the behaviour might cease. Such teaching could take place after a dangerous incident or could be part of training programmes in good parenting.

It is easy to pin blame for tragedies on the social service workers and there are certainly some who lack the skills or knowledge to make adequate assessments of risk. Some staff also suffer from confusion about where their responsibility begins and ends. Nevertheless we need to bear in mind that, according to Macdonald, Sheldon and Gillespie's (1992) review of the research evidence, 75 per cent of social work interventions are classified as good, 17 per cent as mixed and 8 per cent as negative.

The front-line worker is responsible for assessing clients and offering an appropriate and skilled service to those in need. However some workers will find this difficult and some may not be able to distinguish between the different needs of different users. In such instances the skills of the worker need to be linked to the needs of the particular client. This requires skilled supervision, which will enable social workers to use their 'practice wisdom', allow a rigorous check on practice which, in turn will provide support for the worker and protection for the client.

References

Alaszewski, A., Walsh, M., Manthorpe, J. and Harrison, J. (1997) 'Managing risk in the city: The role of welfare professionals in managing risks arising from vulnerable individuals in cities.' *Health and Place 3,* 15–23.

Alaszewski, A. and Manthorpe, J. (1991) 'Literature review: Measuring and managing risk in social welfare.' *British Journal of Social Work, 21,* 277–90.

Bentman, J. and Barwood, A. (eds) (1990) *Services for People with Learning Difficulties.* Taunton: Somerset Social Services Department.

Beresford, P. and Croft, S. (1986) *Whose Welfare: Private Care or Public Service.* Brighton: Lewis Cohen Centre.

Blom-Cooper, L. (1996) *The Case of Jason Mitchell: Report of the Independent of the Inquiry.* London: Duckworth.

Brearley, P. (1980) 'A preliminary framework for risk analysis.' In P. Brearley, F. Hall, P. Gutridge, G. Jones and G. Roberts (eds) *Admission to Residential Care.* London: Tavistock Publications.

Brown, B.J. And Christie, C. (1981) *Social Learning Practice in Residential Care.* Oxford: Pergamon Press.

Burke, P. (1990) 'The fieldwork team response: An investigation into the relationship between client categories, referred problems and outcome.' *British Journal of Social Work 20,* 469–482.

Burke, P. (1997) 'Risk and supervision: Social work responses to referred user problems.' *British Journal of Social Work 27,* 115–129.

Butler-Sloss, Rt Hon Lord Justice E. (1988) *Report of the Inquiry into Child Abuse in Cleveland 1987.* London: HMSO.

Carpenter, M. (1851) *Reformatory Schools for the Children of the Perishing and Dangerous Classes and for Juvenile Offenders.* London: Gilpin.

Dale, P., Murray, D., Morrison, T. and Waters, J. (1986) *Dangerous Families: Assessment and Treatment of Child Abuse.* London: Tavistock Publications.

Kemshall, H. and Pritchard, J. (1997) *Good Practice in Risk Assessment and Risk Management 2.* London: Jessica Kingsley Publishers.

Lane, D.C. and Smart, C. (1994) 'Mad, bad and dangerous to know? The evolution, application and limitations of the 'generic structure' concept in system dynamics.' Working paper: no.161. London: City University Business School.

London Borough of Brent (1985) *A Child in Trust. A report of the Panel of Inquiry into the Circumstances Surrounding the Death of Jasmine Beckford.* London: Brent.

Macdonald, G., Sheldon, B. and Gillespie, J. (1992) 'Contemporary studies of the effectiveness of social work.' *British Journal of Social Work 22,* 615–643.

Manthorpe, J., Walsh, M., Alaszewski, A. and Harrison, L. (1997) 'Developing good practice in risk issues with people with learning disabilities.' *Disability and Society 12,* 1, 511–530.

Parton, N. (1986) 'The Beckford Report: A critical appraisal.' *British Journal of Social Work 16,* 511–530.

Thomas, N. (1994) '"The social worker as a bad object." A response to Maguerite Valentine.' *British Journal of Social Work 24,* 749–754.

Tindall, B. (1997) 'People with learning difficulties: Citizenship, personal development and the management of risk.' In H. Kemshall and J. Pritchard (eds) (1997) *Good Practice in Risk Assessment and Risk Management 2.* London: Jessica Kingsley Publishers.

Valentine, M. (1994) 'The social worker as a "bad object".' *British Journal of Social Work 24,* 71–86.

CHAPTER 5

Assessing Risk in Work with Offenders

Bill Beaumont

> It was generally agreed that the immediate purpose of a prediction scale was to improve the identification by probation officers of offenders ... at risk of a custodial sentence. (Mair and Lloyd 1989, p.6)

This conclusion, from a Home Office workshop on risk and probation practice, proves a lot can happen in ten years! The report acknowledged, in passing, the parole unit's Reconviction Prediction Score (RPS) (Nuttall *et al.* 1977) and growing use of statistically based prediction by American probation departments. However, it asserted that probation services were 'at the forefront of developments in the use of prediction scales in England and Wales' (Mair and Lloyd 1989, p.2) and focused almost exclusively on 'risk of custody' scales. By 1996, they were all but forgotten and Kemshall was able to suggest that: 'risk assessment and effective risk management are likely to become the main preoccupations of the Probation Service.' (1996a, p.134)

The 1991 Criminal Justice Act's emphasis on 'just deserts' sentencing (and targeted use of 'punishment in the community') had been rapidly supplanted by Michael Howard's 'prison works' policy. The decarceration achieved by systems management in the juvenile justice system (without using risk of custody predictions) had been thrown into reverse. A change of government in 1997 has not reduced the punitive pressures on probation and youth justice services. The new home secretary has said there can be no doubt that the probation service's major purpose is protection of the public and his first criminal justice legislation threatened new sanctions against young offenders and their parents. This climate of opinion has facilitated the rise and fall of risk as a major preoccupation in work with offenders.

It is worth reminding ourselves just how recently 'risk' moved centre stage in criminal justice social work, arguably for the first time in its history. The focus moved rapidly from systems goals (such as targeting probation interventions or reducing use of custody) to the risks posed by individual offenders. In this field, the new preoccupation with risk assessment represents a return to a classic theme of criminological study from Lombroso onwards – the classification of offenders, and prediction of offending, reconviction and 'dangerousness'. The reasons for this renaissance are largely political and this chapter aims to keep that in focus while reviewing the state of risk research in this area of social work. Reflecting risk's newly prominent position, there has been a burgeoning of publications on risk and probation work (for instance Kemshall 1995a, 1996a, 1997; Creamer and Williams 1996; Lawrie 1997; Williams 1997). This chapter reviews rather than replicates this recent work.

Dimensions of risk

The major preoccupation in relation to offenders has always been the risks they pose to others. The main research focus has been on statistical prediction and its uses in predicting delinquency, reconviction and 'dangerousness' were reviewed in Chapter 3. Space precludes coverage of all (actual or potential) fields of research interest in relation to risk and offenders. As elsewhere in social work, attention has been paid in recent years to the risks faced by probation staff from threats, aggression and violence by clients (see, for example, Littlechild 1993). Little attention has been paid to risks of self-harm amongst offenders as the discussion in Chapter 2 showed. There is a substantial literature only in the field of self-harm and suicide risk amongst prisoners (for a recent summary see Liebling 1997). A little work has now been done on self-harm amongst probationers (Cox and Pritchard 1995; Wessely *et al.* 1996).

Living Dangerously, the title of Graef's (1992) book exploring young offenders' self-perceptions, neatly encapsulates the very risky lives lead by many offenders. Amongst the risks they commonly run are accidental injury in the course of crime, assault by other offenders, health damage from their own behaviour, police harassment, wrongful arrest and/or conviction, the hazards of imprisonment, alienation from sources of support, social exclusion and financial insecurity. Much might be learnt from a careful study of why people, mainly men, choose and/or are forced to lead such risky lives. There is, of course, much relevant research (though not in the 'risk' paradigm) but these issues have found little place in recent discussions of risk and probation practice.

Another neglected area of research in relation to offender services is risk and organisational behaviour. Probation services have been encouraged and/or forced into reorganisations without adequate analysis of risk. A few examples suffice to make this point – will larger services serve local communities better? will focusing on more serious offenders aid or prejudice organisational survival? will 'case management' prove more effective or efficient? In an anxious, blaming (and privatising) political climate, the risks faced by public service organisations are clearly high but go largely unresearched. Noting these understudied dimensions of risk, it is time to return to our major focus.

Prediction research and probation

The major fields of criminological prediction research were explored fully in the Chapter 3. There has been less research on prediction scales specifically related to offenders on probation but most work done belongs firmly within that same research tradition. This review assumes the reader has already read Chapter 3.

Mair (1989, p.13) pointed out that 'During the 1980s the use of risk prediction scales has become a prominent feature of the work of probation departments in the USA.' He related this to pressure on departments to prove they were offering value for money, particularly in developing intensive probation schemes. This work (for instance Wright, Clear and Dickson 1984; Clear and Gallagher 1985) usually linked level of probation intervention to degree of risk predicted. Clear and Gallagher (1985) claimed most US probation agencies had started to use some form of paper-driven offender classification over the previous ten years. Petersilia and Turner (1987) agree this introduction of prediction devices was resource driven. They suggest probation staff resisted workload decisions based solely on reconviction predictions and demanded a more balanced approach: 'Most probation classification instruments now use a combination of recidivism-prediction and needs-assessment scores to assign levels of community supervision' (p.157).

Risk of custody scales had similar objectives. The best-known British scale (Bale 1987) was developed as a local screening device, intended to ensure community service was used as an alternative to custody. Other scales which followed (Fitzmaurice 1989; Godson 1989; Creamer, Ennis and Williams 1994) were similarly designed to target intensive schemes on offenders otherwise at risk of custody. Their use became briefly popular and was commended by the cost-conscious Audit Commission (1989). They proved controversial – in some areas, Bale's scale (validated on sentencing decisions in Cambridge) was adopted without revalidation and in some urban services the problem of what to do about 'race' (an issue which has dogged American prediction research) quickly surfaced. Mair (1989) had warned:

> American research has demonstrated that it is vital to validate any classification system adopted from another area (Wright, Clear and Dickson 1984). And the situation should always be under review ... revalidation is necessary to keep up with trends in offending and sentencing. (p.19)

This warning was particularly apposite for attempts to predict sentencing behaviour in view of the well-established variations between courts (and even individual sentencers). In relation to sentencing trends, all scales would certainly have needed revalidation to take account of the massive shift towards use of custody which followed Michael Howard's declaration that 'prison works'. It was perhaps not coincidental that interest in risk of custody scales quickly lapsed and attention shifted to risk of reconviction.

The best-known British reconviction prediction device for probationers (Humphrey, Carter and Pease 1992) borrowed its methodology from RPS (Nuttall *et al.* 1977), using a sample of 750 people placed on probation in Greater Manchester during 1985 and a three-year follow-up period. When the prediction device was tested on the validation sample, the authors were satisfied its predictive power was 'of the same order as ... the parole predictor' (p.63). It scores 21 variables (see Table 4.1) and provides a three-year reconviction prediction for eight score bands, ranging from 18 per cent for the lowest risk band to 69 per cent for the highest. The authors hoped the scale would be used to measure whether teams, projects or individual officers were producing outcomes better or worse than predicted. Although enthusiastic about their scale as a crude but robust starting point, they were obviously nervous about the use to which it might be put in a service newly dominated by managerialism and warned: 'Being neither a denial of, nor a substitute for, professional skill and judgement, the predictor is but a complementary tool, capable of enhancing and promoting such attributes' (p.41).

Other probation areas had also started work on reconviction prediction (for example Merrington 1990) and some made use of the Manchester predictor. Wilkinson (1994) reports on work to adapt it for use in Inner London. His validation study, using a small sample (152 probationers) and short follow-up period (13 months), found the Manchester device performed less well on this new sample but still had considerable predictive power. He found the Inner London caseload (of the early 1990s) higher risk than Greater Manchester's (in the mid-1980s). A 'customized' predictor scale was devised with fewer risk bands and using only seven variables readily available from routine monitoring (see Table 5.1).

A significant issue influencing choice of final variables was a wish to avoid personal characteristics which might be considered discriminatory. The 'customized' scale performed slightly less well than the original device but was deemed good enough for routine use. The final phase of the project (not reported) involved collecting reconviction information when orders ended, so real outcomes could be compared with predictions and used to evaluate the work of teams, projects and (perhaps) individuals.

Little routine use of such predictors seems to have followed immediately though some research use is documented. However, building on these developments (and its own experience of parole predictors) the Home Office commissioned work on a reconviction predictor for use by probation services. Copas (1995) reports the development of this device which has since become known as the Offender Group Reconviction Score (OGRS). As in his parole study (Copas, Marshall and Tarling 1996), he used statistical modelling but this time (for simplicity) settled for a more conventional device predicting only risk

Predictor Variables	Parole Study		
Table 5.1 Variables used in prediction studies			
	Humphrey *et al.* 1992	Wilkinson 1994	Copas 1995
Personal			
Age	✓	✓	✓
Sex	✓		✓
Marital status	✓		
Social history			
Employment history	✓ (2)		
Offence	✓	✓	✓
Offences taken into consideration	✓		
Previous convictions	✓	✓	✓
Court appearance rate			✓
Prison sentences	✓	✓	
Suspended sentences	✓		
Custody as juvenile			✓
Longest custodial sentence	✓		
Age at first custodial sentence	✓		
Age at first conviction	✓		
Juvenile supervision orders	✓		
Previous probation orders	✓	✓	
Age at first probation	✓		
Breaches of probation/supervision	✓		
Length of current probation order	✓		
Community service orders	✓	✓	
Social prospects			
Living arrangements now	✓		
Employment position now	✓	✓	

Note: (2) indicates two different factors used in relation to that variable.

of reconviction within two years. OGRS was developed using data from a very large sample of 13, 711 people, comprising four subsamples – people placed on probation without conditions, with (4A/B) conditions, on community service in 1987, and a stratified sample of people released from prison that year. The wide range of variables tested initially were whittled down to six (see Table 5.1). This device suffered little 'shrinkage' when tested on the validation sample and achieved accuracy: 'comparable to the value obtained by Nuttall *et al.* (1977) and in several other studies, most of which also use social as well as criminal history variables' (Copas 1995, p.201). The OGRS is calculated as shown in Table 5.2.

Table 5.2 Calculating OGRS	
Start with 57 (a number chosen to yield simple end values)	
Subtract 9 if female	
Subtract age in years	
Add (number of youth custody sentences × 4)	
Add (total number of court appearances × 2)	
Add (court appearance rate × 11)	
If offence group is:	
Violence	*Subtract 2*
Sex	*Subtract 9*
Burglary	*Add 7*
Theft	*Add 6*
Fraud	*Subtract 1*
Motor	*Add 3*
Criminal damage	*Add 7*
Drugs	*Subtract 5*
Other	*Subtract 5*

Source: Derived from Copas 1995, p.201.

This score is converted into percentage probability of reconviction within two years. OGRS has now been made available to the probation service and greeted with a very mixed reaction, which is discussed later.

The 'What Works' movement, influential in probation services throughout the 1990s (see McGuire 1995), has produced its own variation on risk assessment, combined (as in America) with needs assessment. It claims meta-analyses of effectiveness studies established one feature of successful offender programmes as 'a matching between offender risk level and degree of service intervention, such that higher-risk individuals receive more intensive services, while those of lower risk receive lower or minimal intervention' (McGuire and Priestley 1995, p.14).

These developments draw heavily on the extraordinarily confident psychology-based school of criminology which has emerged from Canada. With characteristic flourish, Andrews (1995, p.35) claims: 'there now exists a psychology of criminal conduct (PCC) that is empirically defensible and whose applications are promising for the design and delivery of effective direct service programmes.' Andrews claims confidently that the research literature identifies a number of risk/need factors predictive of criminal behaviour and specifies six major sets of factors:

- antisocial/procriminal attitudes, values and beliefs
- procriminal associates (and lack of prosocial influences)
- temperamental and personality factors conducive to criminal activity (in which he includes psychopathy, impulsivity, restless aggressive energy and a taste for risk)
- history of antisocial behaviour
- family factors (in which he includes criminality, lack of affection and poor parental supervision)
- low levels of personal achievement in education and employment

and three minor sets:

- lower class origins and upbringing in a poor neighbourhood
- personal distress from various sources
- 'a lot of biological/neurophysiological indicators' yet to be adequately theorised.

This list of predictive factors, said to have emerged from a new series of (still to be published) meta-analyses, is of course in striking contrast to those used so far in mainstream criminological studies (see Tables 3.1 and 5.1).

Andrews and Bonta (1995) have patented their own risk/need assessment instrument, the Level of Service Inventory – Revised (LSI-R). Aubrey and

Hough (1997) say this revises a scale originally developed by the Ontario Ministry of Correctional Services and 'combines risk and needs factors together, to yield a single score indicating both risk of reconviction and the level of supervision required' (p.6). Completion of LSI-R involves use of a structured interview form comprising 54 questions. Scoring is through a combination of yes/no answers and simple rating scales, to produce a prediction score interpreted with the help of a manual. Those involved in promoting its use by probation services in England and Wales claim: 'the weighting system has been devised not by actuarial analysis but by meta-analysis, extrapolating from a large number of research studies which examine predictors of criminal behaviour' (Sutton and Davies 1996, cited in Aubrey and Hough 1997, p.6).

Aubrey and Hough note that Sutton and Davies criticise other reconviction predictors (such as OGRS) because they cannot predict risk in individual cases, presumably claiming LSI-R can. Aubrey and Hough are clearly not convinced this will prove to be the case if empirically tested. Evaluation of the usefulness of LSI-R is impeded by commercialism – like related treatment programmes, it is a patented system and would-be users are obliged to purchase training and manuals from its licensed promoters. Some English probation services have done so and now pay £1 for each LSI-R form used. For commercial reasons, trained users are not supposed to allow unauthorised access to the forms or manual. A well-known academic, Peter Raynor, subsequently received a research grant, funded through his university by the promoters (*The Cognitive Centre Foundation*) in partnership with several probation services, to undertake a validation study and calibrate the device for use in the UK context. It is interesting, in this age of supposed cost-consciousness, that probation managers have been persuaded to hand over large amounts of public money for a system not even validated for use in the UK prior to its introduction.

Aubrey and Hough were commissioned by the Home Office to pilot a separate needs assessment instrument. This research was aimed at developing a 'performance indicator' which would assess impact on clients' offence-related problems as an intermediate measure of achievement (to be considered alongside impact on reconviction rates). Aubrey and Hough adopted the Manitoba scale (Bonta *et al.* 1994) and found probation officers had no difficulty using such scales but had mixed views about their usefulness. They warned against simplistic use of such performance measures – greater clarity (or disclosure) about the scale of a client's problems as supervision progressed might be misinterpreted as a worsening in their situation. They supported development of risk and needs assessments in tandem but argued: 'it is important to mount an empirical test of the proposition that risk of reconviction scales including needs variables are more precise than those which do not' (1997, p.ix).

So the battle lines were drawn – OGRS versus LSI-R! The clash between traditional criminological prediction methods and the psychology of criminal conduct's preferred risk/needs assessment is likely to leave probation services in confusion over statistical risk prediction devices for some time to come. Colombo and Neary (1998) found use of OGRS and LSI-R joined by another contender, ACE – the Assessment, Case Recording and Evaluation system developed by the Oxford Probation Studies Unit. ACE combines the OGRS reconviction predictor with a home-grown needs assessment scale (Roberts *et al.* 1996). Although Colombo and Neary's survey (in the first half of 1998) found more areas relying on in-house risk assessment schemes than any of these measures, services' future plans indicated they were likely to have become the big three by the end of the 1990s.

Organisational approaches to risk

Research findings on statistical prediction have, until recently, attracted little interest within probation and youth justice services. Risk assessment and management rarely appear as index terms in mainstream texts prior to the mid-1990s (see, for example, McGuire and Priestley 1985, Harding 1987, Pitts 1990, May 1991). Harris (1992) only briefly reports Clear and O'Leary's (1983) work on matching risk with levels of probation intervention. A key development was the redefinition (by the Criminal Justice Act 1991) of the purpose of probation supervision from 'advise, assist and befriend' to a three-pronged formulation, including the specific goals of public protection from, and prevention of reoffending by, individual offenders. Even then, the *National Standards* (Home Office 1992) which accompanied implementation gave risk assessment and management a fairly low profile. The probation texts of the early 1990s followed this low-key approach. Raynor, Smith and Vanstone (1994) pay more attention to risk of custody than risk assessment – their short discussion of the 'risk principle' deals only with targeting intensive probation interventions on higher risk offenders. As late as 1996, May and Vass gave little space to risk in their collection of essays on probation work.

However, government pressure on the probation and youth justice services intensified. The irritation which had produced the semantic transformation of probation work into 'punishment in the community' intensified into outright hostility under Michael Howard (Beaumont 1995). National standards were revisited and greater emphasis placed on the service's public protection role. Presentence reports were now to include a specific section on risk, conveying a 'professional judgement of the risk of re-offending and the risk of harm to the public which the offender …. now poses' and such assessments were not to be 'confined to cases of violent or sexual offences where there is a risk of serious harm …' (Home Office 1995, p.11). The age of risk in work with offenders had now arrived.

The fact risk had previously been infrequently discussed in the probation literature does not mean practitioners were oblivious to the issues. Getting a client through their order or licence without reconviction was seen as one (but only one) indication of success. Practitioners had sleepless nights when supervising serious offenders. Supervising life (and hospital order) licences was seen as particularly taxing work reserved for experienced practitioners. However, such work was a small and specialist area – the great bulk of probation and youth justice work was with people who might present a medium to high risk of re-offending but were unlikely to commit a serious offence. Since the 1960s, the probation service in England and Wales has steadily moved away from working with the least serious offenders towards a more heavily convicted client group. However, this change has been more gradual than sometimes claimed (Lacey 1997) and it remains true today that serious offenders form a small proportion of the service's work. The Inspectorate's inspection of work with 'dangerous offenders' (HMIP 1995) estimated that around 14,000 offenders per year are placed under statutory supervision (under 10 per cent of all commencements) having been convicted of serious violence (cited in Lawrie

1997). Although gradual, this development may in time have pushed the service towards a more formal focus on risk. The probation service was alert to the damage done to social services departments by publicity surrounding child protection enquiries. It would also have been influenced by the rising social mood of anxiety and fear of risks (Castel 1991; Luhmann 1991; Beck 1992; Douglas 1992). However, despite these other pressures there seems little doubt that the rise of risk as an issue has been mainly driven by the new punitiveness of government policy.

ACOP's (1994) report *Guidance on the Management of Risk and Public Protection*, provides a useful benchmark against which to measure the impact of this new 'risk' paradigm. It reviewed guidance offered to staff (in all probation areas) in 1993 and concluded it focused on preventing violence to staff, extreme dangerousness (concentrating on particular offences), physical rather than psychological harm and lacked a common approach between services. It argued 'for a culture shift within services to a more active recognition of responsibility for assessing risk to the public and its subsequent management' (p.1). ACOP recommended a two-stage approach, with initial risk assessments done in all cases (including reports) and a more complex procedure applied to offenders likely to cause serious harm. Although recognising the continuing need for staff safety, the emphasis was now on public protection. Staff working with high-risk cases should be offered support (some of which sounded more like scrutiny!) and training. Services should learn from each other, develop common approaches and move towards interagency working (based on child protection experience). The report drew on recent Department of Health work on offences committed by mentally disordered people and appended their draft guidance. ACOP proposed a 13-point risk assessment checklist covering specificity (how much harm to whom), likelihood of harm, precipitating circumstances, offender's views and motivation, information from others and possible preventive measures. Individual service guidelines offered as examples of good practice also adopted the clinical assessment approach and used broad classifications of risk. The ACOP document contains no discussion of statistical risk assessment devices. It does not make clear the sources for its risk indicators (nor empirical evidence of their usefulness) though the influence of ACOP's adviser, Herschel Prins, seems evident. While promoting use of risk assessment and management techniques, ACOP warn probation services to guard against two dangers – a belief that having agreed systems solved the problem, and communicating false reassurance (given the service's limited ability to really protect the public).

Growing academic interest in 'risk' (Beck 1992; Royal Society 1992) produced two ESRC research programmes and one ESRC grant enabled Hazel Kemshall to undertake a major review of 'Risk in probation practice' (1995b). She located revival of interest in risk within a 'new penology', which Feeley and Simon (1992) argue focuses on management of justice (and offenders) and targets offenders most risky to public safety (preferring community surveillance for those deemed 'less risky'). This new penology therefore depends on 'accurate prediction and safe management of risk' (Kemshall 1995a, p.68). She criticised the ACOP report for its limited conception of risk, narrow focus on physical harm and particular categories of offence, inattention to risk perception and situational factors, and failure to move beyond procedures to an emphasis on improved practice.

Kemshall (1996b) asked probation officers, and their managers, to analyse the risk present in a number of case examples. Responses indicated a lack of consensus – practitioners brought their own values, knowledge and experience to bear. She perceived a broad difference between 'client-oriented' officers (less likely to perceive high risk, slower to act, more concerned about clients' rights) and 'community safety' officers (more likely to perceive high risk, quicker to act, less concerned about clients' rights). There was greater uniformity in the highest risk cases involving a particular known victim. She warned managers against a rush into proceduralism, identifying several potential traps – premature policy making (based on inadequate understanding); claiming managerial expertise (her research detected no difference between managers and practitioners); denying the complexity of risk; assuming staff had sufficient information (and privileging quantitative over qualitative information); and a misplaced belief that rules will avert bad outcomes (despite evidence from accident inquiries). Kemshall (1996b, p.7) concluded that 'Fuzzy thinking on risk isn't necessarily dangerous, for risk itself is fuzzy, changing constantly with differing probabilities and differing impacts for different people. Prescription and regulation cannot respond to diversity and fluctuation …'.

Kemshall (1996a) suggested improved practice should seek more certainty about the level of risk and then pay more attention to what could be done to reduce it. She said the probation service had 'found it easier to adopt the clinical method from the mental health arena than the actuarial model from criminological studies' (p.135). Whilst recognising some limitations of statistical predictions, she supported their use as the first stage of her proposed 'alternative risk assessment model', which takes the form of the 14-point checklist (adapted from Brearley 1982) set out in Table 5.3.

Table 5.3 Kemshall's risk assessment checklist
1. General predictive hazards
2. Specific hazards
3. Strengths in the situation, either of the person, of others, or of the environment
4. Danger(s)
5. Level of risk present: 1 2 3 4 5 (1=low risk)
6. Risk of what?
7. Risk to whom?
8. Consequences of the risk? to whom?
9. Costs of acting/not acting? to whom?
10. Action required to minimise the hazards
11. Action to enhance the strengths
12. Consequences of no action? to whom?
13. Recommendation (to include case plan reflecting work proposed on hazards and strengths, and including evidence for level of risk determined)
14. Date for review.

Source: Kemshall 1996, p.140.

Using this, the worker weighs hazards against strengths and decides whether the level of risk is tolerable. Despite the very general nature of her scheme, Kemshall concludes (in a piquant demonstration of the flavour of the times) with an attempt to deflect the risk of her checklist going wrong:

Hazel Kemshall and the University of Birmingham wish to confirm that the model of risk assessment suggested ... is merely one possible method of assessing the risk of an offender and no guarantees can be given that such a model is infallible ...(1996a, p.143)

We do indeed live in anxious times!

Kemshall (1997) subsequently discussed risk in relation to parole supervision, where the highest risk cases may be more often encountered. Here she argues that:

assessments will need to utilise both actuarial factors and careful professional judgement grounded in sound clinical techniques, enabling a dynamic and interactive assessment of:

key demographic factors, predisposing personality and behavioural traits, situational and environment factors, and particular conditional triggers and stressors. (1997, p.241)

She goes on (in keeping with current fashion) to offer an ABC of risk assessment. Where violence is involved (drawing on work by Megargee 1976; Scott 1977; Webster *et al.* 1994) she suggests the following assessment model:

Offender (including analysis of predisposing personality and behavioural traits), *plus*

Victim (access to, proximity to, grooming of),

plus

Availability of Weapons (access to, preparedness to use),

plus

Circumstances (environmental factors, conditions, circumstances and situational triggers),

equals the

Violent Offence. (Kemshall 1997, p.242)

Following the MacArthur risk assessment study approach (Steadman and others 1994), she argues the probation service should target dynamic factors which can be addressed by their intervention. In relation to parole, she suggests the prison service should produce statistical risk assessments while the probation service undertakes clinical assessment of dynamic risk factors.

Hazel Kemshall's work has clearly been very influential in shaping current probation service (and Home Office) policies on risk assessment and management. She has been drawn fully into shaping official developments, running workshops for probation managers and conducting a Home Office/ACOP survey on risk training (Kemshall 1997), as well as proposing her own training course (Kemshall 1996) which has proved popular with local services. Her work has alerted the probation service to the complexity of the issues, the extensive base of research knowledge available and the significance of dynamic as well as static risk factors. She appears to have adopted a thoroughly pragmatic position – risk assessments will continue to be used so they should be as good as possible, and current government policies (of punitiveness and tight constraints on probation resources) are irresistible and justify improved risk assessment and management strategies.

Other academic reviewers have been more critical of recent developments. Creamer and Williams (1996) accept that, since informal risk prediction is inevitable, there can be no objection in principle to more formal schemes. They identify some potential advantages of risk predictors as decision-making aids – they can reduce inconsistencies, promote efficient resource use, ensure appropriate use of community supervision, help avert excessive intervention and could be linked to a progressive penal policy. However, they also highlight some potential disadvantages – their use introduces predictable error rates, they may produce unintended outcomes, the use to which they are put is critical and their apparently objective basis give them a deceptive appearance of ideological neutrality. These problems may be less immediate when they are used for research purposes but remain similar and need to be weighed against their potential usefulness in helping identify effective measures, monitor team practice and compare different approaches. Creamer and Williams are concerned that a simple focus on reconviction rates worryingly over-simplifies the aims of penal policy; that past disadvantage contributes to higher prediction scores and so they perpetuate discrimination; that most reconviction predictors rely almost entirely on past criminal behaviour, making their use inconsistent with a 'just deserts' approach to sentencing; and that risk predictors create an air of unjustified certainty.

Williams (1997) examines the balance between rights and risks in work with prisoners. He argues that not taking risks may also have adverse consequences, in this case exposing prisoners to the continuing risks associated with imprisonment. Amongst the concerns he raises are that:

- use of mechanistic assessment instruments distances decisions from both staff and prisoners, and prejudices prisoners' rights

- prisons are using risk assessment to try to avoid 'the political potential of catastrophes' (Beck 1992, p.24) and erring on the side of caution

- risk assessment is being used to legitimate punitive measures

- risk assessment in the Sex Offender Treatment Programme has caused injustices (Casey 1996)

- cautious release policies (and other injustices) may recreate the conditions for major prison disturbances and also create greater public risk when embittered prisoners are eventually released

- risk assessments introduce new barriers between offenders and staff; greater openness leads to higher scores and adverse recommendations, so greater evasiveness may be the wiser option.

Williams is concerned that in the 'actuarial society',

> decision-making can come to be dominated by the need to 'cover one's back'. In such a climate, border line cases are determined cautiously. Prisoners are thus refused early release, home leave, lower security categorisation and other discretionary goods. (1997, p.262)

The relationship between the use of risk assessment and a more punitive penal system may not be inevitable but appears worryingly close.

Kemshall and Pritchard's two edited volumes on 'good practice in risk assessment and management' (1996, 1997) include four other chapters on particular aspects of work with offenders. McEwan and Sullivan (1996) discuss sex offender risk assessment and suggest a 21-point schedule for clinical assessment (drawing on the work of Wolf 1984, Finkelhor 1986 and Salter 1988). Underlying their assessment scheme are strong assumptions that sex offenders will reoffend, will deny the seriousness of their offending and that 'sex offenders cannot be cured' (p.155). Their thinking is typical of a strand of probation service opinion which contributed to pressures for new legislation, culminating in the rushed introduction of the Sex Offenders Act 1997. Beattie (1997) discusses risk in relation to domestic violence and probation practice. She supports a clinical assessment approach (without mentioning statistical prediction) and reviews a range of suggested risk factors while arguing, like other recent contributors (Morton 1994; Mullender 1996), for increased vigilance by probation officers. Johnston (1997) considers how information from victims can be built into probation service risk assessments. Lawrie (1997) discusses the role and responsibilities of 'middle managers' in relation to risk. Writing as a Home Office Inspector, she interestingly stresses damage limitation:

> The quintessential test of good practice is not whether a person under supervision seriously harms someone else, it is whether the quality and content of work is appropriate on the basis of the known facts … can it be demonstrated that everything is being, or has been, done to try to prevent harm occurring? If the answer is yes, then the practice is or was satisfactory, irrespective of the actual outcome of the case …(Lawrie 1997, p.302)

This emphasis on defensible process, rather than outcome, is unlikely to withstand the tabloid onslaught following an incident of serious reoffending. She urges middle managers to be interventionist and provides a nine-point checklist to help them ensure defensible practice.

In another recent contribution, Tallant and Strachan (1995) have discussed the importance of the way individuals 'frame' situations in reaching risk assessments (drawing on research in occupational psychology). They suggest risk assessments are subject to a number of partially predictable biases, including a tendency to simplify complexity. They suggest ways to reduce practitioner bias and also suggest use of a visual aid to help involve clients directly in their own risk assessments. Despite some evidence (from child protection and mental health inquiries) that offenders have sometimes been aware (and even seeking to convince the authorities) of the danger they posed, there is singularly little other discussion in the offender literature about the prospects for involving people directly in their own risk assessments. Reith (1997) reviewed the outcomes of ten mental health inquiries following homicides (since 1994) which had direct implications for the probation service. The probation service is often involved in providing a care and supervision package jointly with the mental health services in such cases and she argues it plays a useful role.

Risk assessment and management are obviously going to remain prominent on the probation service's agenda for the immediate future. While less has been written about young offenders, it is clear that these concerns are also driving the government's youth justice policies. The echoes of the James Bulger case are still reverberating: the first secure training centre for 12–14-year-old persistent offenders has opened; press reports vying to identify the youngest ever rapists are an ominous sign of building pressures; and curfews for the under-10s (and exclusions of junior-school pupils) indicate that the 'risk society' (Beck 1992) is progressively feeling menaced by the 'dangerousness' of ever younger children.

Many probation services are now expecting officers routinely to complete risk assessment or risk/needs assessment forms on clients. There is considerable confusion amongst staff about the theoretical and empirical basis for such instruments. They have received a mixed reaction from practitioners – some have welcomed (or promoted) this innovation while many others have seen it is as just another example of the new managerialism which has filled their in-tray with forms to be completed. The National Association of Probation Officers (NAPO) has set its face against statistical prediction devices such as OGRS (NAPO 1997) and probably accurately reflects the profession's reluctance to reduce the complexities of people's lives to numerical ratings. The rapid developments in this field have left most practitioners, and much practice, in a confused state. In a telling example, a student on placement locally during 1997 found officers using two different versions of a risk/needs assessment form and had difficulty tracking down instructions for completing (and interpreting) either version. This is therefore a good time to be reviewing the strengths and weaknesses of the research evidence on which risk assessment innovations are based.

Using risk research in practice

This concluding section discusses the usefulness of current research knowledge for management and direct practice in criminal justice social work. Much emphasis has been placed recently on use of statistical prediction. The strengths and weaknesses of the relevant criminological research were appraised fully in the last chapter. The messages drawn out there for other fields of social work apply equally to probation and youth justice services. Statistical prediction does not offer a 'quick fix' solution in assessing the risks posed by offenders. Despite much research, reconviction prediction devices have so far been unable to better 70 to 80 per cent accuracy. This is good enough to make them useful in research and for some administrative purposes (such as providing safeguards against unaided expert judgement) but not as a substitute for expert judgement. Kemshall (1996a) instead proposes they should be used in all cases to underpin expert judgement and I will return to that suggestion later. Prediction devices are at their weakest in relation to serious offences (where risk prediction is most crucial) where they have so far found it hard to improve on 50 per cent accuracy and much work remains to be done if usable systems are to be developed. A strong commercial interest is promoting a risk/needs assessment instrument (LSI-R) within the probation service. Although its proponents argue it is soundly based on outcomes from meta-analyses of the psychological predictors of reconviction, their claims have still to be tested by independent, empirical scrutiny. Pending such evaluation, LSI-R is probably better viewed as one more attempt at structured clinical assessment.

Since statistical prediction is rudimentary in all areas of serious offending and there are no agreed 'gold standard' devices yet available in relation to reconviction generally, services and practitioners have little immediate alternative to relying mainly on expert judgement. There are some interesting hints in the offender research that probation officers' judgements may be quite good – Wilkinson (1994) found good general concordance between officers' estimates and calculated reconviction prediction scores; Bale (1989) recounts his struggle to get his risk of custody scale better than the 75 per cent accuracy achieved on average by officers locally; and Roberts (1989) reported similar average accuracy (higher for some officers) in his risk of custody study. Careful research in this area is required, since statistical predictors are only worthwhile if they can do substantially better than unaided expert judgement. There is little research in the offender field which tests alternative paradigms for expert judgement (or the numerous checklists offered and used by different writers, services and projects) against outcomes. Without such evidence, services and practitioners can do little but opt for the most credible 'best practice' claims they encounter, remembering they remain simply unsubstantiated claims.

It may be more important to understand the social, political and intellectual contexts which have forced risk to the surface as an issue, then to understand the minutiae of prediction research findings. Much else is known about risk perception, assessment, reduction and management. Hazel Kemshall has already introduced into the probation discussion some wider sociological perspectives and research evidence. Brearley's (1982) early text, on risk in social work, drew heavily on approaches taken in the insurance industry and many have followed his example. Other writers have drawn on the health and safety literature, and accident prevention inquiries. Another important area of research is the work on 'risk perception' (see, for example, Pidgeon *et al.* 1992) – why some high-risk activities (such as hang-gliding or smoking) are seen by many as acceptable while low-risk events (like homicide) are so feared. Within this body of research, Slovic, Fischhoff and Lichtenstein (1980) identified crime as a risk area high on their 'dread' scale and therefore perceived as high risk regardless of real levels of exposure. Careful attention to such research may suggest strategies for reducing the fear associated with crime and thereby defusing the recurrent moral panics which so drive criminal justice policy.

Criminal justice researchers, policy makers and practitioners should also draw on the extensive body of research on risk reduction and management in other areas (see Hood *et al.* 1992 for an overview). Probation and youth justice services have worked hard to concentrate on more serious convicted offenders, responding to researchers' warnings about the dangers of premature intervention and 'net widening'. This has been organisationally stupid from the perspective of risk assessment – they are now supervising people with high probabilities of reconviction, their results will seem to be worsening and they are 'set up' to be blamed for failing to protect the public. Probation day centres (according to Mair and Nee 1992 and Lloyd, Mair and Hough 1994), for instance, have succeeded in targeting offenders who have a poorer chance of avoiding reconviction than the prison population! In consequence, day centres had worse reconviction rates than prison and provided Michael Howard with the strongest strand in his claim that 'prison works' better than other penalties. One prudent organisational response would be to return to working with lower risk offenders as quickly as can decently be managed. A more socially responsible course would be to insist that the organisational and research focus needs to move beyond risk assessment to risk reduction and management. Many features of the criminal justice system serve to increase, not reduce, risk of reoffending – the discharge arrangements for prisoners are one obvious example – and some attention to risk reduction strategies may prove productive. Hood *et al.* (1992) highlight tensions within approaches to risk management which cut across very different areas of research and it would be useful to map criminal justice system responses against these wider patterns.

It is also important to try to locate discussions about risk and offending in wider sociological perspectives. Castel (1991) has argued that modern Western societies are undergoing an epochal shift, from a focus on the 'subject' to a focus on 'risk factors' (and concomitant practice shift from the deployment of professional expertise to a managerial/administrative search for efficiency). In this shift the response to 'dangerousness' shifts from 'treatment' to a twin strategy of internment and prevention: 'The modern ideologies of prevention are overarched by a grandiose technocratic rationalising dream of absolute control of the accidental ...' (p.289).

Castel notes the pursuit of a hygienist utopia free of risk plays on alternative registers of fear and security (well illustrated in public debates on crime) and creates a 'delirium of rationality'. He warns that:

> This hyper-rationalism is at the same time a thoroughgoing pragmatism, in that it pretends to eradicate risk as though we were pulling up weeds ... one finds not a trace of any reflection on the social and human costs of this new witch-hunt. (p.289)

It is not hard to detect evidence in support of this theoretical analysis within recent developments in British criminal justice policy – the pragmatism of the 'What Works' movement; the spread of managerialist and technocratic approaches; and sex offenders as one group recently exposed, very literally, to the techniques of the witch-hunt.

There is no space here to elaborate on the importance of sociological analyses of the role the concept of risk may be playing in Western societies (Luhmann 1991; Beck 1992). These issues are explored more fully in other chapters and progress has been made elsewhere in considering their importance for social work (see Parton 1996; Kemshall *et al.* 1997). However, some reflection on these wider themes by managers and practitioners in criminal justice social work may help them understand the policy pressures they are experiencing and avoid a technocratic and pragmatic response. Clearly criminal justice social work services are being buffeted by a 'rhetoric of public protection' greater than the real issues of public protection they face. It may be helpful to illustrate this distinction first with an example from a very different sphere:

> In Sweden it was politically opportune to evacuate a large number of Lapps by helicopter for the duration of missile testing in their area, although the probability and extent of loss in the event of a helicopter crash was far greater than the possibility that a single person in a sparsely inhabited area could be struck by falling missile debris. (Luhmann 1991, p.31)

Here, politicians made the (rationally) riskier choice because *they* would have been blamed had a single Lapp been injured by falling debris from missiles they were choosing to test. In contrast, a helicopter crash could have been portrayed as a tragic and unforeseeable accident (despite the firm data available about the risks of helicopter travel) – no blame would attach to the politicians because they were acting to avert another danger. Closer to our field of concern, American risk researchers still focus mainly on individual prediction factors, rather than pointing out that widespread ownership of handguns might just contribute to rather high incidence of serious violence, because they fear the power of the gun lobby. An example even closer to home might be perceived in recent home secretaries' refusals to release Myra Hindley – this is clearly not based on any assessment of the risk she might pose (on real issues of public protection) but the use successive home secretaries have been able to make of her case as a token of their commitment to the 'rhetoric of public protection'.

The risk paradigm poses considerable dangers for criminal justice social work, which need to be accurately identified and vigorously contested. It is not accidental that the new home secretary, Jack Straw, chose immediately to release to the press figures on the number of serious crimes committed by people under probation supervision. The same facts could have been used as proof that the probation service had responded to government demands to focus on work with higher risk offenders and even as a basis for attributing some credit (possibly spurious!) to the service for the number of high-risk offenders who had *not* committed serious crimes. But the political spin ensured news stories reflected the desired message – the probation service was paying insufficient heed to public protection.

The messages thus delivered to criminal justice social work services are clear. Take no chances, join the ranks of the punitive pessimists. There are no prizes for taking risks, only penalties. There are no political penalties if you err on the side of caution and estimate risks as higher than they are (offenders will suffer, but who cares if the criminal justice social work services don't?).

So don't resist custody in borderline cases; support severe penalties for offenders who might commit further serious crimes; don't press for release of those already in prison or hospital; support intrusive conditions on release for those selected as safest (or who can no longer be detained); don't voice opposition to the excesses of the risk paradigm and public protectionism (such as selective incapacitation, preventive detention, mandatory sentencing and 'life means life'). The consequences can be seen in recent developments in relation to sex offenders. The probation service, even (untypically) NAPO press statements, contributed to a public perception (probably false) that sex offenders pose particularly high risks of reoffending and (possibly false) are particularly evasive, devious and untrustworthy. Probation voices have supported continued detention, long licences and extended supervision for sex offenders, mounting no coherent opposition to the deeply flawed Sex Offenders Act 1997. As that law has given rise to vigilantism (and incidents of serious violence) the probation voice has remained muted and generally pessimistic.

These risks of 'risk' call for a cool and sturdy response from criminal justice social work services. Unfortunately, ACOP's response and the influential work of Kemshall both reflect instead a pragmatic acceptance of the need to adopt more thoroughly a risk assessment and management approach to practice. Too much credence is being given to claims made for statistical reconviction predictors and risk/needs assessment instruments. The main reaction so far has been the managerialist response – to institutionalise use of risk or risk/needs assessment schedules and set up bureaucratic procedures designed more to insulate the organisation from future blame than to improve public protection. Since checklists seem obligatory in the field of risk, here is my 11-point proposal for a more measured response.

1. Recognition that the services' past preoccupation with offenders' welfare leaves some room for improvement in handling risk issues.

2. An appropriate focus on the harm done by offenders; Nellis' (1995) proposal – equal concern for offenders and victims – may offer the appropriate value base.

3. A willingness to engage in public debate to ensure the real risks posed by serious crime are understood.

4. A policy position based on thorough understanding of sociological analyses of the role 'risk' is playing in modern Western social organisation.

5. A training strategy to ensure staff are well informed about the research on risk in all its complexities.

6. Promotion of more research (particularly focused on risk perception, dynamic risk factors and constructive management of risk).

7. Use of a simple risk screening process to apply to all new cases to detect the minority of cases where there is a substantial risk of serious harm.

8. Use of data from reconviction studies to alert staff to cases where reconviction for less serious offences is likely (rather than routine use of a reconviction predictor in all cases which might encourage an unhelpfully pessimistic and defensive practice).

9. Use of a more complex risk assessment process only in those cases where a substantial risk of serious harm has been identified. In such cases, assessment should (where research evidence is strong enough) use statistical

prediction to anchor expert judgement (as suggested by Quinsey *et al.* 1995). Work with these offenders should focus on dynamic risk factors and seek to reduce the risk of serious harm.

10. Practice based on knowledge, and careful assessment, of the risks involved in any action taken to reduce risk (including consequences such as alienation, incarceration, amplification of risk, and substitution of one risk by more serious risks).

11. Support for, and promotion of, styles of work which adopt the optimistic stance that constructive work with offenders can both improve their welfare and reduce risks of reoffending.

Finally, a few thoughts on how developments have affected practitioners. Although management practice has adjusted rapidly to the new demand for risk assessments, it is less clear how much impact this has yet had on practice. Mair (1989) commented on several hurdles routine use of risk instruments might encounter in the probation service – resistance to increased accountability or loss of discretion and professional power; reluctance to let formalised assessment techniques displace individual judgement; and feelings of increased vulnerability to scrutiny, pressure to conform and exposure to blame (for not following procedures even when bad outcomes do not ensue). He pointed to American research which highlighted various resistance strategies employed by main grade staff (Cochran, Corbett and Byrne 1986) and the need for careful work to ensure practitioner support (Clear and O'Leary 1983). These issues have largely been ignored in the rush into 'risk' in this country.

It is of no surprise that clinical approaches have proved more acceptable than statistical approaches. Social work has never been a highly numerate profession, so it is not surprising that opposition has focused on statistical prediction scales – an early article in NAPO News on the piloting of OGRS expressed incredulity that probation officers should be expected to work out square roots (NAPO 1995)! NAPO subsequently went on formally to oppose the use of statistical reconviction predictors for either monitoring or decision-making purposes (NAPO 1997). A more watchful approach to claims for clinical assessment approaches may also be justified.

However, for practitioners the key issue is the struggle to resist a collapse into defensive practice. This theme has been well explored in relation to child protection social work and even the pendulum of official Department of Health policy has begun to swing towards constructive work to lessen the chances of abuse rather than a total preoccupation with risk assessment. Kemshall (1996b) expresses concern about the temptation to 'play it safe' and 'cover your back'. Such practice is easy and comforting, though ultimately not very satisfying. The checklist offered above provides a framework for positive practice which keeps risk firmly in its place and promotes constructive work with offenders. As they resist defensive practices, practitioners could do worse than bear in mind (as a slogan) Frank Bruno's memorable response when Harry Carpenter asked him, in a radio interview, if he wasn't afraid of getting hurt in his next fight: 'If I thought like that Harry, I'd never get out of bed in the morning.'

References

ACOP (1994) *Guidance on the Management of Risk and Public Protection.* Wakefield: Association of Chief Officers of Probation.

Andrews, D. (1995) 'The psychology of criminal conduct and effective treatment.' In J. McGuire (ed) *What Works: Reducing Reoffending.* Chichester: Wiley.

Andrews, D. and Bonta, J. (1995) *LSI-R: the Level of Service Inventory – Revised.* Toronto: Multi-Health Systems.

Aubrey, R. and Hough, M. (1997) *Assessing Offenders' Needs: Assessment Scales for the Probation Service.* London: Home Office.

Audit Commission (1989) *The Probation Service: Promoting Value for Money.* London: HMSO.

Bale, D. (1987) 'Uses of a risk of custody scale.' *Probation Journal 34,* 4, 127–31.

Bale, D. (1989) 'The Cambridgeshire risk of custody scale.' In G. Mair (ed) *Risk Prediction and Probation.* London: Home Office.

Beattie, K. (1997) 'Risk, domestic violence and probation practice.' In H. Kemshall and J. Pritchard (eds) *Good Practice in Risk Assessment and Risk Management 2: Protection, Rights and Responsibilities.* London: Jessica Kingsley Publishers.

Beaumont, B. (1995) 'Managerialism and the probation service.' In B. Williams (ed) *Probation Values.* Birmingham: Venture.

Beck, U. (1992) *Risk Society: Towards a New Modernity.* London: Sage.

Bonta, J., Pang, B., Parkinson, P., Barkwell, L. and Wallace-Capretta, S. (1994) *The Revised Manitoba Classification System for Probationers.* Manitoba: Manitoba Justice Department.

Brearley, C. (1982) *Risk and Social Work: Hazards and Helping.* London: Routledge and Kegan Paul.

Casey, M. (1996) 'Lifers and the Sex Offender Treatment Programme.' *Prison Report 34,* 24.

Castel, R. (1991) 'From dangerousness to risk.' In G. Burchell, C. Gordon and P. Miller (eds) *The Foucault Effect: Studies in Governmentality.* Hemel Hempstead: Harvester Wheatsheaf.

Clear, T. and Gallagher, K. (1985) 'Probation and parole supervision: A review of current classification practices.' *Crime and Delinquency 31,* 3, 423–43.

Clear, T. and O'Leary, V. (1983) *Controlling the Offender in the Community: Reforming the Community-supervision Function.* Lexington: Lexington Books.

Cochran, D., Corbett, R. and Byrne, J. (1986) 'Intensive probation supervision in Massachusetts: A case study in change.' *Federal Probation 50,* 2, 32–41.

Colombo, A. and Neary, M. (1998) '"Square roots and algebra": Understanding perceptions of combined risk/needs assessment measures.' *Probation Journal 45,* 4, 213–19.

Copas, J. (1995) 'On using crime statistics for prediction.' In M. Walker (ed) *Interpreting Crime Statistics.* Oxford: Clarendon.

Copas, J., Marshall, P. and Tarling, R. (1996) *Predicting Reoffending for Discretionary Conditional Release.* London: Home Office.

Cox, M. and Pritchard, C. (1995) 'Troubles come not singly but in battalions: The pursuit of social justice and probation practice.' In D. Ward and M. Lacey (eds) *Probation: Working for Justice.* London: Whiting and Birch.

Creamer, A., Ennis, E. and Williams, B. (1994) *The DUNSCORE: A Social Enquiry Practice and Evaluation Tool for Social Workers and Social Work Managers in Scotland.* Dundee: University of Dundee and the Scottish Office.

Creamer, A. and Williams, B. (1996) 'Risk prediction and criminal justice.' In G. McIvor (ed) *Working with Offenders.* London: Jessica Kingsley Publishers.

Douglas, M. (1992) *Risk and Blame: Essays in Cultural Theory.* London: Routledge.

Feeley, M. and Simon, J. (1992) 'The new penology: Notes on the emerging strategy of corrections.' *Criminology 30,* 4, 449–75.

Finkelhor, D. (1986) *A Sourcebook on Child Sexual Abuse.* Newbury Park, CA: Sage.

Fitzmaurice, C. (1989) 'Predicting risks in courts: The Staffordshire Sentencing Prediction Scale.' In G. Mair (ed) *Risk Prediction and Probation: Papers from a Research and Planning Unit Workshop.* London: Home Office.

Godson, D. (1989) 'The use of "Risk of Custody" measures in Hampshire.' In G. Mair (ed) *Risk Prediction and Probation: Papers from a Research and Planning Unit Workshop.* London: Home Office.

Graef, R. (1992) *Living Dangerously: Young Offenders in Their Own Words.* London: HarperCollins.

Harding, J. (ed) (1987) *Probation and the Community.* London: Tavistock.

Harris, R. (1992) *Crime, Criminal Justice and the Probation Service.* London: Routledge.

HMIP (1995) *Dealing with Dangerous People: The Probation Service and Public Protection.* London: Her Majesty's Inspectorate of Probation.

Home Office (1992) *National Standards for Supervision of Offenders in the Community.* London: Home Office.

Home Office (1995) *National Standards for Supervision of Offenders in the Community.* London: Home Office.

Hood, C., Jones, D., Pidgeon, N., Turner, B. and Gibson, R. *et al.* (1992) 'Risk management.' In *Risk: Analysis, Perception and Management.* London: Royal Society.

Humphrey, C., Carter, P. and Pease, K. (1992) 'A reconviction predictor for probationers.' *British Journal of Social Work 22,* 33–46.

Johnston, P. (1997) 'Throughcare practice, risk and contact with victims.' In H. Kemshall and J. Pritchard (eds) *Good Practice in Risk Assessment and Risk Management 2: Protection, Rights and Responsibilities.* London: Jessica Kingsley Publishers.

Kemshall, H. (1995a) 'Risk in probation practice: The hazards and dangers of supervision.' *Probation Journal 42,* 2, 67–72.

Kemshall, H. (1995b) 'Risk in probation practice.' Unpublished report to the ESRC.

Kemshall, H. (1996a) 'Offender risk and probation practice.' In H. Kemshall and J. Pritchard (eds) *Good Practice in Risk Assessment and Risk Management 1.* London: Jessica Kingsley Publishers.

Kemshall, H. (1996b) 'Risk assessment: Fuzzy thinking or "decisions in action".' *Probation Journal 43,* 1, 2–7.

Kemshall, H. (1997) 'Risk and parole: Issues in risk assessment for release.' In H. Kemshall and J. Pritchard (eds) *Good Practice in Risk Assessment and Risk*

Management 2: Protection, Rights and Responsibilities. London: Jessica Kingsley Publishers.

Kemshall, H., Parton, N., Walsh, M. and Waterson, J. (1997) 'Concepts of risk in relation to organizational structure and functioning within the personal social services and probation.' *Social Policy and Administration 31,* 3, 213–32.

Kemshall, H. and Pritchard, J. (eds) (1996) *Good Practice in Risk Assessment and Risk Management 1.* London: Jessica Kingsley Publishers.

Kemshall, H. and Pritchard, J. (eds) (1997) *Good Practice in Risk Assessment and Risk Management 2: Protection, Rights and Responsibilities.* London: Jessica Kingsley Publishers.

Lacey, M. (1997) 'Training and the future of the probation service: Is the paste out of the tube?' In B. Beaumont and B. Williams (eds) *Criminal Justice, Social Work and Probation Training* (Conference Proceedings). London: CCETSW.

Lawrie, C. (1997) 'Risk: The role and responsibilities of middle managers.' In H. Kemshall and J. Pritchard (eds) *Good Practice in Risk Assessment and Risk Management 2: Protection, Rights and Responsibilities.* London: Jessica Kingsley Publishers.

Liebling, A. (1997) 'Risk and prison suicide.' In H. Kemshall and J. Pritchard (eds) *Good Practice in Risk Assessment and Risk Management 2: Protection, Rights and Responsibilities.* London: Jessica Kingsley Publishers.

Littlechild, B. (1993) *I Needed to be Told I Hadn't Failed: A Research Report into Aggression and Violence Experienced by Probation Staff in Hertfordshire.* Hertford: University of Hertfordshire and Hertfordshire Probation Service.

Lloyd, C., Mair, G. and Hough, M. (1994) *Explaining Reconviction Rates: A Critical Analysis.* London: HMSO.

Luhmann, N. (1991) *Risk: A Sociological Theory.* Berlin: Walter de Gruyter.

McEwan, S. and Sullivan, J. (1996) 'Sex offender risk assessment.' In H. Kemshall and J. Pritchard (eds) *Good Practice in Risk Assessment and Risk Management 1.* London: Jessica Kingsley Publishers.

McGuire, J. (ed) (1995) *What Works: Reducing Reoffending.* Chichester: Wiley.

McGuire, J. and Priestley, P. (1985) *Offending Behaviour: Skills and Stratagems for Going Straight.* London: Batsford.

McGuire, J. and Priestley, P. (1995) 'Reviewing "what works": Past, present and future.' In J. McGuire (ed) *What Works: Reducing Reoffending.* Chichester: Wiley.

Mair, G. (1989) 'Some implications of the use of predictive scales by the probation service.' In G. Mair (ed) *Risk Prediction and Probation: Papers from a Research and Planning Unit Workshop.* London: Home Office.

Mair, G. and Lloyd, C. (1989) 'Prediction and probation: An introduction.' In G. Mair (ed) *Risk Prediction and Probation: Papers from a Research and Planning Unit Workshop.* London: Home Office.

Mair, G. and Nee, C. (1992) 'Day centre reconviction rates.' *British Journal of Criminology 32,* 3, 329–39.

May, T. (1991) *Probation: Politics, Policy and Practice.* Milton Keynes: Open University Press.

May, T. and Vass, A. (eds) (1996) *Working with Offenders: Issues, Contexts and Outcomes.* London: Sage.

Megargee, E. (1976) 'The prediction of dangerous behaviour.' *Criminal Justice and Behaviour 3,* 3–21.

Merrington, S. (1990) *The Cambridgeshire Risk of Reconviction Scale: 1990 Progress Report.* Huntingdon: Cambridgeshire Probation Service.

Morton, F. (1994) *Domestic Violence, Community Safety and Justice for Women.* London: London Action Trust/Inner London Probation Service.

Mullender, A. (1996) *Rethinking Domestic Violence: The Social Work and Probation Response.* London: Routledge.

NAPO (1995) *NAPO News,* September.

NAPO (1997) *NAPO News,* March.

Nellis, M. (1995) 'Probation values for the 1990s.' *Howard Journal 34,* 1, 19–44.

Nuttall, C. *et al.* (1977) *Parole in England and Wales.* London: HMSO.

Parton, N. (1996) 'Social work, risk and the "Blaming System".' In N. Parton (ed) *Social Theory, Social Change and Social Work.* London: Routledge.

Petersilia, J. and Turner, S. (1987) 'Guideline-based justice: Prediction and racial minorities.' In D. Gottfredson and M. Tonry (eds) *Prediction and Classification: Criminal Justice Decision Making.* Chicago, Illinois: University of Chicago Press.

Pidgeon, N., Hood, C., Jones, D., Turner, B. and Gibson, R. (1992) 'Risk perception.' In Royal Society, *Risk: Analysis, Perception and Management.* London: Royal Society.

Pitts, J. (1990) *Working with Young Offenders.* London: Macmillan.

Quinsey, V., Lalumiere, M., Rice, M. and Harris, G. (1995) 'Predicting sexual offences.' In J. Campbell (ed) *Assessing Dangerousness: Violence by Sexual Offenders, Batterers and Child Abusers.* London: Sage.

Raynor, P., Smith, D. and Vanstone, M. (1994) *Effective Probation Practice.* London: Macmillan.

Reith, M. (1997) 'Mental health inquiries: Implications for probation practice.' *Probation Jouyrnal 44,* 2, 66–70.

Roberts, C. (1989) 'The potential of predictive instruments to aid clinical judgement: The case of Probation Officers and their Social Enquiry Reports.' In G. Mair (ed) *Risk Prediction and Probation.* London: Home Office.

Roberts, C., Burnett, R., Kirby, A. and Hamill, H. (1996) *A System for Evaluating Probation Practice.* Oxford: Probation Studies Unit.

Royal Society (1992) *Risk: Analysis, Perception and Management.* London: Royal Society.

Salter, A. (1988) *Treating Child Sex Offenders and Victims.* Newbury Park, California: Sage.

Scott, P. (1977) 'Assessing dangerousness in criminals.' *British Journal of Psychiatry 131,* 127–42.

Slovic, P., Fischhoff and Lichtenstein, S. (1980) 'Facts and fears: Understanding perceived risk.' In R. Schwing and W. Albers (eds) *Societal Risk Assessment: How Safe is Safe Enough?* New York: Plenum.

Steadman, H., Monahan, J., Appelbaum, P., Grisso, T., Mulvey, E., Roth, L., Robbins, P. and Klassen, D. (1994) 'Designing a new generation of risk assessment research.' In J. Monahan and H. Steadman (eds) *Violence and Mental Disorder: Developments in Risk Assessment.* Chicago, Illinois: University of Chicago.

Sutton, D. and Davies, P. (1996) *An Introduction to the 'Level of Service Inventory – Revised' (LSI-R).* Cardiff: Cognitive Centre Foundation.

Tallant, C. and Strachan, R. (1995) 'The importance of framing: A pragmatic approach to risk assessment.' *Probation Journal 42,* 4, 202–7.

Webster, C., Harris, G., Rice, M., Cormier, C. and Quinsey, V. (1994) *The Violence Prediction Scheme: Assessing Dangerousness in High Risk Men.* Toronto: University of Toronto Centre for Criminology.

Wessely, S., Akhurst, R., Brown, I. and Moss, L. (1996) 'Deliberate self-harm and the probation service: An overlooked public health problem.' *Journal of Public Health Medicine 18,* 2, 128–32.

Wilkinson, J. (1994) 'Using a reconviction predictor to make sense of reconviction rates in the probation service.' *British Journal of Social Work 24,* 4, 461–73.

Williams, B. (1997) 'Rights versus risks: Issues in work with prisoners.' In H. Kemshall and J. Pritchard (eds) *Good Practice in Risk Assessment and Risk Management 2: Protection, Rights and Responsibilities.* London: Jessica Kingsley Publishers.

Wolf, S. (1984) 'A multi-factor model of deviant sexuality.' Paper presented at the Third International Conference on Victimology, Lisbon.

Wright, K., Clear, T. and Dickson, P. (1984) 'Universal applicability of probation risk-assessment instruments: A critique.' *Criminology 22,* 1, 113–34.

CHAPTER 6

Assessing Risk in Mental Health

Joan Langan

Introduction

Risk assessment is an intrinsic element in mental health work and knowledge about research on risk factors, known as actuarial data, can be an important source of knowledge for professionals. This chapter reviews some of the research about risk to self and to others, although its primary focus is upon the latter. The chapter also reviews some of the research about professionals' accuracy in predicting risk and then goes on to discuss the implications for social work practice. However, to do that without first outlining the context within which risk assessment takes place would lend credence to the view that it is a technical skill rather than an activity which takes place within a specific political, cultural and social context.

Political, legal and policy context

The 1990s has seen a shift to more powers to control individuals seen as a risk to others. Risk and dangerousness rather than need are becoming the criteria for eligibility for services (Kemshall *et al.* 1997). Many factors are responsible for the current emphasis upon control and protection in mental health: a number of homicides by people in recent or current contact with psychiatric services; the resulting coverage by the media including the demonising of black men as dangerous (Sayce 1995); criticisms of the policy of community care and powerful voices such as the Royal College of Psychiatrists, SANE and the National Schizophrenia Fellowship demanding legislative and policy change (Fennell 1996). Supervision registers have been established; guidance on the discharge of mentally disordered people and their continuing care in the community has been issued which suggest how and when to undertake a risk assessment (NHS Executive 1994). The 1983 Mental Health Act has been amended in the Patients (in the Community) Act 1995 to provide a new power of 'aftercare under supervision', although Fennell (1996) argues that it adds little to existing powers and has serious implications for justice and human rights. A review of the 1983 Mental Health Act is also being undertaken.

Whilst these new measures relate to people who are considered to be a risk to themselves, the main reason for their development is concern about dangerousness to others. Two recent studies of the use of supervision registers bear this out (Cohen and Eastman 1996; Davies and Woolgrove 1998). Although suicide rates in one of the study areas were 17 times higher than deaths from homicide or serious injury, the majority of people placed on registers were defined as a risk to others.

That anyone should be killed by a person with a diagnosis of mental illness is deeply regrettable. We need to learn from and respond to the lessons which repeatedly arise from homicide inquiries (Sheppard 1995; Howlett 1997). However, mental health policy is in danger of being driven by these appalling but relatively rare tragedies. This is despite the fact that Taylor and Gunn's 1990 research on homocides by people defined as mentally ill shows a 3 per cent annual decline in their contribution to official statistics for the period 1957–95. The majority of people diagnosed as having a severe mental illness are not dangerous and are in fact much more likely to harm themselves than others. It is also clear that many who become dangerous when experiencing psychosis are extremely concerned and troubled by their behaviour and want help and support so that they are prevented from harming other people (Campbell and Lindow 1997).

Alongside the increased emphasis upon risk comes the requirement for professionals to develop systematic and coordinated risk assessment and management policies (NHS Executive 1994; Steering Committee 1996; Sheppard 1995). Definitions of risk are left to professional judgement yet professionals are given little guidance, even when using compulsory powers, about the level of risk to self or others which justifies intervention (Langan 1991a). When risks are perceived to be extreme, the lack of guidance or conceptual frameworks for assessing risk may not be so acute. Yet mental health prof-

essionals commonly operate in conditions of uncertainty where risks are unclear and ethical dilemmas are rife. Furthermore, the little research that has been
done on social workers shows that they lack clarity in assessing risk (Fisher,
Newton and Sainsbury 1984; Sheppard 1990) or confidence in developing a
social rather than a medical orientation (Barnes, Bowl and Fisher 1990;
Sheppard 1990).

Selecting risks

Much of the literature on risk in relation to mental health is uncritical about
what is seen as a risk. Risk is commonly seen as a harmful outcome rather than
in its original meaning as balancing probabilities. Mary Douglas (1985)
reminds us that risks are culturally and socially determined and that amongst all
those existing in the world, only some are identified as important, usually
because they accord with the interests of powerful groups. For example,
concern about risk tends to concentrate upon dangerousness rather than upon
suicide or being unnecessarily deprived of one's liberty (Langan 1991b).

The prevailing emphasis upon risk also allows blame to be allocated when
things go wrong (Douglas 1985). There is a widespread perception that
community care is failing (and so therefore are professionals in their duties) and
that we are all at risk from those defined as mentally ill (Rose 1997). This
increases the likelihood of defensive practice, a tendency previously noted by
Fisher, Newton and Sainsbury (1984) where social workers adopted a 'mental
set' in which any risk taking by people with mental health problems was to be
avoided. Trying to work in partnership with service users and develop practice
with risk taking can be extremely difficult when resources are inadequate,
preventative services are in short supply and there is little or no support for risk
taking. As Carson (1990) says, 'time and resources will affect how and how well
the risk is assessed and subsequently managed' (p.3).

The risks arising from mental disorder are important and there has been
much research in this area, as is discussed later in this chapter. However, other
risks, such as the disempowering aspects of much mental health provision; the
predominant emphasis upon medication and the serious side effects, including
death, which can be associated with drug use, are often ignored or underplayed.

Peter Campbell (1992) says that the user movement is incorrectly seen as anti-medication when the 'issue is more correctly one of appropriate and inappropriate use'. A particular risk for people who are black or from minority ethnic groups is the racism within mental health services (Bowl and Barnes 1990; Fernando 1995). As a consequence they experience greater coercion than their white counterparts (Davies *et al.* 1996, cited in Nazroo 1998; Takei *et al.* 1998).

Predictions about risk

Mental health professionals are often involved in assessing risk to self or others. Their judgements frequently have profound and far-reaching implications for the individuals concerned, whether by the curtailment of civil rights or a failure to protect individuals from their own actions. However, studies of how accurate professionals are in predicting risk have shown that they have little predictive ability. Studies tend to concentrate upon medical practitioners, psychologists or nurses generally in hospital rather than community settings. Little research appears to have been done about the ability of social workers to predict risk in mental health settings.

Studies compare prediction against outcome. In relation to suicide, Pokorny (1983, reported in Pokorny 1993) studied 4800 people admitted consecutively to psychiatric hospitals in the USA. In the follow-up period of four to six years 67 people committed suicide and the original predictions showed that there were many false positives and negatives. Pokorny concluded that 'identification of particular persons who will commit suicide was not possible at any practical or useful level, because of the relative rarity of this behaviour (low base rate) and the imprecision of our predictive scales, instruments, and items' (p.2).

A decade later Pokorny (1993) reanalysed his original data but the results were again disappointing. He concluded that the term 'prediction' is unhelpful since its meaning of 'identifying particular individuals is not a feasible goal'. He suggested the use of terms such as 'probability' or 'estimate' and 'estimate the risk of suicide' rather than 'predict suicide'. Other researchers (Goldstein *et al.* 1991, reported in Hughes 1996) also followed up a large sample of people (n=2000) consecutively for two years and concluded that prediction of suicide at the individual level was impossible. These results, and others reviewed by

Hughes (1996, p.417), led him to conclude that 'there are no accurate predictors for suicide and possibly only limited predictors of violence/homicide'. Indeed the National Confidential Inquiry into Suicide and Homicide by People with Mental Illness (based on English data for suicide and English and Welsh data for homicides) found that the majority of people who committed suicide were not seen as a high risk (Appleby 1997).

More research appears to have been carried out on the ability of clinicians (generally doctors or nurses) to predict risk to others than on risk to self. Until recently studies tended to look at hospital rather than community-based samples. According to Webster *et al.* (1994), studies conducted in the 1970s were so disappointing that few were carried out in the 1980s. Indeed Monahan (1981, cited in Monahan and Steadman 1994) concluded, from a review of five prediction studies, that clinicians were inaccurate in two out of three judgements made.

Over-prediction of violence appears to be common and two famous cases in the United States, known as the Baxstrom and Dixon cases, demonstrate this. Against medical opinion, the Supreme Court freed people defined as 'criminally insane' and dangerous from secure into ordinary psychiatric provision. Research on individuals in both groups who moved into the community was carried out (Steadman and Cocozza 1974 and Thornberry and Jacoby 1979, cited in Webster *et al.* 1994) with average follow-up periods of four and a half years for Baxstrom and three years for Dixon (Webster *et al.* 1994). Although age (youth) and previous criminal history were associated with rearrest or hospitalisation due to violence, the link was not strong. Violence was significantly over-predicted leading to high false positive rates – for Dixon only 18 per cent and for Baxstrom only 31 per cent of people predicted to be violent actually were (Webster *et al.* 1994).

Although a second wave of research was carried out which attempted to overcome many of the methodological problems associated with earlier research, Webster *et al.* (1994) describe the results as disappointing, a conclusion supported by findings from the following research studies. In the United States, McNeil and Binder (1991) examined whether accuracy could be enhanced if predictions were made about specific groups and if assessment of risk was conceptualised as 'assessment of a person's level of risk of violence rather than the prediction of risk'. The research focussed upon short-term predictions by nurses and doctors of people recently admitted to one psychiatric hospital in the United States (n=149). Doctors and nurses rated individuals in terms of whether there was a low, medium or high probability of their being physically assaultive and/or aggressive. Whilst nurses were more accurate than doctors, violence was over-predicted. Both groups were more accurate when assigning people to the low-risk group but were much less accurate when it came to people who were aggressive or assaultive. Perhaps this is not surprising given the low base rate for violence. Nurses accurately assigned only one-fifth and doctors only one-tenth of individuals to the high probability of violence group. In a later study, McNeil and Binder (1995) found that although doctors' and nurses' overall accuracy was 69 per cent, they were again most accurate in assigning people to the low-risk group. An interesting finding is that the true positive group was more likely than the true negative group to have a recent history of violence, a diagnosis of serious mental illness and to be considered as hostile and suspicious. Individuals who were placed in the false positive group also tended to be considered as hostile and suspicious, but they were less likely to have a diagnosis of serious mental illness. Overall the risk of violence from people from minority ethnic groups and from men was over-estimated whilst the risk of violence by women was under-estimated.

In another study, Lidz, Mulvey and Gardner (1993) studied a large sample (n=1948) of people being examined in the emergency room of a psychiatric hospital in the United States. Each person assessed as likely to be violent was followed up, as was a matched control group. Professionals were interviewed once whilst individuals in both the predicted to be violent group and the control group, as well as key informants, were interviewed three times over a six-month period. The researchers found that individuals who had caused concern about their potential for violence were 'significantly' more likely to be violent than those who had not (53% versus 36%). Clinicians' judgements were better than chance for male but not for female clients whose likelihood of violence was, in common with McNeill and Binder's study, significantly under-estimated. Lidz, Mulvey and Gardner suggest that this may be due to ignorance about the true base rate for women's violence. The high number of false positives and negatives for both men and women led the researchers to say that there 'is substantial room for improvement'. They also say that their study does not clarify whether clinical judgement is more accurate than merely using past violence to predict future violence. However, they assert that the study demonstrates that clinicians are more accurate than was previously thought in that they did pick out a violent group whose violence tended to be of a more serious nature than that committed by the control group.

The studies cited provide little optimism about the ability of clinicians to predict accurately who will and will not be violent or aggressive and confirm the disappointing findings of previous studies. Over-prediction of violence is common and where predictions reach a better than chance level, it is usually because of the accuracy of predictions about who will not rather than who will be violent (Taylor and Monahan 1996). In relation to offending, Reed (1998) suggests that the best predictors of future offences are those risk factors which are common to the whole population. Steadman *et al.* (1998) also say that we have little idea about how accuracy can be improved.

Risk factors

An understanding and knowledge of factors, known as actuarial data, which identify characteristics which may increase the likelihood of an individual being a risk to self or others is seen as an important element of risk assessment. Indeed, professionals are often told that they should use actuarial data alongside professional judgement, although usually without being given much indication of how they should do this.

Risk to others

In terms of risk to others, the first question to be answered is whether people defined as mentally disordered are more likely to be dangerous than the rest of the population. A large amount of research has considered this question. Until recently, there was consensus that people defined as mentally disordered did not present any increased risks to others. However, that view has shifted recently although there is still a lack of consensus over the interpretation of findings.

Swanson (1994) and Swanson *et al.* (1990) used data from a large (n=10,059) self-report community study into the prevalence of untreated mental disorder – known as the Epidemiologic Catchment Area Survey (EPA). Respondents were asked questions about violent behaviour and were screened for the presence of mental disorder and substance misuse. Swanson's work is widely cited, including within government guidance (NHS Executive 1994). According to Mullen (1997, cited in Howlett 1998) it has, more than any other study, inclined public opinion in America to the view that there is a link between mental disorder and violence. However, the data-set is large and difficult to summarise and different methods of estimating risk are used throughout the study. Swanson also made 'some potentially problematic assumptions' (1994, p.102) to allow data from the various EPA sites to be used.

I shall now attempt to summarise the most significant findings. The relative risk of violence in the preceding year amongst people with a diagnosed mental illness was about 2.5 times higher than that of people without such a diagnosis. The relative risk for people with substance misuse problems was about five whilst for people with both substance misuse and a diagnosed mental disorder the relative risk was six. Yet, since violence in the community is relatively rare, the absolute risk of a person diagnosed as having a major mental disorder being violent within the previous year was low. Swanson states that there is

> compelling evidence that the mentally ill, as a group, do not pose a high risk in absolute terms. Only about 7% of those with major mental disorder (but without substance abuse) engage in any assaultive behaviour in a given year. (1994, p.132)

The findings show the importance of substance misuse as a factor in violence. Another of Swanson's conclusions is that:

> while serious mental illness emerges as one significant factor that helps to explain (or statistically predict) violence, it is only one, (and probably not the most important determinant). Variables such as 'age, gender, marital history, economic status, education and position in social strata all define conditions in which mental disorder may be more or less likely to engender assaultive behaviour'. (1994, p.132)

In another study designed to examine the relative risk of violence by people with a diagnosed mental disorder, Hodgins *et al.* (1996) used a huge sample of everyone born in Denmark over a three-year period (n=322, 401). All psychiatric admissions and convictions for criminal acts were reviewed. The results show increased levels of convictions for both men and women with histories of psychiatric hospital admission. People admitted to hospital with drug or alcohol misuse had higher rates of violence (13% and 10% respectively) than people defined as having a major mental disorder (6.7%) who in turn had higher rates than people without a psychiatric history (1.5%). Interestingly, Hodgins *et al.* found that women diagnosed as having a major mental disorder had higher levels of violence than men. The researchers caution that the extent to which these findings are generalisable depends upon whether other countries have similar criminal justice, mental health and social services systems.

In Australia, Wallace *et al.* (1988) carried out research examining the relationship between prior conviction and contact with psychiatric services by drawing together data on convicted adults with data on psychiatric service use over a two-year period. This resulted in a sample of 4156, of whom 92 per cent were male. The researchers found that one-quarter of people with convictions for serious crimes had had contact with psychiatric services and that most of these individuals had diagnoses of substance misuse or personality disorders. They also found that whilst the chance of a person with a diagnosis of schizophrenia committing a crime was higher than for the rest of the population, the actual risk was 'tiny'.

The finding of elevated rates of violence for people with a diagnosed mental disorder in the studies discussed above is consistent with the results from other studies (Marzuk 1996; Taylor and Monahan 1996). However, what is clear from these studies is that the absolute risk of violence is low and that the majority of people defined as having a mental disorder are not dangerous to anyone else. In fact, as is discussed later, they are much more likely to be a risk to themselves. The magnitude of the relative risk is hard to establish since studies use different research methods, different study populations and different definitions both of violence and mental disorder. Reviewers also differ in the emphasis which they place upon these findings. One of the most important issues of all when analysing the research is whether people who misuse drugs or alcohol are defined as mentally disordered since this significantly affects results. The same could also be said for people defined as having a personality disorder.

As Swanson (1994) observes: 'the magnitude of the observed relationship between psychiatric diagnosis and violent behaviour is influenced a great deal by whether persons with substance abuse and dependence and dual diagnosis are to be counted among those with mental disorders' (p.112).

Recent work by Steadman *et al.* (1998) bears this out. They are comparing rates of violence of ex-psychiatric patients (n=500) with others also living in the community (n=500) (macarthur website). The research focuses upon physical violence and threats involving a weapon only. Early findings are that it is substance misuse which explains any differences in violence. Former psychiatric patients without substance misuse problems had 'about the same' rates of violence as community controls. People who misused substances, whether or not they were former patients, had higher rates of violence. However, ex-patients were more likely than the control group to misuse substances. In addition, within the first few months of discharge, the rate of violence of ex-patients with drug or alcohol problems was 'significantly higher' than rates for the control group who misused substances. The research also found that the type and object of violence as well as where it took place were similar in both groups.

Rather than attempting to establish the 'true' prevalence of dangerousness, Taylor *et al.* (1994) suggests that research might be more profitably directed at examining the nature of the relationship between violence and different aspects of mental disorder. Indeed research is taking place across a number of much more specific areas, some of which is reported here. For example, Taylor *et al.* (1994) review research which suggests that the presence of delusions (false beliefs) increases the likelihood of violence, and cite a study by Hafner and Boker (1982) which demonstrated that amongst psychiatric patients who were homicidal, 89 per cent of those with schizophrenia and 56 per cent of those with psychosis had delusions. Yet three-quarters of non-violent patients with schizophrenia and one-quarter of those with psychosis also had delusions. Taylor *et al.* (1994), who are based in Britain, are developing a research tool to examine the content of delusions to try to distinguish between those who are violent and those who are not.

Another area of research is exploring the content of psychotic symptoms in relation to risk to others. Swanson (1994) found that the presence of recent or current symptoms, rather than just a history of psychiatric treatment, appeared to be an important factor in the development of violence. Also in the United States, Link *et al.* (cited in Link and Stueve 1994) carried out research which suggested that psychotic symptoms were important in the development of violence. Reanalysis (Link and Stueve 1994) indicates that differences between users/ex-users and the control group were largely explained by the 'intrusion of external, uncontrollable and threatening forces'. Indeed, differences in violence between patients who experienced psychosis but who were free of such symptoms and the control group sample were not statistically significant. Link and Stueve describe their findings as preliminary and advise caution in the use of these findings on the basis that a) there may be other reasons for the violence than mental illness, and b) because the association between these symptoms and violence is low since most of the people who experienced them in their study were not violent.

In the United States, Estroff *et al.* (1994) and Estroff and Zimmer (1994) explored the influence of social networks and social support on violence by people diagnosed as mentally ill. Their starting point was that: 'Characteristics of the person's social support system and the members of the person's social network constitute risk factors for violence because they may create or decrease the opportunity or need for defensive, threatening or assaultive behaviour' (Estroff *et al.*, p.669).

One hundred and sixty-nine people, living in the community, and diagnosed as having a serious mental illness, were interviewed over a period of 18 months as were 59 relatives/friends. Fifty-six people (ie about one-third) either threatened violence, committed a violent act or both during this period (nearly twice as many violent threats as acts were made). The majority of the violent acts (70%) were committed by men. Women were the object of their violence in 60 per cent of cases. People with a diagnosis of schizophrenia (40% of the sample) were significantly more likely to commit a violent act but no more likely to threaten violence than the rest of the sample. Whatever the diagnosis, being financially dependent on others increased the risk of violence.

Social network also affected violence, since the larger it was, the more likelihood there was of violent threats occurring. This was also the case for relatives since as their numbers increased, so did the likelihood of a violent threat. The researchers also found significant differences in the social network characteristics of people with different diagnoses and say that this merits further research. More than half of the people who were on the receiving end of violence were relatives, particularly mothers living with their adult sons or daughters. As the researchers say, 'this reflects the predominance of relatives in the social networks of individuals in the sample' (Estroff *et al.* 1994, p.674). They suggest that in particular people with a diagnosis of schizophrenia, who feel 'fearful' and who live with relatives, particularly mothers, need support.

In comparison with the rest of the sample, Estroff and Zimmer (1994) found that those who were violent were more likely to see those on the receiving end of their violence as threatening or hostile and to see themselves as friendly and less hostile. The perception that others were hostile increased the risk of violent actions or threats. As the researchers say, 'people who threatened violence felt threatened'. They believe that the findings show the importance of understanding the social and interpersonal worlds of individuals, the quality of their relationships, their life history and their clinical condition as 'interrelated and independent factors when assessing risk'.

> We think it is a mistake to categorise people as violent or to conceptualise vio-
> lence as a characteristic of a person without considering the interpersonal and
> clinical processes and social contexts that individuals experience over time ...
> (Estroff *et al.* 1994, p.677)

Another conclusion (Estroff and Zimmer 1994) is that violence is not an inherent characteristic of the individual and that containing and controlling individuals whose violence arises from the provocation or actions of others is unjust.

Whilst the research activity in relation to risk to others is huge, there is a sense also in which the nature of any asociation between mental disorder and violence is still unclear and contested. Opinions differ as to whether research suggests an association or a causal relationship between mental disorder and violence (Swanson *et al.* 1990; Hodgins *et al.* 1996; Mulvey 1994; Coid 1996) or even whether it suggests any relationship at all (Wallace *et al.* 1998). For example, factors common to the rest of the population such as youth, being male, being of low socioeconomic status and substance misuse all emerge as significant risk factors in the development of violence. This leads Hiday (1995, p.124) to suggest that 'being a young, adult, single male of lower socio-economic status, and being a substance misuser hold far greater risks of violence'.

However, Hodgins *et al.* (1996) cite work which suggests that whilst substance misuse increases the risk for violent behaviour it does not explain all of the increase: 'in other words, recent findings suggest that the major disorders increase the risk for violent behaviour, and this risk is further elevated by alcohol and drug use' (p.495).

Whilst Taylor and Monahan (1996) agree with Hiday about substance misuse, they disagree with Hodgins. They believe that substance misuse is as important a risk factor in violence as a diagnosis of schizophrenia. In relation to schizophrenia, they assert that it is active psychotic symptoms, particularly the presence of delusions, which are important in increasing the risk for violence. However, Link and Stueve (1994) warn that even if these symptoms are significant, there are dangers associated with their development as clinical or research tools:

> Not only do symptom scales miss all the potent environmental and individual sources of violent behaviour that have nothing to do with mental illness, but their association with violence – both in an absolute sense and compared with other known causes and correlates of violence – is also modest. For the most part, most respondents in our study who experienced threat/control-override psychotic symptoms had not engaged in recent violent behavior, just as most members of other 'high-risk' groups (eg men, young adults, economically disadvantaged individuals) had not done so. (p.156)

Hiday (1995) also argues that the picture is a complex one and that research needs to examine the following.

1. The direction of any association between mental disorder and violence since an assumption is being made that the direction is from mental illness to violence. She hypothesises that this could equally be true in the other direction. Indeed, Wallace *et al.* (1998) found that most individuals with convictions for violent offences generally predated contact with psychiatric services whilst Link and Stueve (1994) suggest that their work supports the opposite conclusion.

2. The situation in which violence occurs since few studies, with the exception of Estroff and colleagues, have explored the social context or interpersonal relationships within which violence takes place.

3. The role of alcohol and drug abuse.

4. The role of dual diagnosis and particularly the importance of a diagnosis of antisocial personality disorder.

Hiday also suggests that a diagnosis of antisocial personality disorder rather than the presence of mental illness or active psychosis might be the most significant factor in the development of violence. Indeed, Webster *et al.* (1994) found that the best variable for predicting dangerousness in high-risk men (ie those found guilty of criminal offences or mentally disordered offenders with previous histories of violent behaviour) was the diagnosis of personality disorder. Wallace *et al.*'s (1988) work also shows the significance of this diagnosis in the development of serious criminal behaviour.

Hiday has developed a causal model which argues that serious mental illness, even where the person is experiencing a psychotic episode, does not provide sufficient cause to explain violence. She believes that poverty and 'social disorganisation' provide the additional reasons. Whilst I would take issue with her focus upon social disorganisation rather than discrimination and oppression, the identification of social factors is welcome. Hiday hopes that her model will refocus research away from violence being seen as emanating from the individual to 'towards social forces which link severe mental illness and violence indirectly through multiple pathways' (1995, p.130).

The above accounts give a flavour of some of the research currently being undertaken, much of it in the United States. One issue is that different research teams focus on discrete aspects of individuals' mental states, behaviours or situation. As a result, the reader can be left unsure about the relative importance of the various risk factors or their interrelationship. The ongoing research project by Steadman *et al.* (1994) represents one way forward since it aims to gather information about how the following four 'domains' interrelate and effect the development of violence.

1. Dispositional factors – the individual's demographic characteristics and their personality, for example how they handle anger, how impulsive they are.

2. Clinical factors – the effect of mental disorder, substance misuse, psychotic symptoms, delusions and hallucinations on the development of violence.

3. Historical factors – family or education history, including history of abuse.

4. Contextual factors – level and type of support, social networks.

Researchers working within these areas (some of whose work is described above) are developing a risk assessment schedule derived from research findings.

Risk to self

Another major area for risk assessment is assessing the risk of suicide or parasuicide, which has been defined as 'a deliberate non-fatal act ... done in the knowledge that it was potentially harmful and in the case of overdosage the amount that was taken was non fatal' (Morgan, Pocock and Pottle (1975), cited in Gunnell 1994). Whilst attempted suicide represents an unsuccessful attempt to commit suicide, parasuicide describes an action which did not have suicide as its aim. However, the research cited uses parasuicide as a term to cover both types of non-fatal act.

The incidence of parasuicide is between 10 and 20 times higher than for suicide (Gunnell *et al.* 1995) and whilst more women than men commit parasuicide there is some evidence of a trend towards greater parity between the sexes (Payne *et al.* 1997). Parasuicide is the best predictor of subsequent suicide, although the linkage is not particularly strong since less than 10 per cent of individuals who commit parasuicide later commit suicide (Payne *et al.* 1997). However, roughly one-third to a half of people who commit suicide have a history of parasuicide (Gunnell *et al.* 1995) and the risk of suicide increases with the number of parasuicide attempts (Payne *et al.* 1997).

Within England and Wales, the overall rate of male suicide has risen since the 1980s whilst female rates have declined. For the first time in the UK the ratio of male to female suicides is approximately three to one (Gunnell 1994). Rates of suicide differ between age groups and the male rate of suicide has increased for those under 45. The rise is most pronounced for men aged 35–44 (a two-thirds increase), slightly lower for men aged 15–24 (almost doubled) and for men aged 25–34 there has been a 50 per cent rise (Pritchard 1996, cited in Payne *et al.* 1997). The suicide rate for men aged between 45 and 74 is stable whilst the rate for men aged 75, who used to have the highest suicide rate, is decreasing (Payne *et al.* 1997). Amongst women suicide rates increase with age, although differences between age groups are reducing.

In terms of ethnicity, Soni Raleigh and Balarajan (1992) found low suicide rates amongst men from the Caribbean and the Indian subcontinent. Rates for East African men and women (most of whom are of Indian descent) were high. Rates for Indian women, and particularly young Indian women between the ages of 15–34, were also high. The researchers note that this finding is consistent with the high suicide mortality rate of young women in India. The authors suggest that 'levels and causes of psychological stress among young Indian women, in particular, need further detailed study' (p.367). The confidential inquiry into homicides and suicides by mentally ill people (the Boyd Report) also found that black psychiatric patients had a higher suicide rate that their white counterparts (cited in Payne *et al.* 1997).

Other risk factors for suicide and parasuicide are marital, economic and employment status. Suicide risk is higher for people who are divorced, widowed or single (Gunnell and Frankel 1994; Payne *et al.* 1997); for those who experience socioeconomic deprivation (Gunnell *et al.* 1995) and those who are unemployed. There is also research emerging on the links between childhood trauma and parasuicide, mental health problems and substance misuse. For example, Mullen *et al.* (1993) found a relationship between abuse and later suicidal behaviour.

An increased risk of suicide is associated with a diagnosis of mental disorder. Harris and Barraclough (1997) analysed 249 research reports on suicide and mental disorder. They summed up the results of studies which compared expected suicide rates with those observed to arrive at a standardised mortality ratio (SMR) for 44 mental disorders, including various forms of substance misuse. Thirty-six disorders had SMRs higher than expected. Of particular note is the risk for people defined as having a serious mental illness. The SMR for major depression was 20 times that expected; for manic depression the comparable figure was 15 times that expected. Whilst the overall risk of suicide in people defined as having schizophrenia was 8.5 higher than for the general population, the figure was higher for people who were under 30 or who were experiencing a psychotic episode.

Harris and Barraclough also found that opiate dependence increased the risk of suicide to between 14 to 20 times, whilst a history of attempted suicide combined with drug misuse magnified the risk for women to 87 times that expected (Harris and Barraclough 1997). Neeleman and Farrell (1997) suggest that the rise in suicide rates amongst young men may be related to their substance misuse and Hawton *et al.* (1993, cited in Payne *et al.* 1997) found that substance misuse was the strongest indicator of subsequent suicide amongst men aged 20–24 who had attempted suicide. Although more men than women misuse substances (Payne *et al.* 1997), women who abuse alcohol have a suicide rate 20 times higher than expected. The comparable figure for men is four times higher (Harris and Barraclough 1997).

Gunnell and Frankel (1994) review research which estimates suicide risk by psychiatric patient status. They demonstrate that the majority of suicide is committed by people in current or recent contact with psychiatric treatment, who have a history of parasuicide or who abuse drugs or alcohol. Findings in relation to people who use or have used psychiatric services for England and Wales are that:

- current or past psychiatric patients (including out-patients) form 50 per cent of the suicides
- those in current or recent (6–12 months) contact with psychiatric services form 25 per cent of the suicides
- people in the four weeks since discharge from psychiatric hospital form 10–15 per cent of suicides.

Harris and Barraclough's review leads them to a similar conclusion: 'Treatment in a psychiatric setting is, in these studies, consistently associated with high risks of suicide. The recently discharged and the recently admitted are at especially high risk' (1997, p.219).

Payne *et al.* (1997) alert us to the differences which gender makes to this overall picture in the 12 months after discharge. Male suicide rates have not increased for those in the 12 months after discharge as much as the overall rate of increase for men in the population. However, the opposite appears to be the case for women, whose rate of suicide after discharge is high when compared with overall rates of female suicide. Women also appear to be more at risk of suicide during an in-patient stay than men.

Harris and Barraclough (1997) found that a complex mix of factors increased the risk of suicide: how recent was the prior attempt to commit suicide; a history of attempts; substance misuse; a history of current or past psychiatric treatment; a diagnosis of schizophrenia or depression. Many social characteristics, including insecure housing, a poor employment record and being orphaned at a young age, were also associated with an increased risk of suicide. Their study and Gunnell and Frankel's (1994) provide clear evidence of the increased risks of suicide and attempted suicide for people who are defined as mentally disordered. However, as Gunnell and Frankel state, 'there is no single, readily identifiable, high risk population that constitutes a sizeable proportion of overall suicides and yet represents a small, easily targeted group' (p.1232). They conclude that the most easily definable groups to focus upon are people recently discharged from psychiatric hospital, young men or those with a history of parasuicide.

Conclusion

People diagnosed as having a mental disorder have higher rates of suicide and parasuicide than the rest of the population. However, the picture is much less clear when considering risk to others. Research in the last decade has suggested that there is a link, albeit a modest one, between mental disorder and violence or dangerousness. It also suggests that looking beyond broad diagnostic categories to factors such as the presence of particular psychotic symptoms may be important. However, the picture is now complicated by some recent research which suggests that diagnoses of severe mental illness such as schizophrenia may have little if any predictive power. Substance misuse may be the most important risk factor, with 'psychopathic disorder' another strong contender.

A key focus in current social welfare provision is to identify accurately and target individuals who are seen as a high risk (Parton 1996). Although in mental health this encompasses people who are a suicide risk, a greater emphasis on individuals who may be a risk to others is clearly evident. Indeed, research activity mirrors this emphasis and this in turn reflects the concerns of legislators, policy makers and practitioners to reduce the likelihood of individuals, defined as mentally disordered, harming others. Yet it is unclear how much research about risk factors helps professionals working with individuals on a day-to-day basis. The current state of knowledge about risk factors is a changeable one and furthermore many individuals who fit into high-risk categories are not a risk to themselves or others. Moreover, professionals have consistently been shown to be poor at predicting risk accurately and we have little idea about how accuracy can be improved (Steadman *et al.* 1998).

Actuarial information is also 'static' (Grubin 1997) in that it cannot take into account information about individual characteristics or circumstances which may depress or increase risk. Such information also generates 'probability statements' about groups of individuals which may be of limited use at the level of individual prediction (Grubin 1997). Perhaps the best use for actuarial information is that it can sensitise professionals to factors which may represent an increased risk for individuals and lead to their developing practices which seek to reduce risk for all service users. To do that, professionals need to keep up to date with research about risk factors as well as current opinion, since that shifts over time. Findings about risk also have a significant effect on the remedies being suggested, whether they have the aim of protecting or con- trolling individuals. As Wallace *et al.* (1988, p.483) say:

> The haste to criticise deinstitutionalisation and to advocate for more legal powers of restraint and more enforced drug compliance has obscured the reality that among our patients it is not those with schizophrenia or severe affective illnesses who are responsible for the vast majority of offending, but substance misusers and people with severe personality disorders.

Much research on risk to others has also been carried out from a clinical or medical perspective focusing narrowly upon an individual's mental state or behaviour. Here the focus tends to be upon individual risk factors, often divorced from contextual considerations such as socioeconomic, demographic and social factors. The research tends to accept unquestionably the concept of mental illness or disorder and the benefits of orthodox ways of treating people defined as mentally disordered. Ensuring an individual's compliance with traditional psychiatric treatment, primarily medication, is seen as the best means of reducing dangerousness. As Goodwin (1997, p.271) states, mental health is a contested area where there are 'competing premises over the nature of mental health problems, and ... divergent views on the value of psychiatric treatment'. By contrast, little research on risk to others appears to have been conducted from a social perspective which seeks to understand the development of violence within its social, cultural and interpersonal context. Moreover, whether considering risk to self or others, risk factors emerge which should be of concern in a wider policy arena than mental health alone – socioeconomic conditions, youth, male gender and being a substance misuser.

The one voice missing from research on risk to others is that of the service user. Sayce (1995) states that users' experience of being violent, their perceptions of causes, triggers and help required as well as their ability to predict violence are under-researched. Estroff and Zimmer (1994) also say that we have little knowledge or interest in the views of service users about how and why violence occurs and that 'their fears and perceptions are too often considered to be symptoms rather than legitimate concerns' (p.292). One reason may be that there is less acknowledgement that social, economic, demographic and interpersonal factors may be significant in the development of behaviour or mental states which are seen as irrational and frightening. As Klassen and O'Connor (1994) say, research traditionally works from the assumption that the 'dangerous' can be identified and that society can ignore the social processes within which violence is generated:

> We need not consider prenatal and neonatal health risks, socialisation and education of children, stressors and supports in the general population, and issues of mental health and optimal functioning common to us all, and we need not consider prevention or treatment ... Thus we have separated violence research from the body of our knowledge about human behaviour. (p.250)

Indeed it is surprising that we have little or no research about the 'protective factors' (Appleby 1992) in individuals' lives which serve to reduce risk, whether that be to self or others.

Social work professionals need to keep up to date with research about risk factors, since knowledge is not fixed but is changing as new research findings become available. They also need to develop confidence in the specific contribution they make in approaching risk assessment from a social rather than a medical perspective, and some of the research cited provides information about the importance of an individual's social and interpersonal context. Such information may confirm what professionals already know from their practice or sensitise them to other factors which may be significant in an individual's life. It may also allow them to counter unwarranted assumptions about the nature of any association between risk and mental disorder. But they also have to continue to live with uncertainty, since research will not allow them to predict who will or will not be a risk. As Parton (1996) says, the current focus upon risk may erroneously allow us to believe that certainty is possible when it is not.

References

Appleby, L. (1992) 'Suicide in psychiatric patients: Risk and prevention.' *British Journal of Psychiatry 161,* 749–58.

Appleby, L. (1997) *National Confidential Inquiry into Suicide and Homicide by People with Mental Illness.* London: Department of Health.

Barnes, M., Bowl, R. and Fisher, M. (1990) *Sectioned: Social Services and the 1983 Mental Health Act.* London: Routledge.

Bowl, R. and Barnes, M. (1990) 'Race, racism and mental health social work: Implications for local authority policy and training.' *Research, Policy and Planning 8,* 2, 12–18.

Campbell, P. (1992) 'A survivor's view of mental health.' *Journal of Mental Health 1,* 117–22.

Campbell, P. and Lindow, V. (1997) *Changing Practice: Mental Health Nursing and User Empowerment.* London: The Royal College of Nursing and MIND Publications.

Carson, D. (1990) 'Risk-taking in mental disorders.' In *Risk-taking in Mental Disorder: Analyses, Policies and Practical Strategies.* Chichester: SLE Publications.

Cohen, A. and Eastman, N. (1996) 'A survey of the use of supervision registers in South Thames (West) Region.' *Journal of Forensic Psychiatry 7,* 3, 653–61.

Coid, J.W. (1996) 'Dangerous patients with mental illness: Increased risk warrants new policies, adequate resources and appropriate legislation.' *British Medical Journal 312,* 965–9.

Davies, S., Thornicroft, G., Leese, M., Higginbottam, A. and Phelan, M. (1996) 'Ethnic differences in the risk of compulsory psychiatric admission among representative cases of psychosis in London.' *British Medical Journal 312,* 533–37.

Davies, M. and Woolgrove, M. (1998) 'Mental health social work and the use of supervision registers for patients at risk.' *Health and Social Care in the Community* 6, 1, 25–34.

Douglas, M. (1985) *Risk Acceptability According to the Social Sciences.* USA: Russell Sage Foundation.

Estroff, S.E. and Zimmer, C. (1994) 'Social networks, social support and violence among persons with severe, persistent mental illness.' In J. Monahan and H.J. Steadman (eds) *Violence and Mental Disorder: Developments in Risk Assessment.* Chicago, Illinois: University of Chicago Press.

Estroff, S.E., Zimmer, C., Lachicotte, W.S. and Benoit, J. (1994) 'The influence of social networks and social support on violence by persons with severe mental illness.' *Hospital and Community Psychiatry 45,* 7, 669–79.

Fennell, P. (1996) 'Community care, community compulsion and the law.' In M. Watkins, N. Hervey, J. Carson and S. Ritter (eds) *Collaborative Community Mental Health Care.* London: Arnold.

Fernando, S. (1995) *Mental Health in a Multi-Ethnic Society.* London: Macmillan.

Fisher, M., Newton, C. and Sainsbury, E. (1984) *Mental Health Social Work Observed.* London: George Allen and Unwin.

Goldstein, R.B., Black, D.W., Nasrallah, M.A. and Winokur, G. (1991) 'The prediction of suicide.' *Archives of General Psychiatry 48,* 418–22.

Goodwin, S. (1997) 'Independence, risk and compulsion: Conflicts in mental health policy.' *Social Policy and Administration 31,* 260–73.

Grubin, D. (1997) 'Predictors of risk in serious sex offenders.' *British Journal of Psychiatry 170,* 32, 17–21.

Gunnell, D.J. (1994) *The Potential for Preventing Suicide: A Review of Literature on the Effectiveness of Interventions Aimed at Preventing Suicide.* Bristol: University of Bristol, Health Care Evaluation Unit.

Gunnell, D.J. and Frankel, S. (1994) 'Prevention of suicide: Aspirations and evidence.' *British Medical Journal 308,* 1227–33.

Gunnell, D.J., Peters, T.J., Kammerling, R.M. and Brooks, J. (1995) 'Relation between parasuicide, suicide, psychiatric admissions and socioeconomic deprivation.' *British Medical Journal 311,* 226–30.

Hafner, M. and Boker, W. (1982) *Crimes of Violence by Mentally Abnormal Offenders.* Translated by Helen Marshall. Cambridge: Cambridge University Press.

Harris, E.C. and Barraclough, B. (1997) 'Suicide as an outcome for mental disorders.' *British Journal of Psychiatry 170,* 205–28.

Hawton, K., Fagg, J., Platt, S. and Hawkins, M. (1993) 'Factors associated with suicide after parasuicide in young people.' *British Medical Journal 306,* 1641–644.

Hiday, V.A. (1995) 'The social context of mental illness and violence.' *Journal of Health and Social Behaviour 36,* 122–37.

Hodgins, S., Mednick, S.A., Brennan, P.A., Schulsinger, F. and Engberg, M. (1996) 'Mental disorder and crime: Evidence from a Danish birth cohort.' *Archives of General Psychiatry 53,* 489–96.

Howlett, M. (1997) 'Community care homocide inquiries and risk assessment.' In H. Kemshall and J. Pritchard (eds) *Risk Assessment and Risk Management 2: Protection, Rights and Responsibilities.* London: Jessica Kingsley Publishers.

Hughes, D.H. (1996) 'Suicide and violence assessment in psychiatry.' *General Hospital Psychiatry 18,* 416–21.

Kemshall, H., Parton, N., Walsh, M. and Waterson, J. (1997) 'Concepts of risk in relation to organisational structure and functioning within the personal social services and probation.' *Social Policy and Administration 31,* 3, 213–32.

Klassen, D. and O'Connor, W.A. (1994) 'Demographic and case history variables in risk assessment.' In J. Monahan and H.J. Steadman (eds) *Violence and Mental Disorder: Developments in Risk Assessment.* Chicago, Illinois: University of Chicago Press.

Langan, J. (1991a) 'Unfit for the job.' *Community Care,* 17 October.

Langan, J. (1991b) 'A common practice?' *Community Care,* 24 October.

Lidz, C.W., Mulvey, E.P. and Gardner, W.P. (1993) 'The accuracy of prediction of violence to others.' *Journal of the American Medical Association 269,* 1007–11.

Link, B.G. and Stueve, A. (1994) 'Psychotic symptoms and the violent/illegal behaviour of mental patients compared to community controls.' In J. Monahan and H.J. Steadman (eds) *Violence and Mental Disorder: Developments in Risk Assessment.* Chicago, Illinois: University of Chicago Press.

McNeil, D.E. and Binder, R.L. (1991) 'Clinical assessment of the risk of violence among psychiatric inpatients.' *American Journal of Psychiatry 148,* 10, 1317–321.

McNeil, D.E. and Binder, R.L. (1995) 'Correlates of accuracy in the assessment of psychiatric inpatients: Risk of violence.' *American Journal of Psychiatry 152,* 6, 901–6.

Marzuk, P.M. (1996) 'Violence, crime and mental illness: How strong a link?' *Archive of General Psychiatry 53,* 481–6.

Monahan, J. (1981) *The Clinical Prediction of Violent Behaviour.* Washington, DC: Government Printing Office.

Monahan, J. and Steadman, H.J. (1994) 'Towards a rejuvenation of risk assessment research.' In J. Monahan and H.J. Steadman (eds) *Violence and Mental Disorder: Developments in Risk Assessment.* Chicago, Illinois: University of Chicago Press.

Morgan, H.G., Pocock, H. and Pottle, S. (1975) 'The urban distribution of non-fatal deliberate self-harm.' *British Journal of Psychiatry 126,* 319–28.

Mullen, P.E. (1997) 'A reassessment of the link between mental disorder and violent behaviour and its implications for clinical practice.' *Australian and New Zealand Journal of Psychiatry 31,* 3–11.

Mullen, P.E., Martin, J.L., Anderson, J.C., Romans, S.E. and Herbison, G.P. (1993) 'Childhood sexual abuse and mental health in later life.' *British Journal of Psychiatry 163,* 721–32.

Mulvey, E.P. (1994) 'Assessing the evidence of a link between mental illness and violence.' *Hospital and Community Psychiatry 45,* 7, 663–8.

Nazroo, J.Y. (1998) 'Rethinking the relationship between ethnicity and mental health: The British fourth national survey of ethnic minorities.' *Social Psychiatry and Psychiatric Epidemiology 33,* 145–48.

Neeleman, J. and Farrell, M. (1997) 'Suicide and substance misuse.' *British Journal of Psychiatry 171,* 303–4.

NHS Executive (1994) *Guidance on the Discharge of Mentally Disordered People and Their Continuing Care in the Community.* HSG(94)27.

Parton, N. (1996) 'Social work, risk and "the blaming system".' In N. Parton (ed) *Social Theory, Social Change and Social Work.* London: Routledge.

Payne, S., Lart, R., Gunnell, D. and Doyal, L. (1997) 'Understanding gender issues in suicidal behaviour.' Unpublished report to the NHS South and West Research and Development Directorate.

Pokorny, A.D. (1993) 'Suicide prediction revisited.' *Suicide and Life-threatening Behaviour 23,* 1, 1–10.

Pritchard, C. (1996) 'New patterns of suicide by age and gender in the United Kingdom and western world 1974–1992: An indicator of social change?' *Social Psychiatry and Psychiatric Epidemiology 31*, 227–34.

Reed, J. (1998) 'Risk assessment and clinical risk management: The lessons from recent inquiries.' *British Journal of Psychiatry 170* (suppl. 32), 4–7.

Rose, D. (1997) 'Trial by television.' *Community Care,* 4–10 December.

Sayce, L. (1995) 'Response to violence: A framework for fair treatment.' In J. Crichton (ed) *Psychiatric Patient Violence.* London: Duckworth.

Sheppard, D. (1995) *Learning the Lessons.* London: The Zito Trust.

Sheppard, M. (1990) *Mental Health: The Role of the Approved Social Worker.* Sheffield University: Joint Unit for Social Services Research.

Soni Raleigh, V. and Balarajan, R. (1992) 'Suicide and self-burning among Indians and West Indians in England and Wales.' *British Journal of Psychiatry 161*, 365–8.

Steadman, H. and Cocozza, J. (1974) *Careers of the Criminally Insane.* Lexington, Massachusetts: Lexington Books.

Steadman, H.J., Robbins, P.C., Monahan, J. Appelbaum, P., Grisso, T., Mulvey, E.P. and Roth, L. (1998) *The MacArthur Violence Risk Assessment Study (1) Executive Summary.* http://ness.sys.Virginia.EDU/macarthur/violence.html.

Steadman, H.J., Monahan, J., Appelbaum, P., Grisso, T., Mulvey, E.P., Roth, L., Clark Robbins, P. and Klassen, D. (1994) 'Designing a new generation of risk assessment research.' In J. Monahan and H.J. Steadman (eds) *Violence and Mental Disorder: Developments in Risk Assessment.* Chicago, Illinois: University of Chicago Press.

Steering Committee of the Confidential Inquiry into Homicides and Suicides by Mentally Ill People (1996) Report of the Confidential Inquiry into Homicides and Suicides by Mentally Ill People. London: Royal College of Psychiatrists.

Swanson, G. (1994) 'Mental disorder, substance abuse and community violence: an epidemiological approach.' In J. Monahan and H.J. Steadman (eds) *Violence and Mental Disorder: Developments in Risk Assessment.* Chicago, Illinois: University of Chicago Press.

Swanson, J., Holzer, C., Ganju, V. and Jono, R. (1990) 'Violence and psychiatric disorder in the community: Evidence from the Epidemiological Catchment Area surveys.' *Hospital and Community Psychiatry 41*, 761–70.

Takei, N., Persaud, R., Woodruff, P., Brockington, I. and Murray, R.M. (1998) 'First episodes of psychosis in Afro-Caribbean and White people.' *British Journal of Psychiatry 172*, 147–53.

Taylor, P.J. and Gunn, J. (1999) 'Homicides by people with mental illness: Myth and reality.' *British Journal of Psychiatry 174*, 9–14.

Taylor, P.J. and Monahan, J. (1996) 'Commentary: Dangerous patients or dangerous diseases?' *British Medical Journal 312*, 967–9.

Taylor, P.J., Garety, P., Buchanan, A., Reed, A., Wesseley, S., Ray, K., Dunn, G. and Grubin, D. (1994) 'Delusions and violence.' In J. Monahan and H.J. Steadman (eds) *Violence and Mental Disorder: Developments in Risk Assessment.* Chicago, Illinois: University of Chicago Press.

Thornberry, T. and Jacoby, J. (1979) *The Criminally Insane: A Community Follow-up of Mentally Ill Offenders.* Chicago, Illinois: University of Chicago Press.

Wallace, C., Mullen, P., Burgess, P., Palmer, S. Ruschena, D. and Browne, C. (1998) 'Serious criminal offending and mental disorder.' *British Journal of Psychiatry 172*, 477–84.

Webster, C.D., Harris, G.T., Rice, M., Cormier, C. and Quinsey, V. (1994) *The Violence Prediction Scheme: Assessing Dangerousness in High Risk Men.* Toronto: University of Toronto Institute of Criminology.

CHAPTER 7

Assessing Risks for Children

Kay Sargent

Introduction

The need to assess risk has been a dominant feature of social work with children and families in the United Kingdom in the past decade (Parton 1985, 1991). Childhood involves a long period of vulnerability and dependency on the adequate care of adults, and child welfare services have assumed responsibility for the protection of children from the harms to which they might be exposed (Corby 1993). They have also needed to balance the detection of risk of these harms with the desire to support families in becoming safer places in which children can grow to adulthood (Parton 1997).

Ideas about risk are closely linked with the idea of significant harm, which is central to the Children Act 1989. The possibility that the child is suffering or is likely to suffer from significant harm is the threshold condition for asking the court to make a care order in respect of a child (Children Act 1989 s.31) and for undertaking an enquiry into their circumstances (Children Act 1989 s.47). In both these cases the social worker would be expected to undertake an assessment of current and likelihood of future harm. Initially the parts of the Act dealing with the need to detect and rescue children at risk of harm seemed to take precedence in practice over those sections offering family support. A government review of research reports into the implementation of the Children Act indicated the need for a reassessment and rebalancing (Department of Health 1995), but it is still true that social workers spend much of their time undertaking assessments of the risks to which children are exposed to enable them to plan services and make decisions about their future.

While concerns have traditionally centred on the risks of harm to children from adults, there has been growing awareness of the risks to children from other children and young people. Children can be seen as childhood innocents who are victims rather than victimisers (Stainton Rogers 1989), but we know children are also capable of inflicting harm on other children. While there is less research information available about children who harm other children, this is growing, tending to concentrate on the issue of bullying and physical harm (Miles 1994) and sexual abuse (Bentovim, Vizard and Hollows 1991; Calder Martin, Hanks and Epps 1997). These aspects will not be covered in this chapter. There are difficulties in making links between assessments of child and adult behaviour in this area. While children who may damage other children raise complex questions for practitioners and managers, their behaviour, even more than that of adults, needs to be seen in the context of their development, and the possibility of their own maltreatment. It is doing them a disservice to concentrate solely on the risk they present.

This chapter will look at the nature and extent of the risk to children from adults, at approaches to assessing risk and uncertainty including prediction studies, at the current body of research into their effectiveness, and their usefulness for practitioners and managers.

The nature and extent of risk

Research shows that children's experience of maltreatment can have a profound effect on their development and future life. Abuse of children in childhood affects their physical growth (Iwaniec 1995), their emotional wellbeing (Erickson, Egeland and Pianta 1989; Briere 1992), and their social and educational attainment (Howes and Epinosa 1985; Mueller and Silverman 1989). While some children appear to be more resilient than others (Mrazek and Mrazek 1987), abuse always has some impact on development, limiting and diminishing potential. In extreme cases it can result in death. Although some children do die at the hands of strangers, a great many more do so because of the physical abuse or neglect of parents or carers (Creighton 1995). Adults who have experienced abuse and ill-treatment in childhood are over-represented in groups of adults who suffer mental health problems (Carmen, Reiker and Mills

1984), and in those who are dependent on drugs and alcohol (Cohen and Densen-Gerber 1982) or are involved in prostitution (Silbert and Pines 1981).

The measured extent of child abuse is dependent on its definition. A broad base of sources of harm is reflected in the definition of abuse given by the recent report of the National Commission of Inquiry into the Prevention of Child Abuse (1996, p.4):

> Child Abuse consists of anything which individuals, institutions or processes do or fail to do which directly or indirectly harms children or damages their prospects of a safe and healthy development into adulthood.

This definition includes direct and acute forms of abuse, but also indirect forms such as poor housing, family health problems and poverty, and social processes such as child labour or prostitution.

While social workers are involved in the impact of indirect social abuse on families, most child protection work has been concerned with individual cases of abuse of children defined under the four categories of physical, sexual and emotional abuse and neglect, as outlined in the guidelines *Working Together under the Children Act 1989* (Department of Health 1991). These more precise definitions form the basis of each local authority's child protection procedures and establish the threshold for registration of children thought to be at risk of significant harm on area child protection registers.

The perceived nature of risk to children will depend on which definition of abuse is being used, and the estimation of the extent of risk on how the abuse is recognised and recorded. Susan Creighton (Creighton 1995) suggests five levels of possible awareness and recognition of all cases of child abuse and neglect. These range from those cases which are known and reported to child welfare agencies, through those known to professionals in other disciplines or to friends and neighbours, but not to those agencies dealing specifically with children, those cases known only to child and abuser/perpetrator, and those which are not recognised by anyone at all. An understanding of the extent of abuse needs to take account of all of them.

Incidence and prevalence studies which try to estimate the extent of abuse measure different parts of this spectrum. Incidence studies, which record the actual number of cases recorded in a given population over a certain period of time, will primarily record cases at the first level, while prevalence studies, which attempt to measure the proportion of a population thought to have experienced abuse over a much longer period of time, will also have access to cases at the other levels.

The most recent figures available from the Department of Health (DoH) show an actual figure of 32, 351 children registered on 31 March 1996 (DoH 1997), which represents a small proportion of the estimated 13 million children in the UK, and which might be thought to indicate low levels of abuse in the population as a whole. Comparisons with incidence figures from other countries show considerable variation. Estimates of incidence per 1000 children of all kinds of abuse vary from 17.8 in the USA to 0.17 in the Netherlands, with that in England, Scotland and Wales averaging around 2 (Creighton 1995).

Prevalence studies give greater estimates of the numbers experiencing abuse, but also show considerable variation. They have looked more often at sexual abuse. Examples include those surveys undertaken for MORI (Baker and Duncan 1985) and Childwatch (BBC 1987). Prevalence studies also show wide variation. Comparison studies of sexual abuse involving direct contact rates in the United Kingdom and the USA vary from 3 per cent to 27 per cent (Creighton 1995). Those which include non-direct contact are considerably higher.

Given the difficulties in establishing and recording the exact extent of those children who may be suffering maltreatment it is reasonable to assume that

> in spite of the varying estimates produced by the different studies, there can be no doubt that there is a large base group of children who have been, or are being, maltreated … [and] … only a fraction of them are being reported to child protection practitioners. (Creighton 1995, p.19)

Awareness of this, and of the extreme consequences for a small number of these children, have made social workers conscious of the need for accurate ways of trying to identify those children most at risk.

Definition of risk assessment

The most commonly used definition of risk assessment in literature relating to protecting children is Wald and Woolverton's 'A process for assessing the likelihood that a given person (usually a parent) will harm a child in the future' (Wald and Woolverton 1990, p.486). This definition incorporates the key ideas of the harm being located in the family, that it will take place at some future point, and that an assessment can be made of how far this is likely or predictable and, by implication, preventable.

Risk assessments are usually trying to prevent a recurrence of harm after an incident has already occurred, but can also try to isolate those most likely to harm their children before any harm has taken place. This kind of preventive and predictive assessment tries to screen out of whole populations those most likely to abuse their children, with the aim of targeting services to them. It can be seen as a useful way of identifying and addressing early problems and making sure that scarce services reach those most in need of them (McCurdy 1995), but its limitations have been analysed by Dingwall (1989) who sees the process as inaccurate, statistically unreliable and socially discriminatory, singling out lower-class parents and the disadvantaged for ever closer scrutiny. Furthermore, large-scale screening for possible abuse requires levels of social policing which are not likely to be acceptable (Dingwall 1986; Horne 1990).

In practice, risk assessments most often follow an incident which has already identified concerns about a child's welfare, either because of harm already inflicted on that child or to another child in the family, or where an adult known to have already harmed a child is having close contact. There is an assumption that because of this harm or injury there is a risk of further harm. This belief lies at the core of child protection work and distinguishes it from other kinds of child welfare. It is why the analysis of risk is central to current child protection practice.

> This means that the work is focused on very specific aspects of family life, namely the provision of remedies for those identified aspects of functioning which are perceived as an immediate or potential threat to the well-being of children. (Parton, Thorpe and Wattam 1997, p.155)

Risk assessment can take place at an initial investigative stage, where it is more likely to involve concern about the child's immediate safety, or at a later stage when decisions are being made about the child's longer-term future.

The assessment of risk and decision making processes are interlinked. Time is an important variable in assessing risk (Carson 1995). Acute risks over a short space of time, such as the risk of recrimination from parents or carers if they remain at home for a child who has just indicated physical or sexual abuse, may be more easily identified than the longer-term ones of what sort of care can be provided by those parents and carers in the future.

Approaches to assessing risk

Assessing risk is a mixture of art and science. A scientific approach needs more and better ways of accurately identifying children who are most at risk, and proving that the methods used for identification are both consistent and reliable. The art of risk assessment lies both in the application of available instruments and in the use of practitioners' judgement and experience. Ways of making risk assessments can be broadly grouped into different categories.

1. Checklists of predictive factors

Checklists of predictive factors rely on the study of information from cases where abuse has already occurred in order to compile lists which will indicate those cases where abuse is most likely to occur in the future. The best-known model is Greenland's (1987) list of characteristics of parents and of children most at risk of severe physical injury, which was compiled from a study in Canada and the United Kingdom of 107 child deaths from physical assault by parents. Greenland identified nine characteristics of parents and nine characteristics of children which he felt were most likely to indicate future abuse (1987, p.185).

Characteristics of parents

- Previously abused or neglected as a child
- Age 20 years or less at the birth of first child
- Single parent/separated; partner not biological parent
- History of abuse/neglect or deprivation
- Socially isolated – frequent moves – poor housing

- Poverty – unemployed/unskilled worker; inadequate education
- Abuses alcohol and/or drugs
- History of criminally assaultive behaviour and/or suicide attempts
- Pregnant – post partum – or chronic illness.

Characteristics of children

- Previously abused/neglected
- Under five years at the time of abuse or neglect
- Premature or low birth weight
- Now underweight
- Birth defect – chronic illness – developmental lag
- Prolonged separation from mother
- Cries frequently – difficult to comfort
- Difficulties in feeding/elimination
- Adopted, foster or stepchild.

This list is given in full because it contains similar factors to other studies and identifies characteristics which indicate general social disadvantage. Reder, Duncan and Grey's analysis (1993) of 36 inquiry reports into the death of children on the child protection register between 1973 and 1979 lists comparable features and adds information about the relationship between family and the professional organisation to the characteristics of individuals. They are, however, both based on worst-case scenarios of child death, and there are difficulties in transferring this to more general use in other cases of physical abuse, let alone sexual or emotional abuse. Taken at face value they can also imply that everyone in a certain group, single parents, those abused in their own childhood, or children who are fostered or adopted for instance, are likely to abuse their own children, which is of course not true.

In the United States predictive checklists have been refined and developed into sophisticated tools, based on an actuarial model of analysing information from large numbers of individual cases, and then identifying a small number of factors which forecast events with a fair degree of accuracy. Some models give these factors individual weightings, which, added together, give a numerical estimate of risk (Johnson, L'Esperence and Baird 1984). Claims are made for the checklists' statistical reliability, tested against long-term case studies and applied to all kinds of abuse, which range from 65 to 80 per cent (Johnson 1996). This is well above chance, but raises the question of what is an acceptable level of error, given the consequences of identifying cases as false positive (potentially abusive when they are not) and false negative ('safe' when further abuse does occur).

Predictive checklists also depend on consistent application to be effective, and the evidence from the USA is that practitioners do not use them consistently (Dueck, Bronson and Levin 1992). This may, in part, reflect a healthy scepticism of the extent to which the complex behaviour patterns found in situations where children are maltreated can be reduced to statistical formulations. This is the main criticism of this kind of research. Its main advantage is that it can reduce opportunities for individual practitioner bias to influence assessment.

2. Assessment and analysis of child and family functioning

Another way of assessing risk is by looking at aspects of child/parent relationships and family functioning. This approach rests on the belief that some individual parents, some family systems and some kinds of child/parent relationships are more likely than others to be damaging to children. Assessments can identify these families. This is the approach taken by *Protecting Children: A Guide for Social Workers Undertaking a Comprehensive Assessment* (DoH 1988a), which has been the basis of practice in local authorities. This suggests eight dimensions which need to be considered, including the nature of the abuse and causes of concern, the child, the family, the parents as individuals and family interactions.

The belief that abuse is more likely to occur in families where relationships are not functioning optimally and that some families are inherently more dangerous places for children than others stems from work done by the NSPCC in Rochdale in the mid-1980s (Dale *et al.* 1986) and is rooted in family therapy theory. This sees families as interactive systems in which the response of one person to the initiative of another will, in turn, influence that other person. Individual behaviour, including abusive behaviour, can only be understood in this context. Systemic ideas were also used in the work at Great Ormond Street Children's Hospital, London, with families where sexual abuse had occurred (Bentovim *et al.* 1988).

Criticisms have been made of the assumption of family norms in ideas about dysfunctional families and, particularly by feminist writers, of systemic family therapy's avoidance of power dynamics or acceptance by adults in the family of responsibility for abusive actions (Driver and Droisen 1989). Nevertheless the idea that assessments need to be made of the way family patterns are established and continue across generations is important given the intergenerational nature of much abuse (Buchanan 1997).

Assessments of family functioning are primarily made in a subjective way, based on broad family interviews and consideration of family members' own histories, beliefs and relationships, but there have been attempts by psychologists and family therapists to formulate standardised procedures, based on systematic questioning (Wilkinson 1993), or observation of families undertaking different tasks (Epstein, Bishop and Baldwin 1983). In practice, apart from the format found in *Protecting Children* (DoH 1988a) of suggested questions, genogram and family history, social workers are not likely to use more formal tools, although they may seek the advice of other professionals such as psychologists and psychiatrists who do so.

Other theoretical bases have been used in family assessment, particularly in assessing how well parents and carers are meeting children's needs currently and their potential to meet them in the future. Physical progress in terms of height, weight and growth can be measured via growth charts. Assessments of capacity to meet emotional needs make use of attachment theory (Bowlby 1969, 1988), which stresses the importance of the development of a strong emotional bond between child and caregiver to ensure optimum emotional health and development: 'The importance of a secure attachment for a young child cannot be overemphasised. It provides the child with a secure base from which to explore the world and to which the child can return when anxious or distressed' (Adcock 1995, p.204).

Assessments of attachment in young children are primarily made by observation of children and carers (particularly mothers), especially in new situations (Ainsworth *et al.* 1978). Jenner and McCarthy (1992) use observations of parents and children in a different way in the Parent–Child Game, which uses social learning and cognitive behavioural theory. Some parental behaviours are observed as more child centred and positive than others which are more directive and negative. The Parent–Child Game aims to be an intervention and an assessment, attempting to measure and encourage more child-centred behaviour and thereby change parent/child relationships. Parents can also be assessed individually in terms of psychological functioning or more specific behaviours which may harm children, such as drug and alcohol abuse or sexual offending.

The information gathered from these kinds of assessment gives a detailed, but complex, picture of individual children and their families and the way children might be suffering abuse. However, they are less helpful in assessing the risk of the abusive behaviour being repeated. Emphasis is placed on the evidence of the parent or family's willingness and ability to change existing patterns of behaviour. In contrast to the predictive factors checklist approach, and with the possible exception of the Parent–Child Game, they have no standardised way of measuring this capacity; individual professional judgement is crucial.

3. Consensus-based models

Consensus-based models of assessing risk rely on the shared opinions of practitioners rather than of expert individuals. Individual professional knowledge, opinions and interpretation of events are combined to make a joint decision about the nature and severity of the risk. This method of assessing risk is an active process, and is the model which is used throughout the child protection system in England and Wales, in multidisciplinary case conferences. Parents are also included, although their contribution and experience is different from that of the professionals (Cleaver and Freeman 1995; Thoburn, Lewis and Shemmings 1995). Conferences make decisions about whether or not the risk of harm to a child is sufficient to warrant registration, and can also make comments, but not final decisions, on whether or not it is safe for children to remain at home.

It is possible to identify the factors which are seen as increasing risk by analysing the decision-making process. Studies of conference decisions in relation to physical abuse and neglect have been undertaken by Corby and Mills (1986), to sexual abuse by Waterhouse and Carnie (1992), and to all forms of abuse by Farmer and Owen (1995). The main factors contributing to a decision to register recorded by Farmer and Owen were:

- the perceived severity of the abuse
- the existence of secondary concerns/evidence of more than one kind of abuse
- the prior involvement of the family with social services or other agencies
- mothers being believed to be involved in the abuse.

Conferences spent the majority of their time discussing the particular nature of the incident, and much less on planning to protect the child. The attitude of parents, and particularly mothers, to the abuse is identified as important in all three studies. Mothers are expected to take responsibility for protecting their children, even though this involves difficult decisions about their own relationships with partners, friends and other family members. This assumption is based on sexist ideas about the position of mothers in families, and they may not get support in their own right to help them. It is an interesting further finding of Farmer and Owen's study that 20 months after registration the needs of the primary carer were met 50 per cent less well than those of the children.

Farmer and Owen also make some interesting comments about the approaches taken in different conferences to assessing risk. Conferences took note of the number of causes of concern mentioned, of the context of past abusive incidents as predictors of future ones, and of how far conference members believed that abuse had occurred (whether or not this was accepted by carers). Very few assessments fully explored the dynamics of the child/carer or child/family interaction, or referred to theories of the causation of abuse or research evidence which supported professionals' opinions.

Research, such as these studies, which look at risk evaluation and decision making in conferences, are useful in showing how assessments are actually being made and used. Farmer and Owen (1995) take this a step further and try to relate the process of risk assessment and evaluation to the eventual outcome for the child and the family. Their main conclusion is that risk assessment is only one part of family assessment and can fail to take account of the wider needs of the child.

4. Critical path analysis: child abuse inquiries and case reviews

Child abuse inquiries and case reviews requested by local authorities or central government reconstruct risks with hindsight. They are extensive examinations of a particular case which has had an unfortunate outcome, either because a child has died (see for example London Borough of Brent 1985; London Borough of Greenwich 1987; Bridge Child Care Consultancy 1995) or because children have been removed from their parents' care in a way which is later presumed unnecessary (DoH 1988b). They are examples of analysing risk by a critical analysis of the path of events. They consider how the risks were regarded by those involved at the time, but have the advantage of knowing what happened subsequently. This puts them in the unique position of being retrospective studies of prospective events. While this may seem a negative way of reviewing risk, especially when the idea of blame and accountability is present as it is in many child abuse reviews, there are lessons to be learned about the nature of risk, and suggestions of possible steps to reduce it (Reder, Duncan and Grey 1993; Corby 1996).

The Bridge Child Care Consultancy, which has undertaken several of the more recent reviews in the United Kingdom, repeatedly highlights the need for an accurate chronological account of events on case files, and in particular of injuries and incidents involving the child. These are often missing before the review, but when they are compiled after the child's death can show a pattern of individual events which have more significance viewed together than singly. Other key recommendations for practice from inquiry reports are the need for training and supervision for staff, the need for good professional communication systems, and the importance of seeing, considering and listening to the child(ren) involved.

Research into the effectiveness of risk assessment

In the UK there has been no specific research into the effectiveness of different ways of assessing risk, although there has in the USA, where risk assessment models are in use in over 40 states (Berkovitz 1991). These have been assessed individually for their effectiveness, both for validity (their accuracy in predicting harm tested by looking at later case outcome) and their reliability (their consistency in predicting harm when used in different case situations). Actuarial models, drawing on factors identified in past cases for use as predictors, score higher in both areas than consensus- or family assessment-based models (Johnson 1996).

Comparative studies of different models can also be made, on the same two parameters. Lyons, Doueck and Wodarski (1996) compared ten models in use in several states, which they chose because they had been tested for validity and reliability, and presented to peer review at conferences or via journals. This research has relevance to the United Kingdom, because although these particular models are not in use here, they fall into groups which mirror the approaches described above. Three of the ten models were actuarial models – that is using past indicator checklists to predict abuse – the others relied on different kinds of family assessment and child assessment. One of these models, the Child At Risk Field System, is similar to *Protecting Children* (DoH 1988a) in approach, looking at the child, the parents, the family, the kind of maltreatment and the agency involvement to make an assessment.

Lyons, Doueck and Wodarski (1996, p.148) conclude that when tested solely on their ability to predict abuse, 'So far there is too high a rate of error or uncertainty to recommend exclusive reliance on any risk assessment instrument for predictive purposes'. They found that the use of risk assessments did, however, lead to a greater standardisation of evaluation among child protection workers, and that assessments which used more than one parameter were more successful. As would be expected, there was greater agreement about high- and low-risk cases than those in the middle range.

British research studies have attempted to evaluate the effectiveness of how social workers assess risk less directly; by assessing outcomes for those children who have experienced abuse, or by wider evaluations of the child protection system. The 20 studies commissioned by the Department of Health, and summarised in *Child Protection: Messages from Research* (DoH 1995), make interesting comments about the process of deciding which children are most at risk of harm, and on the outcomes for these children and their families. Just two of these studies will be highlighted here.

Gibbons, Conroy and Bell (1995) found that only a very small number of children about whom concerns are expressed are the subjects of case conference, and even fewer of these are actually offered services within or outside of the registration process. This would seem to suggest that the system for assessing those at risk does not target those who need services and support as adequately as might be expected. This research also found that the character- istics of the parents and families of children on the register were still similar to those found by Greenland. Forty-seven per cent had been subjects of earlier investigations, and a substantial minority had histories of criminal behaviour, substance abuse or mental illness.

Farmer and Owen (1995) followed up the outcomes for children who were placed on the register for the next 20 months. They found that although 70 per cent of their sample of 44 children were considered to be protected from harm 20 months after registration, for only 23 per cent was the outcome satisfactory in terms of protecting the child, improving their general welfare and meeting the needs of their carers. Furthermore, after this short lapse of time 40 per cent of the children were being looked after away from home. This would seem to imply that for a sizeable number of children their protection rested on separation from their carers, that is by total removal of the perceived source of risk, rather than by intervention and work with families. It is not possible to tell from this study whether or not this means that social workers correctly assessed that the risks to these children were so great that only separation from parents could protect them.

Evaluation

Research can support practice with children who are at risk of abuse by giving us information about the children who abused and those who abuse them, by assisting the development of methods of working with children and families based on this information, and by testing out the ways practitioners use these tools. The above summary of available tools and approaches to risk and their success in identifying children and ensuring their safety raises several points for future dicsussion.

First, the evidence available from the research into models and methods of assessing risk does not at first sight seem very encouraging. If even those models which have been most thoroughly tested are still too unreliable to be used regularly, as Lyons, Doueck and Wodarski (1996) conclude, how useful can they be in practice? Part of the problem lies in the lack of separation of the aims and limitations of different methods and approaches. The expectation that social workers can find tools which can be totally accurate in predicting outcomes is unreasonable, but if models and methods of assessing risk are seen as aids to collating and using all available information about families, then they do have a part to play. A combination of available approaches and greater clarity about what is being assessed and how, may well prove to be the most successful, but this needs to be further researched.

Second, research information of any kind is of little use if not disseminated and applied. There is evidence that practitioners do not seem to make direct use of research information in formulating their decisions. Practitioners need to be convinced that practice using research is better than practice which relies purely on practice wisdom and professional judgements. Interviews with a small sample of social workers by Fisher (1996) showed that they did not read much, and received little post-qualification training which addressed research explicitly. Nevertheless, practitioners did make use of ideas which resonated with research findings in making decisions about which children were most at risk, and predicting outcomes. These ideas were often circulated via government guidelines interpreting research. There are dangers in accepting others' interpretations of research findings rather than seeking the information first hand.

It is difficult for social workers to make assessments and judgements based on an accurate knowledge base if this is not updated. Without this they are unlikely to acquire confidence in their practice themselves or inspire it in others. There is clearly a need for more first-hand information from research to be readily available to managers and social workers. Closer links need to be developed between academic researchers and practitioners, and post-qualification training needs to encourage this.

Third, the current norms of assessments of risk of harm are still rooted in white, middle-class, gendered ideology. It has already been indicated how expectations are placed on women to protect their children and how checklists can prejudice judgement about families which are socially disadvantaged by factors such as having a low income, containing a single parent, or being from an ethnic minority group. The tools of risk assessment, with few exceptions (Tabbert 1994), do not take account of cultural factors in their construction or their interpretation.

> Race has always been an important variable in the way which services have been provided to black families, but the years of accumulated research and guidance which disseminates the impact of racism on child care services to black families has had little impact on the development of policy and procedures in the child protection field. (Dutt and Phillips 1996, p.159)

Few research studies identify the race or ethnicity of the children studied, and where they are included the numbers are very small. Future research needs to be more explicit in investigating both the experience of black children and their families, and the validity of the methods used to work with them.

Finally, child protection aimed at the detection and prevention of incidents of harm is choosing to look through a narrow window. The debate over the benefits and drawbacks of this are well rehearsed (Parton, Thorpe and Wattam 1997). It may give clarity of purpose, but can miss many of the complexities of child and family relationshps, and the nature both of harm and of life experience for children. Furthermore, the aims of risk detection and reduction as currently expressed are confused, and this is reflected in the research. Are we trying to isolate all incidents of possible harm, or only those children at risk of the most severe harm? Are we trying to use the research to develop practice which will prevent cases of child death because of their parents' actions, or to raise standards of care for all children? How does risk research relate to decision making? There is considerable pressure on social workers and managers to make good decisions, which can be judged as such before and after the event. Again this is giving them an impossible task. Practice which puts safety at a very high premium has considerable costs for workers and for families (Sargent 1996).

Research which focuses only on risk has limited application, and needs to relate to the wider child welfare perspective.

Nevertheless, there are good reasons to continue research which will develop ways of making assessments of children and their families. There needs to be more research into the way social workers make short- and long-term assessments, and the factors which influence them. It is also important to include the children and their families both in the making of the assessments and research into their effectiveness. The stakes are high for practitioners, but still higher for the families and the children involved, and it is important to continue to produce research which can be used in supporting better practice.

References

Adcock, M. (1995) 'Assessment.' In K. Wilson and A. James (eds) *The Child Protection Handbook*. London: Balliere Tindall.

Ainsworth, M., Blehar, M., Waters, E. and Wall, S. (1978) *Patterns of Attachment: A Psychological Study of the Strange Situation*. Hillsdale, New Jersey: Erlbaum.

Baker, A.W. and Duncan, S.P. (1985) 'Child sexual abuse. A study of prevalence in Great Britain.' *Child Abuse and Neglect 9*, 453–67.

BBC (1986) *Childwatch: Overview Results from 2530 Self-Completion Questionnaires*. London: BBC Broadcasting Research.

Bentovim, A., Elton, A., Hildebrand, J., Tranter, M. and Vizard, E. (eds) (1988) *Child Sexual Abuse Within the Family: Assessment and Treatment*. London: Wright.

Bentovim, A., Vizard, E. and Hollows, A. (1991) *Children and Young People as Abusers*. London: National Children's Bureau.

Berkovitz, S. (1991) *Key Findings from the State Survey Component of the Study of High Risk Child Abuse and Neglect Groups*. Washington, DC: National Center on Child Abuse and Neglect.

Bridge Child Care Consultancy (1995) *Paul – Death through Neglect*. London: Chapman and Chapman.

Briere, J.N. (1992) *Child Abuse Trauma: Theory and Treatment of the Lasting Effects*. California: Sage.

Bowlby, J. (1969) *Attachment and Loss. Volume1, Attachment*. New York: Basic Books.

Bowlby, J. (1988) *A Secure Base: Parent–Child Attachment and Healthy Human Development*. New York: Basic Books.

Buchanan, A. (1997) *Cycles of Child Maltreatment*. Chichester: Wiley.

Calder Martin, C., Hanks, H. and Epps, K.J. (1997) *Juveniles and Children who Sexually Abuse.* Lyme Regis: Russell House Publishing.

Carmen, E., Reiker, P. and Mills, T. (1984) 'Victims of violence and psychiatric illness.' *American Journal of Psychiatry 141,* 378–83.

Carson, D. (1995) *Risk Taking with Special Reference to Child Protection.* Southampton: University of Southampton.

Cleaver, H. and Freeman, P. (1995) *Parental Perspectives in Cases of Suspected Child Abuse.* London: HMSO.

Cohen, F. and Densen-Gerber, J. (1982) 'A study of the relationship between child abuse and drug addiction in 178 parents.' *Child Abuse and Neglect 6,* 383–87.

Corby, B. (1993) *Child Abuse: Towards a Knowledge Base.* Buckingham: Open University Press.

Corby, B. (1996) 'Risk assessment in child protection work.' In H. Kenshall and J. Pritchard (eds) *Good Practice in Risk Assessment and Risk Management 1.* London: Jessica Kingsley Publishers.

Corby, B. and Mills, C. (1986) 'Child abuse: Risks and resources.' *British Journal of Social Work 16,* 153–42.

Creighton, S. (1995) 'Patterns and outcomes.' In K. Wilson and A. James (eds) *The Child Protection Handbook.* London: Balliere Tindall.

Dale, P., Davies, M., Morrison, T. and Waters, J. (1986) *Dangerous Families: Assessment and Treatment of Child Abuse.* London: Tavistock.

Department of Health (1988a) *Protecting Children: A Guide for Social Workers Undertaking a Comprehensive Assessment.* London: HMSO.

Department of Health (1991) *Working Together Under the Children Act 1989.* London: HMSO.

Department of Health (1995) *Child Protection: Messages from Research.* London: HMSO.

Department of Health (1997) *Children and Young People on Child Protection Registers. Year Ending 31 March 1996.* London: Government Statistical Service.

Department of Health (1998b) *Report of the Inquiry into Child Abuse in Cleveland.* London: HMSO.

Dingwall, R. (1986) *The Jasmine Beckford Affair.* Oxford: Oxford Centre for Socio-legal Studies.

Dingwall, R. (1989) 'Some problems about predicting child abuse and neglect.' In O. Stevenson (ed) *Child Abuse: Public Policy and Professional Practice.* Hemel Hempstead: Harvester Wheatsheaf.

Dutt, R. and Phillips, M. (1996) *An Overview of Existing Literature, Research and Guidance on Child Abuse and its Impact on the Protection of Black Children in Childhood Matters 2.* Report of the National Commission of Inquiry into Child Abuse. London: The Stationery Office.

Driver, E. and Droisen, A. (1989) *Child Sexual Abuse: Feminist Perspectives.* London: Macmillan.

Dueck, H.J., Bronson, D.E. and Levin, M. (1992) 'Evaluating risk assessment implementation in child protection.' *Child Abuse and Neglect 16,* 637–46.

Epstein, N.B., Bishop, D.S. and Baldwin, L.M. (1983) 'The McMaster Family Assessment Device.' *Journal of Marital and Family Therapy 9,* 171–80.

Erickson, M., Egeland, B. and Pianta, R. (1989) 'Effects of maltreatment on the development of young children.' In D. Cichetti and V. Carlson (eds) *Child Maltreatment: Theory and Research on the Causes and Consequences of Child Abuse and Neglect.* Cambridge: Cambridge University Press.

Farmer, E. and Owen, M. (1995) *Child Protection Practice. Private Risks and Public Remedies.* London: HMSO.

Fisher, T. (1996) *Child Protection: What Knowledge do Social Workers Use?* York: Social Work Research and Development Unit, University of York.

Gibbons, J., Conroy, S. and Bell, C. (1995) *Operating the Child Protection System.* London: HMSO.

Greenland, C. (1987) *Preventing CAN Deaths: An International Study of Deaths Due to Child Abuse and Neglect.* London: Tavistock.

Horne, M. (1990) 'Is it social work?' In Violence Against Children Study Group (eds) *Taking Child Abuse Seriously.* London: Routledge.

Howes, C. and Epinosa, M. (1985) 'The consequences of child abuse for the formation of relationships with peers.' *Child Abuse and Neglect 9,* 397, 196404.

Iwaniec, D. (1995) *The Emotionally Abused and Neglected Child.* Chichester: Wiley.

Jenner, S. and McCarthy, G. (1993) 'Quantative measures of parenting: a clinical developmental perspective.' In P. Reder and C. Lucey (eds) *Assessment of Parenting: Psychiatric and Psychological Contributions.* London: Routledge.

Johnson, W. (1996) 'Risk assessment research: Progress and future directions.' *Protecting Children 12,* 2, 15–19.

Johnson, W., L'Esperence, J. and Baird (1984) 'Predicting the recurrence of child abuse.' *Social Work Research and Extracts 20,* 2, 21–26.

London Borough of Brent (1985) *A Child in Trust. Report of the Panel of Inquiry into the Circumstances Surrounding the Death of Jasmine Beckford.* London: London Borough of Brent.

London Borough of Greenwich (1987) *A Child in Mind. Report of the Commission of Inquiry into the Circumstances Surrounding the Death of Kimberley Carlile.* London: London Borough of Greenwich.

Lyons, P., Doueck, H.J., Wodarski, J.S. (1996) 'Risk assessment for child protective services: A review of the empirical literature on instrument performance.' *Social Work Research 20,* 3, 143–55.

McCurdy, K. (1995) 'Risk assessment in child abuse prevention programs.' *Social Work Research 19,* 2, 77–87.

Miles, R. (1994) *The Children We Deserve.* London: HarperCollins.

Mrazek, P. and Mrazek, D. (1987) 'Resilience in child maltreatment victims: A conceptual exploration.' *Child Abuse and Neglect 11,* 357–66.

Mueller, E. and Silverman, N. (1989) 'Peer relations in maltreated children.' In D. Cicchetti and V. Carlson (eds) *Child Maltreatment: Theory and Research on the Causes and Consequences of Child Abuse and Neglect.* Cambridge: Cambridge University Press.

National Commission of Inquiry into the Prevention of Child Abuse (1996) *Childhood Matters. Vol.2, Background Papers.* London: The Stationery Office.

Parton, N. (1985) *The Politics of Child Abuse.* London: Macmillan.

Parton, N. (1991) *Governing the Family: Child Care, Child Protection and the State.* London: Macmillan.

Parton, N. (ed) (1997) *Child Protection and Family Support. Tensions, Contradictions and Possibilities.* London: Routledge.

Parton, N., Thorpe, D. and Wattam, C. (1997) *Child Protection: Risk and the Moral Order.* London: Macmillan.

Reder, P., Duncan, S. and Grey, M. (1993) *Beyond Blame: Child Abuse Tragedies Re-Visited.* London: Routledge.

Sargent, K. (1996) 'Safety first? Risk and assessment in child protection.' Unpublished conference paper, Oslo.

Silbet, M. and Pines, A. (1981) 'Sexual child abuse as an antecedent to prostitution.' *Child Abuse and Neglect 10,* 283–91.

Stainton Rogers, W. (1989) 'The social construction of childhood.' In W. Stainton Rogers, D. Hevey, J. Roche and E. Ash (eds) *Child Abuse and Neglect: Facing the Challenge.* London: Batsford.

Tabbert, W. (1994) 'Culturally sensitive risk assessment.' In T. Tatara (ed) *Eighth National Roundtable on CPS Risk Assessment. Summary of Highlights.* Washington, DC: American Public Welfare Association.

Thoburn, J., Lewis, A. and Shemmings, D. (1995) *Paternalism or Partnership? Family Involvement in the Child Protection Process.* London: HMSO.

Wald, M. and Woolverton, M. (1990) 'Risk assessment: The emperor's new clothes?' *Child Welfare 69,* 6, 483–512.

Waterhouse, L. and Carnie, J. (1992) 'Assessing child protection risk.' *British Journal of Social Work 22,* 47–60.

Wilkinson, I.M. (1993) *Family Assessment.* New York: Gardner Press.

CHAPTER 8

Old People at Risk

Olive Stevenson

This chapter explores the related concepts of risk and abuse and their implications for assessment; it also considers issues which arise concerning old people who live in the community and those who live in residential and nursing care.

During the course of this discussion, some reference will be made to the available research. However, as we shall see, risk is a multifaceted concept; the research which bears upon it is diverse, coming from many different fields: – medical, technological and social – and the quality and volume is variable. From the point of view of readers of this book, research on abuse as an aspect of risk is likely to be most useful. Although there is a paucity of well-founded empirical research compared, for example, with child abuse, there has been a significant growth in the last decade. In Britain, we are indebted to McCreadie (1995) who has comprehensively summarised and discussed the available evidence on elder abuse in all its forms. Reference in this chapter will frequently be made to McCreadie's work. There are, however, two other distinct dimensions of risk, self-neglect and environmental risk, which are also of significance to workers in this field. These merit a similar review of research, which would need to draw together a wide range of material from many different disciplines. Unfortunately, these reviews have not yet been undertaken.

Both 'risk' and 'abuse' are complex and contested concepts. Risk is inherent in life itself, a necessary component in the exercise of personal autonomy. In childhood, in any given society, there is a fair degree of agreement about acceptable degrees of risk, with subtle gradations as children grow towards maturity. This is much more difficult to achieve in relation to old people, for two reasons. There is no homogeneity in the ageing process, as there is in childhood. Furthermore, there is a strong presumption that older people should exercise choice and self-determination as adults – and hence, take risks – unless or until their capacity to do so is seriously impaired. To assess 'incapacity' is ethically and practically difficult, most of all in those cases in which incapacity is partial and only in some domains of daily living.

There are two aspects of risk of particular relevance to old people. First, there is unnecessary or avoidable risk brought about by the failure of society to adapt the environment to the needs of people who are frail. This is an exceedingly important matter which cannot be explored here in the depth which it merits. It is, however, pertinent that this raises arguments similar to those put forward in relation to disability generally, in what is described as 'the social model'. It is self-evident, for example, that the built environment, in and out of the home, is risky for many of the increasing number of very old people. There is much European interest in this issue, in which partnerships between designers, engineers and social scientists can flourish (Wild and Kirschner 1994; Stevenson 1995). Underlying practical activity to improve the safety of the environment are fundamental matters which make a debate about risk of particular importance to old people. Quite simply, it is evident that Western society has only begun to explore the impact on our social arrangements of changes in the age structure of the population. Many old people are exposed to unnecessary risk, either through lack of imagination and empathy in the younger generation, or through unwillingness to commit resources to rectify the position. This raises uncomfortable questions about the attitudes towards, and value accorded to, old people.

The second aspect of risk concerns its extent and nature. Since risk is a part of life, how do we draw a line between 'acceptable' and 'unacceptable'? The Law Commission (1995), in considering the implications of mental incapacity, borrowed the term 'significant harm', as used in the Children Act 1989, as the criterion for deciding on unacceptable risk. This focuses the analysis on consideration of the damage which the risk has caused or may cause. The likelihood of physical risk is self-evident in many cases, especially when old people live alone. The assessment of risk may not be in itself difficult, rather it is the decision to intervene to protect which may pose painful dilemmas. This usually turns on mental capacity. The more capable old people are mentally, the less likely it is that others will interfere in the choices which they make. When an old person is intellectually competent and wishes to exercise choice to remain in an environment which presents risk of significant harm, most professionals accept this, albeit an important task is to reduce the risk, as far as is possible. However, for relatives, these decisions may provoke anxiety and guilt. In such situations, the capacity of the individuals concerned, both carers and cared for, to tolerate the possibility of significant harm becomes an important factor in the process. Nor is it always easy in very old people to distinguish between a realistic choice of independence against which risk is weighed, and unrealistic denial. This last is often seen when discharge from hospital is imminent and the old person has not tested out how they will cope after illness.

The notion of risk does not, of course, centre solely on harmful events, such as falls. There are also longer-running risks, as when an old person living alone is self-neglectful over diet or hygiene to an extent which may prove damaging to health. Decisions to intervene in such cases are taken with reluctance by professionals, usually at a point when the degree of self-neglect is severe and when others such as neighbours are also adversely affected. Again, however, the situation of involved relatives is very difficult and is likely to lead to earlier action to protect or attempts to do so. Not infrequently, professionals see relatives as over-protective – 'she fusses too much' – and may inadequately appreciate feelings of anxiety about a loved person.

Within residential care, the issue of risk is ever present; it may indeed loom larger in day-to-day anxieties of workers and managers because of their responsibility to provide a 'safe' environment for those whose very reason for entering residential care was their frailty. Failure to do so may lead to accusations of negligence. Indeed, it is possible that, in an attempt to create an environment in which risk is cut to a minimum, the regime becomes too constrictive and adversely affects quality of life. Fire precautions which involve the installation of heavy doors in corridors are an obvious example. (However, were resources available, automatically opening doors would presumably resolve that problem.) As in the community, the issue of mental capacity is critical in the decisions which are taken on risk. A large number of old people in residential care have a significant degree of dementia and the regime of the home has to take account of that. Perhaps the most important of these concerns is the use of restraints to prevent 'risky' wandering by some patients. Whilst it is clear that some restraints are unacceptable – for example, tying to chairs – the use of electronic tagging is controversial but not inherently undesirable if it provides the resident with a degree of freedom.

Although the notion of risk which causes 'significant harm' moves us towards more precise consideration of the kind of physical risk about which health and social care professionals are legitimately concerned, it still leaves us with a huge question – what *kind* of harm are we thinking about? Here again, the analogy with child abuse has some relevance. It is generally accepted that child abuse is a socially constructed concept and, therefore, assumptions about acceptable and unacceptable risk vary across cultures and over time. None the less, as international communication about these issues has developed, it has become clear that, in two ways, there is a degree of consensus which transcends time and space. First, there is a recognition that children require a protective environment of some kind within which to develop; this presumably derives from a biological imperative for the survival of the species. Second, there is a partial consensus about the parameters of protective activity; for example, the 'nurturing' of infants, with all that the word implies, and the existence of sexual taboos. The implication is that significant harm will be caused to children's development without protective action.

Put baldly, and in a simplified form, such an analogy immediately raises questions about society's 'duty of care' towards elderly people. There is nothing comparable with the fierce protectiveness of adults for their young, which, however idealised and 'moralised', has primitive roots in survival. This is not simply a debating point. It prompts us to ask whether there is the same societal imperative to protect old people from harm as there is with children. How far does talk of choice and autonomy for them in fact mask an unwillingness to devote attention and resources to their protection? No doubt, many would argue for the intrinsic value of a 'good enough' quality of life for all citizens and the moral responsibility which this places upon us. But whilst it remains the case that public outcry about child abuse is so many decibels higher than about old people, there must remain a doubt about the extent of the social commitment to action to prevent or alleviate significant harm to old people.

When we turn to the question of what constitutes unacceptable harm to old people, there are even more difficulties than in the case of children. In both, cultural variations are great, but in the case of old people, there is not a clear developmental structure against which to measure harm. For example, whilst both direct physical and sexual assault may be socially prohibited, there is a coherent knowledge base of what is necessary to children's healthy, physical, emotional, social and intellectual development, which offers a yardstick against which to make an assessment of risk. (It has to be said, however, that it is not always fully utilised, for example, in cases of neglect) (Stevenson 1998). With old people, the idea of norms of development towards the goal of maturation is not appropriate in everyday discussion of assessing risk. (Although some aspects of ageing may indeed demonstrate developmental progress – intellectual, emotional or spiritual. But that is a different issue.) For practical purposes, we mainly focus on the maintenance, so far as possible, of the *status quo* by avoiding damage to the established norms and quality of their lives. Obviously, the decline in some people of their physical and mental powers also produces a decline in their quality of life for which there cannot be complete compensation. For many professionals and relatives, the objective is damage limitation. But it is very important that the avoidance of significant harm is seen in holistic terms, in terms of human needs throughout life, rather than simply avoidance of adverse events.

Professionals in the child care field will be familiar with the materials produced by the Department of Health for 'Looking after Children' (Department of Health 1991, 1995) in which a number of dimensions of healthy development are identified. One of these is 'identity'; the development of a sense of identity is accepted as a key issue for children. We are also familiar with the impact of the sociological theory, following Goffman (1961), which traces the effect on adults who are deprived of the symbols and markers of their uniqueness. That is readily transferable to the situations in which (for example) old people in residential care find their past is unknown and uncherished, the clothes which they wear not their own, and so on. Is it just a sense of outraged morality that makes us concerned about this or are we intuitively fearing that the person, as a person, is *damaged* by these experiences? That is to say, that we fear they may be at 'risk of significant harm'? Unfortunately, with this, as with other significant issues, I know of no research to test the effects for very old people of adverse environments on what might be described as the integrity of the personality.

So far, I have considered, first, the idea of risk itself; second, the notion of risk involving 'significant harm', emphasising that 'harm' should be seen in holistic terms which span physical, intellectual, emotional and social factors. Third, however, this raises particular difficulties when we do not have clear yardsticks by which to assess those aspects of harm which are not physically demonstrable.

This discussion of risk and harm has not yet focused on abuse, that is on acts of commission or omission which cause harm. However, abuse is a very important element in risk. If this term were interpreted very widely, one could move to a position in which much harm suffered by old people could be seen as abuse, because society, through its agents, has failed adequately to protect them against risk. But although that analysis has the merit of drawing attention to general social responsibility and to the standards of care to which we should aspire, it may divert us from consideration of more directly abusive behaviour.

A number of definitions of elder abuse have been given by McCreadie (1995); the one used here is that adopted by Action on Elder Abuse, cited by McCreadie.

> Elder Abuse is a single or repeated act or lack of appropriate action, occurring within any relationship where there is an expectation of trust, which causes harm or distress to an older person.

The categories used to differentiate between kinds of abuse are similar to those used for child protection in registration, that is, physical, sexual and emotional abuse and neglect, with the addition of financial abuse. There are similar difficulties in establishing criteria and thresholds of risk especially in relation to the less specific areas of emotional abuse and neglect. None the less, the importance of continuing to develop these criteria is underlined by the accept-ance, discussed above, that in maintaining 'a good-enough life' risk should be considered in relation to the totality of human experience. Despite certain similarities, however, there are two striking differences in comparing abuse of children with that of old people. The first of these concerns family relationships. Reading across from child abuse to the abuse of old people, it is immediately apparent that we cannot make similar assumptions about the responsibilities of relatives. Whereas both in law and in terms of social norms there is no doubt that parents are responsible for their children, there is no parallel certainty in our culture that adult children are responsible for their parents.

There are wide cultural variations in this matter, even between European countries, but most graphically illustrated in Eastern traditions of 'filial piety' which persist in the modern societies in that region, even if weakened. The traditional concept of filial piety (a combination of respect and duty) made it an absolute social requirement for children to take care of their parents. Men were usually formally ascribed these responsibilities; however, as in the West, actual caring tasks were often carried out by women.

In recent years, in our culture, there has been a growing assumption that those adult children who care for older relatives do so as part of a kind of unspoken intergenerational contract; that reciprocity-over-time is the value on which later care is offered. ('What was given to me, I give back'.) Yet this is not clear-cut or absolute (Stevenson 1993). Our contemporary society is character- ised by ambivalence. For example, there is no legal obligation to support parents financially, no 'household means test' as in the past. Yet many are under heavy pressure to do so at least in part – by 'top-up fees' for residential care, for instance, or by paying for home services when they are not otherwise available. More subtly, but no less pervasive, there is still an expectation from society that adult children will and should play a part in the care of their parents. For example, although there is no firm research evidence, it is well known that the physical availability of 'carers' may play a part in the allocation of support by social services. It is clear that we swing between notions of filial obligation and those of earned reciprocity. Just as there is no clear consensus in the society about this, so the conflict is internalised in individuals.

These social attitudes have a direct bearing on one of the most significant findings in the USA confirmed to an extent in the UK (see for example, Pillemer and Finkelhor 1989; Homer and Gilleard 1990). This body of research strongly indicates that most relatives who abuse old people in their homes have long-standing personality or relationship problems. The abuse does not arise simply from the stress of caring, including current interpersonal tensions. It is likely to be rooted either in the emotional and psychological difficulties of the carer, for example in mental illness or addictions, and/or in long-established antagonisms or deficits in parent–child relationships. This is not to deny that 'ordinary' carers, well within the boundaries of normal behaviour, may on occasion feel themselves in danger of abusing and sometimes step over a line which they themselves draw. The research, however, does seem to indicate that such people may be more likely to fear loss of control than actually to lose it. McCreadie (1995) suggests that abuse problems may be exacerbated by the return to the family home of adult children who in former days might have been hospitalised and for whom alternative housing is not now available.

If one puts together societal ambivalence about caring responsibilities and wide variations between individuals in their capacity to care, we are drawn to ask whether there has been a convenient social collusion to reify the word 'carer' and to include within the term some who have little or no motivation to perform that role or whose personal difficulties make them unsuitable to do so. Of course, the same might be said of a subset of 'parents' who cannot undertake that role successfully. But such people are generally accepted as socially deviant. Bringing children into the world, it is felt, places the onus of responsibility fairly and squarely on parents, though much more on mothers than fathers. In the UK today, one has an uncomfortable feeling that it has been convenient for professionals to describe a very heterogeneous group of people as 'carers'. This may engender a false sense of security and may appear to minimise the need for formal provision.

In contrast, but superficially, one can say that the staff who perform 'tending' work in residential care have chosen the work, whereas some relatives have it thrust upon them. However, that ignores the fact that many of the women who enter this work do so because it is local, convenient, the only work that is available and requires no formal qualifications. Whereas in children's homes, all staff must be checked with the police, in adult homes, only the proprietor and/or manager is subject to such queries. Fortunately, the chances of appointing positively dangerous staff are fewer than in children's homes, although this should not blind us to the fact that mentally unbalanced, even sadistic people have been employed in old people's homes. More frequently, however, there is a need to protect old people from staff who are ill-equipped, by temperament, intellect or training, to deal with the problems which old people with various forms of dementia or mental impairment may exhibit. The likelihood of abuse by staff who are bewildered, angered, repelled and even frightened by some behaviour is obviously greater when they are ill prepared for the work. The physical aspects of care and the emotions which are expressed through it, have a profound effect on the wellbeing of old people.

Thus it is evident that some old people, both in the community and in residential care, may be placed at risk of significant harm by those who are not motivated to undertake caring roles. This applies to direct maltreatment but can also be seen in relation to money matters – when, for example, an old person may find themselves under pressure to sell their house against their wishes.

The foregoing discussion is not intended to under-estimate or devalue the good care offered by many at great personal expense or the entirely benign care offered by some staff. Nor are the old people simply 'objects' whether of care or of abuse. There is a dynamic and often intense interaction between carer and cared-for, in which the needs and attitudes of the latter are as significant as the former. McCreadie (1995), for example, points to research findings concerning the risk to carers from old people with dementia or with long-standing problems of excessive control or domination of their children or partners. Furthermore, long-standing patterns of interaction can persist unchanged into later years. For instance, domestic violence involving sexual and physical assaults on an old woman may become visible or more problematic because of the frailty of the old person. In contrast, the onset of dementia can bring about atypically aggressive behaviour in an old person and bring new stresses to a carer who was formerly able to offer adequate support. At a deeper level, the presence of dementing illness may mean that a carer is deprived of the sense of relationship based on shared experience, past or present. The loss of 'personhood' in the old person may strike at the root of human concern, one for the other, paradoxically when the ethical responsibility for their care and protection is greatest.

Thus far, we have considered the distinct but related concepts of risk and abuse and definitional issues which arise from them. Such an analysis takes us into fundamental matters concerning the balance between protection and autonomy for adults who are deemed to be 'at risk' (Parsloe and Stevenson 1993) and the responsibilities of those described as 'informal carers' to their elderly relatives.

These complex, subtle and important problems are being debated in the context of significant developments in legal, political and professional spheres. Two aspects of these are of particular importance to our theme. The first of these concerns the probabilty of legal change in relation to the protection offered to people deemed to be mentally incapacitated. The second concerns the growth across the country of awareness of and anxiety about abuse of adults amongst professionals.

Winds of legal change in England began to blow strongly from 1991 onwards, when the work of the Law Commission on the subject started to emerge, culminating in 1995 with the full discussion paper (Law Commission 1995, 1997). Their deliberations and a draft Bill have formed the basis for the Green Paper *Who Decides?* (Lord Chancellor's Department 1997) which states:

> The Government believes that there is a clear need for reform of the law in order to improve the decision making process for those who are unable to make decision for themselves or who cannot communicate their decisions. These are some of the most vulnerable people in our society. (p.1)

It is to be expected, however, that the debate on such change will be contentious and it is as yet unclear how far the Law Commission's original proposals will be modified in legislation; reservations on some points are apparent in the Green Paper. The Law Commission in its discussion document emphasised the need for certain principles to underlie an assessment of mental incapacity, to ensure that decisions were taken with the utmost responsibility. There was to be a dual test of the 'lack of capacity' and 'the best interests' of the person concerned and four requirements for assessment:

- a person's 'ascertainable, past and present, wishes and feelings'
- 'the need to permit and encourage the person to participate'
- the views of other people concerned with the person
- whether the required action or decision can be achieved by less restrictive methods.

The section of the Green Paper which most concerns readers of this book is entitled 'Public law protection for people at risk' (Chapter 8). The Law Commission recommended that social service authorities should have a new duty to investigate cases of possible neglect or abuse and that they should have short-term powers to protect people whom they believe to be at risk. (It was not envisaged that residential and nursing homes would need to be covered by these provisions because of existing powers under the Registered Homes Act. It is far from clear that this is the case.)

The Green Paper asserts that: 'The government considers that there may be some merit in some of the recommendations made ... but is not convinced that there is a pressing need for reform' (p.68). Accepting that it is important to protect vulnerable adults, it points out that individuals have the right 'to live in isolation if they so choose, even at some degree of risk' (p.68). This observation, however, sidesteps the issues which concern professionals most: first, risk not caused by living in isolation, but by the behaviour of others; second, risk brought about by *extreme* cases of self-neglect.

Despite the tenor of the quotation above, the discussion of detailed proposals which follows does not give an impression of outright political rejection of these powers. Rather, it reads as if there is hesitation partly because empirical evidence on abuse is lacking, partly because of doubt about the social will for change and partly for pragmatic reasons – legislative time, resources and so on.

The principal concern which has been expressed by some practitioners is that without carefully drawn new legislation, vulnerable people who do not readily fall within the provisions of existing mental health provisions will not be safe; specifically, in the case of elderly people, those who are at risk of abuse from others may be intimidated by them and have some degree of physical or mental fragility, but may not be regarded as fully mentally incapable, within the parameters outlined by the Law Commission.

We cannot predict the outcome of this public and professional debate and the nature of the subsequent legislation. This decade may, however, come to be seen as a turning point in social and political acceptance that our present arrangements for the protection of vulnerable people have not been adequate. The uncertainty and ambivalence surrounding this are to an extent understandable because by far the majority of persons who might be affected by changes in law and policy are very old people with a degree of mental fragility, for whom society has had little experience of developing protective systems.

Such an observation leads us to the second theme – the growth of professional involvement in abuse of old people. This has been charted in recent publications. (See for example Pritchard 1995; Department of Health 1995; Kingston and Penhale 1995; Stevenson 1996). In the 1980s, the interest in this issue was raised by the efforts of certain individuals, notably Eastman (1984). But the time was not ripe and it did not catch the imagination of the majority. During the 1990s, we have seen a new coherent and effective campaign by particular individuals, taken forward by the creation of a national organisation, Action on Elder Abuse, and mirrored, albeit unevenly, across the country by the development at local level of policies and procedures in adult abuse. The political and governmental response throughout the 1990s has been hesitant, although not indifferent, but it is of interest that, unlike child protection, the thrust towards development and changes in adult protection, including the field of learning disability, seems to have come from the 'bottom up' rather than the 'top down' and to have come from a range of professionals. It is not surprising that those in the higher levels of management are cautious about the development of protective assessment and intervention which has been shown to require such high resourcing in child protection, and in the absence of a clear legislative framework. But, in my view, action to protect vulnerable older people against harm is on our social agenda to stay.

The implications of the preceding discussion for the assessment of risk are far reaching. Since life is inherently risky, assessment must focus upon the notion of *unacceptable* risk, even although, as we have seen, this will be subject to social definition in different times and cultures. In England, it seems likely that the government will frame 'unacceptability' in terms of 'significant harm', if and when introducing legislation for the protection of adults. This is taken from the Children Act (England and Wales) 1989. Hence assessment of risk focuses on the question: is the person exposed to, or likely to be exposed to, risk of significant harm? As in the case of children, such a phrase opens the door to much legal debate and at times, no doubt, some irritating logic chopping. The experience with children is that it is easier to agree on 'significant harm' in cases where physical manifestations, such as injuries, are clear-cut than in subtler but more pervasive conditions, such as neglect. However, it is increasingly recognised that, for children, neglect may be as – or more – damaging than more specific incidents (Stevenson 1998). It seems highly likely that neglect, both by self and by others and in residential and community contexts, will assume an increasingly higher priority in assessment of old people.

There is as yet little significant research on the processes of risk assessment of old people. Writing of abuse, Bennett and Kingston (1993) acknowledge that even 'the recognition of inadequate care ... is still at a basic level' (p.32). Practitioners obviously need a coherent body of knowledge, clinical experience and research upon which to draw. Some progress is being made (Decalmer and Glendenning 1993; Pritchard 1995).

In the context of practice today, however, the anxiety may centre more on assessment of *capacity* than of risk itself. That is to say, (and this is a crucial difference between child and adult protection), practitioners are frequently uncertain as to the extent to which an old person is capable of exercising choice.

Most, if not all, practitioners accept in principle the right of an old person, who is mentally capable, to make decisions concerning their own lives, even if these expose them to danger of various kinds. At the other end of the continuum, there is little difficulty about taking over these decisions when a person has lost capacity. As we have earlier described, the Law Commission has set ethical parameters for making assessment in the best interests of the person. We are left with the inescapable fact that there are a significant number of cases in which the evidence of incapacity is insufficient to over-ride the autonomy of the person. Most of these cases involve a degree of mental infirmity, often (but not always) associated with the early stages of dementia. There is an increasing body of literature to guide practitioners both in the assessment of the condition and in its implications (for example, Jacques 1988; Hunter 1997).

But there is a long way to go. Nor can the attitudes and feelings of those undertaking the assessment be ignored. The leanings of individual practitioners towards protection or autonomy are bound to play a part.

There is a further dilemma in relation to capacity if the old person is not suffering from mental infirmity, but is afraid, perhaps emotionally paralysed, by an abuser. Physical frailty plays a part in this. An assessment of such a state of mind does not resolve legal or ethical difficulties but is a very important element in the process. These observations remind us how skilled the practitioner needs to be in listening to and communicating with the person and those around them if risk and capacity are to be adequately appraised.

Most risk assessments are done as part of a more general assessment of need. It seems very important that the interaction of need with risk be at the heart of the process. In this way, the implications of the assessment, including the elements of risk, will be considered creatively, with a search for imaginative solutions to the tensions between autonomy and protection. This sounds idealistic but was at the centre of the principle of 'needs-led' assessment, sadly distorted and impoverished by current resource constraints and the mental set of workers caught up in over bureaucratic systems.

With so much that is unknown and untried, there is much to be learnt, both positive and negative, from the child protection experience of the last 20 years (Stevenson 1996). On the positive side, the development of interagency and interprofessional cooperation has much to offer and is being taken up in different ways across the country. A few authorities are initiating 'Adult protection committees', parallel to child protection committees, and many have in place interagency procedures. On the negative side, there is some danger, already identified in the field of child protection, of galloping ahead with procedures when the nature of practice required and the research base for it is still rudimentary. Such considerations pinpoint the need for understanding and analysis of the factors involved in professional judgements, which require the application of values, knowledge and skills. The earlier discussion in this chapter surely indicates that this field of work, with the old people at risk, should involve high-quality professional judgements, comparable with, but not identical to, work with children. It is, therefore, sad and highly regrettable that post-war social work in this country has never established an effective specialism in such work, concerning adults, which would have been compatible and congruent with demographic and social trends. That said, however, it must also be recognised that the day-to-day protection of old people, whether in their own homes or in residential care, will largely depend on the quality of 'hands-on' care offered by workers, both in residential and community settings.

The implications for management, supervision and training are profound and far reaching (Stevenson 1999).

The manifest inadequacies of our present general provision, the near collapse of community care in some areas and the mushrooming of independent residential and nursing home care without clear training requirements provide a difficult and depressing climate in which to attend properly to old people at risk. It is all the more creditable that, despite such difficulties, there is a persisting drive to improve matters. The task is now to gain national commitment to the four prerequisites for progress: research, especially concerning the family relationships of older people; training, especially concerning values and judgements; legal change, to ensure a framework designed to do this work properly; and the development of sensible local policies and procedures. We do not aim to close off risk for old people. Rather, the objective is to minimise risk of significant harm.

References

Bennett, G. and Kingston, P. (1993) *Elder Abuse. Concepts, Theories and Interventions.* London: Chapman and Hall.

Decalmer, P. and Glendenning, F. (1993) *The Mistreatment of Elderly People.* London: Sage.

Department of Health (1991, 1995) *Looking After Children: Research into Practice.* London: HMSO.

Department of Health, Social Services Inspectorate (1995) *Abuse of Older People in Domestic Settings. A Report of Two Seminars.* London: Department of Health.

Eastman, M. (1984) *Old Age Abuse.* London: Age Concern.

Goffman, E. (1961) *Asylums.* London: Penguin.

Homer, A. and Gilleard, C. (1990) 'Abuse of elderly people by their carers.' *British Medical Journal 301,* 1359–62.

Hunter, S. (ed) (1997) *Dementia: Challenges and New Directions.* Research Highlights in Social Work 31. London: Jessica Kingsley Publishers.

Jacques, A. (1988) *Understanding Dementia.* London: Churchill-Livingstone.

Kingston, P. and Penhale, B. (eds) (1995) *Family Violence and the Caring Professions.* London: Macmillan.

Law Commission (1995) *Mental Incapacity.* Law Commission No.231. London: HMSO.

Lord Chancellor's Department (1997) *Who Decides? Making Decisions on Behalf of Mentally Incapacitated Adults.* London: HMSO.

McCreadie, C. (1995) *Elder Abuse: Update on Research.* London: Institute of Gerontology, King's College London.

Pillemer, K.A. and Finkelhur, D. (1989) 'Causes of elder abuse: Caregiver stress versus problem relatives.' *Journal of Orthopsychiatry 59,* 179–87.

Pritchard, J. (1995) *The Abuse of Old People,* 2nd edition. London: Jessica Kingsley Publishers.

Stevenson, O. (1993) 'Informal social care and its implications for formal care.' In D. Hobman (ed) *Uniting Generations, Studies in Conflict and Cooperation.* London: Age Concern.

Stevenson, O. (ed) (1995) *Community Care for Very Old People: Technology for Living at Home.* Cost A5 (Committee on Science and Technology European Community), Volume 10. Kregsei: Akon Press.

Stevenson, O. (1996) *Elder Protection in the Community. What Can We Learn from Child Protection?* London: Institute of Gerontology, King's College London.

Stevenson, O. (1998) *Neglect: Issues and Dilemmas.* Oxford: Blackwell Science.

Stevenson, O. (1999) *Elder Protection in Residential Care. What Can We Learn from Child Protection?* London: Department of Health.

Wild, C. and Kirschner, A. (eds) (1994) *Technology for the Elderly.* Cost A5 (Committee on Science and Technology European Community), Volume 10. Kregsei: Akon Press.

CHAPTER 9

Training Professionals in Risk Assessment and Risk Management

What Does the Research Tell Us?

Mike Titterton

> Sometimes it is necessary to take a gamble – to put something at stake in the hope of gaining a better quality of life. (S. Pritchard and P. Brearley in Brearley 1982, p.93)

Introduction

A noticeable resurgence of interest in 'risk' in the welfare field can be detected after a period of relative neglect following pioneering forays by Brearley (1979, 1982) and Norman (1980). The relationship between training and risk work has, however, received little scrutiny. Training is often advocated as *the* solution to the difficulties and dilemmas faced by welfare professionals. Reed (1997) and Stanley and Manthorpe (1997) have, for example, drawn our attention to the 'chorus of demands' for training emanating from recent inquiries in the field of mental health. In this chapter we explore the contention that training provides us only with a starting point, and that training needs to be acknowledged in research accounts of risk work, rather than as something which is simply tacked on as an afterthought.

Concerns about the training of social workers surface regularly, particularly after adverse publicity in cases of child abuse (Parton 1996; Parton *et al.* 1997). Issues relating to training and risk work tend to emerge surrounded by a powerful set of negative connotations, arising from the risk situations which are singled out for media attention: where children have been severely abused or killed, when people have been discharged from mental hospital into the community with unfortunate consequences, or when social workers have been attacked or even killed by clients in the course of their duties. The impact of the negative construction of 'risk' for the training and development of social workers and other professionals provides a key motif for this contribution.

Some central issues for the training of welfare professionals, including social workers, in the fields of risk assessment and risk management will be addressed here. The chapter consists of two parts. The first half provides a short review of some of the relevant literature on risk; some of the implications for the training of practitioners and managers are concidered. The second part briefly outlines an approach to assessing and managing risks used in the training of over 300 staff in Scotland and then reports some findings from some modest research into the effectiveness of this training. Finally, an attempt is made to pull together some emerging issues and offer some tentative conclusions.

Overview of the literature

This part provides a brief review of the knowledge base as represented by the diverse literature on risk assessment, risk management and related topics. Some of the implications for training professionals in the welfare field are unpacked. The original intention had been to explore research findings on training and risk work, but this topic produced such a singularly unpromising yield that the limits of the search were broadened to incorporate a number of key topics.

The literature search was undertaken online using BIDS social science databases for the periods 1988–93 and 1994–97 and a health database held by the library of the Development Group of the NHS in Scotland. Keywords selected for the search included risk assessment; risk management; risk and training.

There is a startling absence of solid, empirical research on the topic of risk and social welfare, particularly in relation to vulnerable adults. This chapter would be better subtitled 'what the research does *not* tell us'. There is insufficient evidence of a robust nature about how practitioners in a range of settings conceive of risk, how they operationalise the concept, the problems they face in so doing, the impact on practice and the outcomes for the individuals for whom they are responsible.

Instead, the researcher is forced to widen his or her search, to dip into a range of readings, to make connections and comparisons and to make sense of findings from diverse sources. This is a major task in itself and what follows is but a small and modest start in this enterprise. It does not pretend to be comprehensive but instead picks up on some selected findings of particular relevance for social workers and other professionals.

Five topics are examined: definitions and conceptions of 'risk'; risk assessment; risk management; the law, rights and responsibilities; risk and training.

The definition and conceptualisation of 'risk'

The first topic is that of the definition and clarification of the concept of 'risk'. The practical aspects of this should be clear: how we deal with a social problem is influenced by how we define that problem (Manning 1987). The clarity of our language is essential, particularly for the training of practitioners. Yet the term 'risk' is often used indifferently at best and carelessly at worst.

Risk, we are told, has 'always been central' to professions like social work (Manthorpe *et al.* 1995, p.20). However 'risk' in the care of vulnerable people is typically taken to mean the threat to the wellbeing or welfare of the individual, their relatives and members of the public and staff alike. The concept is often interpreted as dealing with the probability of an unfortunate incident occurring. Such incidents result from a conjunction of circumstances which may have harmful consequences. According to this view, the likelihood of such an incident occurring represents its risk (East 1995).

A key development has been the changing perception that risk is 'not, as it is often taken to be, an evil in itself' (Norman 1988, p.82). In her study of the risks older people can face, Wynne-Harley writes: 'Risks and risk taking are commonly seen in a negative light. For example, a thesaurus identifies risk with hazard, menace, peril and danger' (1991, p.1; see also Douglas 1992 and Prins 1996). Equally it can be argued that an 'over cautious life style can bring its own hazards', so an appropriate balance between risk and safety is desirable (Wynne-Harley 1991, p.1). However, as Norman (1980, 1988) has noted, this negative view of risk can also be accompanied by stereotypes and prejudices about old age and old people. One of the authors of the opening quote, Paul Brearley, explicitly rejected the conflation of the term 'risk' with 'hazard' in an influential analysis (Brearley 1982; Carson 1995; Pilgrim and Rogers 1996). Brearley argued that risk taking should be recognised as important for the quality of life of older people. This applies to all contexts of living, whether residential or non-residential.

According to Norman, people take risks every moment of their lives, 'weighing the likely danger of a course of action against the likely gain' (1988, p.82). For the authors of the Counsel and Care document, *The Right to Take Risks*, life is full of risks; risk taking 'adds a sparkle' to people's lives (Counsel and Care 1993, p.1). Some writers suggest that we now inhabit a 'risk society'; risk has become a central category for understanding contemporary society (Beck 1992, 1998; Douglas 1992). Risk is being, in that inelegant jargon, 'norm-alised': it is being redefined as part of everyday discourse in a way which challenges rational scientific assumptions about prediction and control of the natural and social worlds (Lash *et al.* 1996; Parton 1998).

A more balanced definition of 'risk' is called for, one which emphasises its positive as well as its negative nature. The early cues provided by Brearley and Norman are at last being picked up by some of the more recent texts on risk taking (Alberg *et al.* 1996; Carson 1995; Manthorpe *et al.* 1997). Risk taking can have beneficial as well as harmful outcomes. The task for professionals is to identify the types of benefits and harms which may occur, as well as their likelihood. Further, they need to be more specific about the range of factors which affect the likelihood or probability of certain kinds of outcomes; we can also attempt to specify the timescale within which the risk taking activity is intended to take place. A particularly helpful definition of 'risk' is: 'the possibility of beneficial and harmful outcomes and the likelihood of their occurrence in a stated timescale' (Alberg *et al.* 1996, p.9).

As pointed out by various writers, risk taking is all about uncertainty (e.g. Parton 1996, 1998). The possible outcomes of a proposed course of activity could in theory be infinite and it is impossible to predict something with absolute certainty. In the complex world of human interaction we should not expect to do so. Instead, the professional art of risk taking lies in the weighing up of likely outcomes and the use of professional judgement, guided by a systematic method of risk assessment and management.

Language is important: the terms 'children at risk' or 'elderly at risk' really mean that they are 'at risk of harm'. For people to grow and develop as creative and autonomous beings, they have to engage with risk. The concept of risk taking as a 'right' has been discussed by Counsel and Care (1993) for older people and explored further by Herring and Thom (1997) in the case of older people and alcohol. The implications of this have still to be thought through and can provoke lively debate in training sessions, particularly in the fields of dementia, learning disability and children.

There is a pronounced problem in the literature which was surveyed: while a growing number of authors acknowledge the potential for differential outcomes in risk situations, they often then proceed to analyse 'risk' as a threat. The implications of defining risk in a more positive way are rarely explored. There is a dearth of materials for professionals and their trainers to get to grips with. This is particularly marked in the mental health and psychiatric literature, where risk is treated as equivalent to a threat of violence or harm.

Four points emerge from the foregoing review.

- risk is undergoing a process of 'normalisation', identified as necessary to life, and as part of ordinary living
- risk as having differential outcomes is still to be explored
- a more positive conception of risk is called for
- professionals have to be careful about the language we use, e.g. 'risk' is used interchangeably with 'danger' or 'hazard'.

Risk assessment

A burgeoning literature can now be found for risk assessment in health and social care but the overwhelming emphasis remains on assessing for the risk of harmful or adverse outcomes. In the field of mental health, risk assessment has become, as Gunn (1997, p.163) notes, a 'fashionable buzz phrase'. Here the concerns are with 'dangerousness' and risk in terms of violence to self or others (Monahan 1988; Steadman *et al.* 1993; Potts 1995; Howlett 1997; Reed 1997).

Discussions of suicide risk can readily be found (Gunn 1997; Lyon 1997; Rossau and Mortensen 1997; Inskip *et al.* 1998). Latterly there has been an increase in interest in assessing negative risks in relation to 'deviant' populations: sexual offenders (Barker and Morgan 1993; O'Callaghan and Print 1994; Campbell 1995; McEwan and Sullivan 1996; Scottish Office 1997a); those who are or who have been involved in the criminal justice system and who may reoffend (Kemshall 1996; Scottish Office 1998); and drug misusers (Griffiths and Waterston 1996; Argall and Cowderoy 1997).

This preoccupation with assessing negative risks such as potential harm or danger is particularly marked in respect of children (Department of Health 1988; Berkowitz 1991; Waterhouse and Carnie 1992; English and Pecora 1994; Corby 1996; Scottish Office 1997b; Scott 1998). A greater ambivalence about risk may be discerned for adolescents in relation to 'risk behaviours' (Plant and Plant 1992; Maggs *et al.* 1997). A more limited literature is to be found for people with learning disabilities (Manthorpe *et al.* 1997; Tindall 1997) and older persons (Counsel and Care 1993; Lawson 1996; Littlechild and Blakeney 1996; Pritchard 1997; see also the bibliography compiled by Jackson 1992) but here there is a readier acknowledgement of the need to assess for positive or beneficial outcomes.

There are, in general, few research accounts of positive risk assessment, with guidelines to match. While Alberg *et al.* (1996) set out with a balanced understanding of risk as quoted above, the risk assessment guidelines that follow their discussion are based on negative risks, as are the accompanying case studies. Some of the difficulties evident in the risk assessment literature arise from definitional problems and a failure to clarify rigorously the concept of risk to be operationalised. The problems are compounded by a preoccupation with checklists, often divorced from the values and principles which informed them in the original context; sometimes clinical and actuarial models sit awkwardly together.

An influential model for risk assessment has been that provided by Brearley (1982) with its differentiation of 'strengths' and 'hazards', and 'background hazards' and 'situational hazards', which can be listed alongside the feared, undesirable outcome, i.e. 'dangers'. This has been taken up by Sheppard (1990) and Prins (1996) for mental health and simplified somewhat by Kelly (1996) for child abuse. The advantage of this approach is that it encourages practitioners to be more analytical in their approach. A disadvantage from the training point of view is that practitioners can get confused by the terms, a finding also noted by Stanley and Manthorpe (forthcoming). A further difficulty identified by Kelly is that it is a static approach. A key challenge for trainers is getting practitioners to take on board the importance of dynamic risk assessment: as Grubin (1997) points out, risk changes over time, place and circumstances.

The trainer is also faced with professionals working with a diversity of guidelines. There is much reinventing of wheels and duplication of effort: one of the biggest problems is to produce guidance which is clearly linked to a coherent policy framework. Another issue is the growth of assessments involving multidisciplinary teams. A major problem for such teams is the need for standardised procedures for identification of risk and response among team members; Feaviour *et al.* (1995) have proposed a common checklist approach to iron out inconsistencies in assessment and follow up. In the author's experience, the question as to where responsibility lies in multiagency and multidisciplinary settings is increasingly being raised. Kennedy and Gill (1997) have asked: are team members equally liable? These writers point out that while, for example, the psychiatrist and social worker are responsible under the mental health legislation, in circumstances of voluntary care it is less clear.

Some authors argue that the apparent concentration on risk assessment in the literature is misplaced. This argument has two main forms. First, writers like Carson (1995) argue that the emphasis needs to shift to the managing of risks, away from an obsession with assessment. Second, authors such as Wald and Woolverton (1990) writing about child protection contend that risk assessment methodologies are deficient and caution against the view that there is a magical cure-all. Moreover, they criticise the inadequate research basis on which such methodologies rest. However they are generally supportive of the concept of risk assessment.

It is important to be clear about what risk assessment is, what it does and what it cannot do. It may be defined, following Brearley (1982) and Alberg *et al.* (1996), as the process of estimating and evaluating risk, understood as the possibility of beneficial and harmful outcomes and the likelihood of their occurrence in a stated timescale. Risk estimation includes a) estimating the probability that an outcome will occur and b) recognising that a number of possible outcomes will occur. Risk evaluation involves attaching a value to each of the identified outcomes and balancing the relative values of each outcome. Risk assessment cannot offer certainty or precision, as was emphasised above; it does offer challenges for professional judgement making. The trainer has to encourage practitioners to work with the ambiguity which authors like Parton (1998) highlight, but to do so within a systematic and principled approach.

Practitioners can, furthermore, be helped by the trainer to identify the assumptions which underpin risk assessment models. For example, two models of risk assessment can be contrasted, the safety first model and the risk taking model, each with a range of distinguishing features. The first model, safety first, has traditionally been dominant in the case for vulnerable people. This approach is subject to growing criticism (Counsel and Care 1992, 1993; Crosland 1992). The second model, risk taking, attempts to build on key principles developed in response to perceived deficiencies of the first model. The focus of this model is primarily on the *person* and his or her needs. There has to be a balance in looking at what he or she can do, their potential for change and managing their own lives, alongside whatever difficulties he or she might have in day-to-day activities.

'Taking risks', according to Carson, 'involves deciding that the potential benefits of a proposed act outweigh the potential drawbacks' (1988, p.248). The whole process of risk assessment involves this weighing up. Decisions about risks, the Counsel and Care (1993) authors note, are a balance between the right to choice and the competence of the individual. Staff can try to enhance competence, or compensate for it or offer extra support to allow the individual to do an activity with an acceptable degree of risk.

The important point to make here is that there should be a clearly understood and shared policy and philosophy to provide a supportive framework for staff and vulnerable individuals alike to make informed decisions about risks, however large or small. What has been missing from the literature is a sense that risk taking is a learning experience, entailing the sharing of key experiences within and between professions.

The key points emerging from this review are as follows:

- the implications for more positive conceptions of risk are rarely developed, leading to unbalanced assessment frameworks

- a clearer conception of risk assessment, in terms of its limits and function, is called for

- the need for multidisciplinary inputs into the risk assessment framework is essential, and training formats need to reflect this: however clarification of responsibilities is needed

- research accounts have neglected developing risk assessments as a learning experience for practitioners and their clients.

Risk management

Risk management remains a relatively under-developed area of study compared with risk assessment. One of the key problems here is that identified by authors such as Ryan (1996) who argue that risk management is often seen as minimising risk. Ryan then proceeds, as he admits, to deal with risk minimisation as synonymous with management of danger to the public. The problem is acute in the field of mental health where whole models such as the care programme approach are based on a restrictive view of risk (Harrison 1997). There is though a different, and more radical, view emerging according to Davis (1996), the risk taking approach; this has been developed by practitioners with an explicit agenda to involve and empower mental health service users with a more positive perception of risk. These two approaches provide 'contrasting orientations to risk' for social workers (Davis 1996, p.116).

Negative definitions of risk management abound in the literature. This can be evidenced in the mental health field, which Soltys argues has 'unique risk management challenges' (1995, p.473; see also Kaliski 1997). Soltys cites and deploys Reed and Swain's definition of risk management as the 'systematic ... effort to eliminate or reduce harm to persons and the threat of financial losses' (p.473). Similarly Secker-Walker (1997, p.367), writing more generally about health care, focuses on the need for a framework which addresses the 'varied causes of latent and active human failure'. It is hard to find a view of risk management which encompasses achievement as well as failure. Similarly the

Royal Society (1992) has produced a rather limited conception of the potential of risk management.

The research literature has little to say about the limits of risk management; its stages, including where assessment stops and management starts; practical guidance about intervention; and, importantly, when not to intervene. The challenge facing trainers is considerable. Lawson (1996) rightly notes that risk management is not equivalent to getting rid of risk. As Tindall (1997) points out, it can provide a more systematic way for helping people with learning difficulties take more control over their lives. There is a need to work to increase benefits, as well as minimising harms, and this needs to be emphasised in training for managers and practitioners.

Managing risk in the lives of vulnerable people, then, should not mean elimnating risk. This would run counter to the whole philosophy which is being advocated in the risk taking model. Instead it means providing a *process* for ensuring that potential benefits identified by the risk assessment are increased and that the likelihood of harms occurring as a result of taking a risk are reduced.

Nor does risk management mean anticipating every single potential risk and responding accordingly. This would be impossible and again would run counter to the risk taking approach. Rather it involves developing a systematic approach which allows for the planning of risk taking strategies and for monitoring and reviewing. A good risk management process will help to ensure accountability, clarity and support for staff involved in decisions concerning risk. The risk management process must both facilitate risk taking and empower care professionals to make key decisions. What it can do is to place risk management issues at the heart of considerations in the assessment of health and social care needs, care plans and care programmes. The management of risk, as Littlechild and Blakeney (1996) state, must be adaptable. People do not stay constant: changes can take place in the ability to cope. The risks can change too, as has been noted. Monitoring is important to keep abreast of any such changes. This involves working closely with the individual, with their family and carers and with other care staff. Everyone should have a clear idea of what the main risks are and what can be done about them. This is about clarifying expectations and arriving at a realistic, negotiated understanding of risks and how they can be managed. This is where the professional expertise of the welfare worker needs to be focused: *not* on a futile attempt to identify every single potential problem and to control the situation to reduce every single danger.

The key points emerging from this review are these:

- risk management is more than simply risk minimisation: it involves working to increase potential benefits

- it is about providing a process for planning risk taking strategies and for monitoring and reviewing the results

- any risk management process must be flexible and adaptable: trainers and teachers face a key challenge in promoting achievement-oriented visions of risk management.

The law, rights and responsibilities

In promoting a more positive approach towards risk taking, trainers and educationalists have to encourage welfare professionals to take into account the legal implications of risk decisions. As Brearley (1982) argues, the best protection for the social worker lies in good practice and in recognising the potential of the law for use in dangerous situations. The law not only protects clients, it protects the worker and the agency too. Carson (1996) goes further to suggest that use can be made of legal concepts and the operation of the legal system to help improve risk decision making and justify decisions. He contends that practitioners can use the concepts of the law and its procedures for their own purposes, before harm occurs. The law will not yield direct answers but it can help provide procedures and frameworks.

One area which remains under-studied is the legal implications of risk taking. One writer who, with determination, has ploughed something of a lone furrow is David Carson (1994, 1996, 1997). Carson has been influential in promoting the positive side of risk taking and encouraging professionals to use the concepts of the law to justify and improve their risk decisions. He supplies useful arguments for overcoming the 'cover our backs' attitude so prevalent among managers in the social services: he contends that such managers may well find themselves sued for not tackling risks and for not ensuring that their staff are trained. He is a critic of the defensiveness and unimaginative practice which such an attitude produces. However, Carson may under-estimate the resistance of professionals and managers which may have its roots in cultural and organisational factors, rather than just a lack of clarity about the law.

The notion of a 'duty of care' is ripe for exploration. Kennedy and Gill (1997) explore legal considerations arising from patient homicides and speculate on some of the implications for assessment and management of risk. They point to the danger of defensiveness, particularly if patient-as-plaintiffs cases succeed. Since this article was written the outcome of the Christopher Clunis case has been decided: the Court of Appeal has just turned down Clunis's application for damages, with no leave for further appeal. However more claims along similar lines will no doubt be put forward for consideration by the courts.

Harrison (1997) has written about the problems facing risk assessment in a 'climate of litigation'. She argues that there has been a 'seachange' in the attitudes of professionals towards the use of litigation in medicine, and towards the assessment of risk to themselves of an untoward incident. She criticises the tendency of a new form of institutionalisation, where patients become 'entangled in webs of overcautious surveillance by mental health professionals' and the new bureaucracy arising from the care programme approach and defensive practices (1997, p.37). An instructive debate has been taking place in the United States, where concerns about professional duties and responsibilities, litigation and risk assessment in 'managed care' settings have been mounting (Simon 1998).

There are differences within the UK and this is often overlooked, in terms of policy and legal learning. Scotland, for example, has a distinctive legal framework, although some of the issues remain the same. There have also been concerns expressed about the need to revise the Mental Health (Scotland) Act 1984 and the need to tighten up the law around the rights of 'incapable adults'. The Scottish Law Commission (1996) recently published a report which sets out general principles for intervention in the life of someone unable to make decisions for him or herself and which received a favourable welcome.

Social workers and other welfare professionals have to operate within a patchy and ill-defined context. There are two issues to consider here. The first is that much of the legislative provision that does exist tends to deal with constraints and restraints on individuals, such as compulsory admission to care.

'Risk', to the extent that it features at all, is largely conceived of in a negative and constraining manner.

The statutory framework of rights governing vulnerable adults tends to be defined in a likewise manner. For example, there is no clear statutory framework for older people. The problem, in the eyes of some people such as those who lobby for the rights of older people, is that there is no coherent legislative framework for vulnerable adults comparble with that which exists for children. There is nothing equivalent to the Children's Acts, which are based on principles which have been widely agreed and which rely, at least in part, on internationally defined agreements such as the United Nations Convention on the Rights of the Child (Hill and Aldgate 1996).

The second issue, considered in Chapter 8, concerns the question as to whether there are lessons from the field of children's rights, legislation and risk for the field of vulnerable adults. Some people have attempted to draw out the messages from child protection for the protection of older people from abuse or for mental health risk management (Stevenson 1996; Bond 1998). It is important to be clear about the kinds of risk models imported from the area of child abuse. Attempting to protect older people from risky situations would be contrary to the risk taking model. Indeed, it is possible to go further and criticise some child protection approaches as limited in their narrow focus on risk as 'danger'. The rights and risks for older people and other vulnerable adults have to be considered, before there is a rush to accept an all-embracing framework for the 'protection' of adults.

At the heart of many of the issues arising from risk taking lies the issue of rights. Should these form the framework for risk taking to work successfully? There are some provocative issues for policy makers and professionals to consider here.

The main points from this section are as follows:

- professionals need to be trained to be familiar with the law and be prepared to use it in risk decisions
- the notion of a 'duty of care' deserves further study
- the concept of 'the right to take risks' remains to be developed and tested

- caution is required in the extension of prevailing models of child protection to vulnerable adults.

Training and risk

The literature is largely silent on the topic of the effectiveness of training in risk work with vulnerable individuals. The searches produced little of direct relevance. Some general writings on health and safety issues can be found (Toye 1992; Corfield 1994; Oakley and Taylor 1994; Murphy 1996) and there is a growing body of work on training effectiveness and evaluation (Rae 1986, 1995; Talbot 1992; Fowler 1993; Pearce 1995, 1997; Oliver and Scott 1996). In a relatively unusual article, Walton (1978) explores some of the issues of training staff in residential care in taking risks. Stanley and Manthorpe (forthcoming) also present a rare account of a short training course in risk assessment in mental health work. The authors suggest that risk assessment can strengthen communication between professionals and others. However, the impacts of the training were not explored by the writers.

As was noted at the outset, many calls for training have been emerging from inquiries (e.g. North West London Mental Health NHS Trust 1994; Ritchie *et al.* 1994) as Stanley and Manthorpe (1997) note, and from other literature (Harrison 1997). Indeed, Reed claims, in his review of the lessons from recent inquiries, that '[a]ll these reasons for failure are, essentially, amenable to better training – and particularly training in a multidisciplinary, multiagency setting' (1997, p.6). He pinpoints the areas of risk assessment, the use of the Mental Health Acts and the use of security. Sometimes this is targeted towards particular groups such as keyworkers. Harrison calls for a modularised curriculum which is 'applicable to all professional groups' (1997, p.39).

Little of substance in the literature can be found concerning the kinds of training, including methods and formats, which work most effectively with different kinds of professionals. The issue of training of trainers is also a key lacuna. Harris (1997) looks at this problem in relation to psychiatrists. He raises a concern about the wide variation in the methods of teaching; he also claims there is a lack of audit of the effectiveness of the training. Harris points to the value of including other professionals in this training, such as community psychiatric nurses. However he limits himself to three methods, lectures, seminars and national conferences, which represent a limited view of training methods.

Taylor and Meux (1997) note that translating research findings in the area of risk assessment into daily practice is problematical. They write, for example, that different clinicians will interpret research findings and act differently in risk assessment and management, since they are individuals whose judgements are shaped by their own temperament, experiences and professional backgrounds. This point can be extended to other professionals such as social workers, who rely on fine judgements. Taylor and Meux also contend that decisions will be affected by factors such as culture, health care and legal systems and the availability of resources. These authors use a case vignette method to compare and contrast approaches to risk assessment in psychiatry by three different professionals from different countries for each of three case studies. They found that, despite the variety of professional and national backgrounds, all recognised some degree of risk but there were differences of emphasis which 'illustrate again that aspect of risk management which can never be under-emphasised: the importance of a multidisciplinary input' (p.301). This again points up the importance of multidisciplinary and multi-agency training for practitioners and managers across a range of settings using imaginative formats (Titterton 1994).

The issue of appropriate social work competences has still to be properly considered: a recent collection on the topic by Vass (1996) contains no references to risk work in its index. Kelly (1996) has highlighted some of the core competences for social workers, for example those advocated by CCETSW's Revised Paper 30; these include assessing and planning, communicating and engaging and so on (see also the further revision by CCETSW, 1996). However, a more explicit acknowledgement of the specific kinds of competences required for risk work (reflected in the sort of skills which are discussed in the second part of this chapter) is now called for. This lack of explicit recognition by CCETSW is mirrored in the absence of discussion in general social work texts, as Alaszewski and Manthorpe (1991) have noted.

As suggested above, training of professionals is frequently invoked as the answer to problems associated with risk situations with potentially adverse outcomes. The sheer weight of expectations now placed on training is alarming, not least at a time when training budgets are being cut back in the social services. Training has to be seen as part of a longer process of learning. The trainer will often furnish the trainee with reference points for the start of this process. Training has also to be recognised as only one piece of the bigger puzzle that constitutes good practice in risk work. Other pieces include: the development of risk policies; the involvement of informal carers and users; the influencing of professional standards and expectations; and the changing of public and media perceptions of risks. There is, moreover, a range of organisational issues to consider (Alaszewski and Manthorpe 1998; Kemshall *et al.* 1997), as well as a broader set of cultural and political factors (Franklin 1998).

From this section, these key points have emerged:

- there is a pressing need to find out more about appropriate training methodologies in risk work; in particular, there is a necessity to test the effectiveness of training in relation to different kinds of professionals
- training which is multidisciplinary and multiagency in nature can be particularly beneficial; this should be protected from budget reductions
- a better understanding of the learning process and development of risk competences is required
- realistic perceptions of training and its context are needed.

Training and its impacts

Description of the training

This section describes an approach to training and developmental work with social work and other staff. The course has been developed over the last four years and over 300 professionals have participated in Scotland; in addition variations on the course have been run outwith Scotland, and have included both carers and users in workshop sessions. The learning objectives of the course are: to examine issues of risk taking; to explore ways of assessing and managing risks; to develop a multiagency awareness; to provide guidance for managers, workers, users and their carers; to help increase choice in the daily lives of service users.

The course introduced the Person-Centred Risk Assessment and Management System, PRAMS, which is a systematic approach developed by the author for the assessment and management of risk in community and long-stay settings. It provides a comprehensive yet flexible framework for promoting good practice in risk taking in the field of welfare with which care professionals and other staff, vulnerable individuals and their families can work. It is based on research and training exercises with a range of welfare professionals from different disciplines in social work, health care and housing. It embodies an explicit philosophy of risk taking which seeks to enhance the quality of life of individuals in need of support and to improve the quality of risk decisions made by practitioners. It is intended to cover all vulnerable persons, however severe their disability or illness.

PRAMS involves work on five distinct yet related stages. The first stage entails the establishing of principles; participants discuss and agree key statements intended to guide the assessment and management process and its intended outcomes. In the next stage, issues for developing risk policies in the workplace are examined and the rationale, function and content of these policies are discussed. The third stage involves participants considering different assessment models, as well as the key steps for the identification and assessment of risk. They also work on specially constructed vignettes, case studies and scenarios designed to explore dilemmas and develop skills for making decisions. In the following stage, the notion of 'risk planning' is introduced and participants devise planned responses to assessments. The fifth stage deals with models of risk management and the key steps for managing risks; here again participants are set to work on cases designed to test decision making skills. PRAMS is an interlinked system; participants are encouraged to consider the connections between the stages and to continually review what they have learned. Another key theme is that of developing skills: each stage entails work on particular skills. To take an example, the art of making 'judgement calls' is explored in depth at the assessment stage.

Evaluation of the training

This section describes an evaluation of the training course outlined above and addresses some issues from a piece of small-scale research into the effects of training in risk assessment and risk management. The first part describes the feedback from participants in comments written on evaluation forms used by the trainer, filled in immediately on completion of the course.

The great majority of participants who completed an evaluation form felt the course met the aims and objectives stipulated and found it enjoyable and challenging. However, some did not feel it lasted long enough, particularly the short (one-day) version of the course, since the difficult dilemmas which were emerging needed longer time for discussion. They enjoyed coming together and learning together; in this respect it is evidently important that the training format encourages this. Participants benefited not only from working in small groups with colleagues but also with those from different settings and those dealing with different care groups.

What participants found most helpful were: a logical and systematic approach to risk assessment and management; a clear focus on practical under-standing; exchanging ideas; well-structured and well-presented information. They also enjoyed listening to different views of risk and the involvement of different professions. Participants also reported that they enjoyed: risk planning; how to develop an effective policy; defining boundaries between risk assessment and risk management; the right to take risks and treating people as individuals; not being afraid to take risks; thinking through the issues. Case studies, group work and the training manual for further reference were also identified as helpful.

The aspects which some training participants found the least helpful were: the negativity of some people who were not prepared to take risks; people raising issues specific to their workplace; grey areas and boundaries; a mix of backgrounds making it hard to discuss specific issues. However, there were other respondents who evidently found the latter two situations useful.

Other points raised by participants were: senior managers also needed training; training needs to be on a continuing basis; managers need to discuss policy expectations with workers; agreements on confidentiality wanted. There was also a demand for involving the different sectors in training: social work, health, housing and voluntary. Participants also wanted feedback on cases where something 'goes wrong', as well as support of workers by managers on these occasions.

The follow-up evaluation

The second part of this section describes research to examine some of the longer-term impact of the training on professionals and the individuals they look after. The following analysis is based on 40 completed returns from a self-completion questionnaire distributed to social work, health and housing professionals who had attended the course in the preceding nine months. Respondents were asked about the effects of the training in a number of areas. The first of these concerned the impact on practice. How far was the training incorporated and what examples could they provide? Next, what effects did the training have on their clients? Again, could any examples be provided? They were then asked about obstacles to taking risks. A question was also posed about other training or support which might be useful. Finally, they were asked to comment on the difficulties in involving users in risk decisions.

THE IMPACT ON PRACTICE

The respondents for the most part suggested that the training had made a 'substantial impact' on practice. This can be divided into effects on individual practice and on agency practice. On the former, comments included: it 'forces you to work through things in a logical order'; it 'made me more confident in dealing with other professions, made me feel more secure'; it 'allowed me to view risk in a new light', and encouraged the assessing of positive benefits as well as dangers.

Comments on agency practice included: 'found the key steps a very useful tool in carrying out assessments'. Some informants noted that the benefits of training were being passed on to others in the agency and in some follow-up training that was being planned; others reported the production of informal guidelines; others stated that there was a search for consensus on risk taking in multidisciplinary settings, as well as for ways of dealing with conflicting views. Consideration of risk was reported by at least one informant as being a regular part of discussions about and with service users. Some others stated that their agency's definition of risk was being broadened to include more positive risk taking.

THE EFFECT ON CLIENTS

A small number reported that it was still 'early days' for risk taking, others were prepared to comment about the effect on clients. One of the social workers noted that a risk taking approach, developed following the training 'has helped build self-esteem and confidence' and another that her 'client is more relaxed, with a more positive attitude and awareness'. One of the most notable findings was that some social workers and care staff claimed to be involving clients more and consciously making efforts to allow them to take decisions, pointing out the consequences of actions but encouraging them to feel in control. Another worker stated that he was 'now more likely to ask service users to identify risks for themselves' and to work with users' perceptions of risks.

Some respondents said their clients were making more choices for themselves. One support worker pointed to an example of a young female tenant having more control over budgeting and shopping; the tenant was occasionally over-spending and getting into debt which may lead to the decision being reviewed in the future, but the worker still felt it right to allow the young person to try to manage by herself.

One respondent gave the example of a client assuming a role supporting others in a project and becoming more confident, which was seen as important for the individual's self-development; another used the example of a young man with learning disabilities and severe epilepsy being encouraged to do more with less supervision, while yet another pointed to the example of an older client taking risks with cooking. More than one informant pointed out that calculated risk taking was boosting the self-esteem and confidence of their client. A few respondents emphasised that this approach was no easy option and, in the words of one, that it is 'difficult to move with some clients and carers'.

OBSTACLES TO RISK TAKING

A small number of informants stressed that there were no obstacles to risk taking in their work settings, and noted that they had good management support. However this appeared to be a minority view, with most replies detailing a number of barriers. These can be grouped into four main categories.

First, respondents pointed to general fears about letting people make choices, and here cultural and professional factors were implicated. One social worker complained about 'the tendency to wrap people in cotton wool', while a housing support worker wrote about 'our own fears of letting tenants take risks'. Second, the lack of support from management was identified as a major stumbling block. Third, differences between professionals and the lack of a shared enterprise between disciplines were highlighted. More than one person asked for more joint training, for example involving home care and health care professionals such as GPs, consultants, and hospital staff, as well as more training 'at different levels'. Fourth, organisational factors were cited: one informant noted that the 'culture of the organisation' can militate against a risk taking approach, with another arguing that the 'whole organisation needs to take on risk taking' before it can succeed.

In addition, a range of miscellaneous factors was identified. Difficulties in devising standardised policies due to the diversity of clients and their needs and abilities were mentioned. Some pointed to problems with registration and ins-pection staff who were reluctant to countenance risk taking, as well as 'difficult parents'. One person wrote that a key barrier was the attitude that 'staff were there just to "look after" and not to let people face risks'. Others stated that senior management tended to have a more reactive approach to risk and one respondent complained of the 'feeling of being out on a limb' when taking a risk decision. The influence of the media was commonly cited as an obstacle.

SKILLS FOR RISK TAKING

Respondents were asked about the kinds of skills which they felt were impor-tant for developing risk taking approaches.

The first group of skills involved communication skills, such as the 'ability to communicate risk calculation effectively to others, and provide support for risk taking partnerships'. One informant noted that 'the word "risk" is alarming for staff and clients', while another identified the need to put over issues in a way which clients can understand as essential, and yet another emphasised the importance of getting family and friends to see the benefits of risk decisions. A second set of skills involved 'identifying what risks are and what has made them risks'; judging risks and weighing up benefits; analysing risky situations; cultivating new ways of thinking for risk taking; 'thinking things through in greater depth'; and developing the ability to look at the consequences of decisions from a long-term perspective.

Another group of skills consisted of interprofessional and interagency skills, including working with other professionals on risk decisions and, in the words of one informant, 'how to convey our perception of risk to other agencies'. A fourth set concerned planning skills such as forward planning and developing suitable risk plans, as well as the writing of and documentation of plans. The final cluster can be termed negotiation skills, such as balancing the various, and sometimes conflicting, rights of clients and their carers and reaching agreements over decisions about risks.

OTHER TRAINING AND SUPPORT REQUIRED

Respondents made a variety of comments under this heading. Some made clear a desire to expand the basis of the training, with comments like the 'whole organisation needs to get involved'. Joint training was commonly cited as a potentially valuable exercise, for practitioners and managers alike. There was a demand to know more about 'what works and what does not work'. One informant advocated workshops to allow people, working in similar situations and with similar clients, to discuss issues. Some requested updates on the risk taking practices of other staff: what they have found and what have been the clients' views afterwards.

Further training was identified as desirable in specific areas: individual support and risk plans; overcoming difficulties in securing risk decisions and agreements; recording; group leadership skills; and helping clients develop risk taking skills.

Finally, continuing support from peers, supervisors and managers was emphasised for workers and teams where a risk taking approach was being developed. This was identified as particularly important 'where complex risks are involved' and 'especially when things go wrong'.

DIFFICULTIES IN INVOLVING USERS

A small number of staff reported no difficulties in attempting to get users involved in risk decision making. The features which were identified as helpful here included the presence of multidisciplinary discussion with users; the clear recording of decisions; and taking into account the relevant guidance and legislation. The majority of respondents, nevertheless, pinpointed a range of problems. These can be grouped as follows.

The first group of problems involved communication difficulties, for example in not being able to explain risk taking well enough to clients. Involvement was found to be very difficult where users have profound mental and physical disabilities, with little or no verbal communication, and there were issues raised by staff acting as advocates for risk. One informant noted that it depends on capacity relative to the stages of risk management; another 'gloomily' noted that it was difficult to support people in choices which were likely to fail. Others pointed to factors such as: possible difficulties with management; developing methods of common understanding of processes used in assessment; difficulties in reaching consensus.

Conflict with carers and parents, such as in those instances involving 'relatives disputing risk decisions', formed the second set of difficulties. Negative attitudes held by carers could act as a major stumbling block for client and staff. A third group consisted of the difficulties entailed in negotiating acceptable risk. Continuing support was seen by some respondents as necessary for people to accept decisions and the consequences; it would also help overcome problems caused by fear, lack of knowledge, disempowerment and unrealistic expectations. The fourth and final group revolved around problems with public perceptions, where the risks of harmful or dangerous occurrences were often wildly exaggerated, making it sometimes difficult to engage constructively with local communities. This theme often appeared in training sessions and provided much scope for discussion and debate.

Conclusions

In the first part of this chapter, the literature review revealed some significant gaps in research in the area of risk work and some of the implications for training were discussed. How a positive risk taking approach can develop good professional practice and enhance the quality of life of vulnerable individuals remains a particularly pertinent question to answer. The small-scale research reported in the second part suggests that training in risk work can have a substantial impact on practice in at least two ways: it provides individual workers with the confidence and knowledge to take risks; and there are benefits for agency practice, which can be passed on to others. There were direct benefits for clients as reported by social workers and other staff: these included the building of self-esteem and confidence, as well as greater involvement in decisions and choices. However it is clear that there are difficulties in involving users meaningfully in risk decisions, because of communication problems and conflicts with carers and parents. Risk taking approaches could be enhanced through recognising the need for management and the whole agency to take risk taking seriously and the need to develop a shared enterprise with other professionals. The social workers and other staff wanted to develop skills in communication, risk decision making, planning, working with other agencies and negotiation. In this respect, joint training and continuing support for practitioners from peers, supervisors and managers were identified as important.

There are lessons also for the training and development of professionals, of which two may be singled out. First, the things they find most helpful are the chance to think through the issues clearly with colleagues and professionals from other agencies and exchange ideas, and to do so in the context of a systematic approach to risk work. The experience of the training described here has revealed that there are some difficult and complex dilemmas for risk taking for which there is no easy resolution. The fine art of professional judgement involved is still being developed in both residential and community settings. The competences which underpin these 'judgement calls', and the processes by which the latter are made, have yet to be properly researched.

Second, the question of how practitioners can best learn risk assessment and management skills has to be addressed by managers, trainers and educationalists alike. Practitioners learn from each other and from working with other professions, and they require more learning opportunities involving imaginative formats and stimulation through a variety of training methods. A judicious mixture of theory and practice is essential; the need for supervision must also be acknowledged (Burke 1997). Risk taking is not an area which can be learned theoretically; experiential learning is best. Reflection is a critical skill for risk takers, as captured by the notion of the 'reflective practitioner' (Schon

1983; Gould and Taylor 1996). The idea that the development of risk assessment and management skills should be part of a gradual, and reflective, learning process has to be emphasised. A system such as PRAMS encourages people who use it to focus more sharply on skills development and to constantly review what they have learned.

Training is merely the start, not the end, of this process. Research studies of how practitioners learn and develop risk taking skills, and what contribution trainers can make, would make a welcome addition to the literature surveyed in this chapter.

References

Alaszewski, A. and Manthorpe, J. (1991) 'Literature review: Measuring and managing risk in social welfare.' *British Journal of Social Work 21,* 277–90.

Alaszewski, A. and Manthorpe, J. (1998) 'Welfare agencies and risk: The missing link.' *Health and Social Care in the Community 6,* 1, 4–15.

Alberg, C., Bingley, W., Bowers, L., Ferguson, G., Hatfield, B., Hoban, D. and Maden, A. (1996) *Learning Materials on Mental Health: Risk Assessment.* Manchester: University of Manchester Department of Health.

Argall, P. and Cowderoy, B. (1997) 'We can take it: Young people and drug use.' In H. Kemshall and J. Pritchard (eds) *Good Practice in Risk Assessment and Management 2: Protection, Rights and Responsibilities.* London: Jessica Kingsley Publishers.

Barker, M. and Morgan, R. (1993) *Sex Offenders: A Framework for the Evaluation of Community-based Treatment.* London: Home Office.

Beck, U. (1992) *Risk Society: Towards a New Modernity.* London: Sage.

Beck, U. (1998) 'Politics of risk society.' In J. Franklin (ed) *The Politics of Risk Society.* Cambridge: Polity Press.

Berkowitz, S. (1991) *Key Findings From the State Survey Component of the Study of High Risk Child Abuse and Neglect Groups.* Washington, DC: National Center on Child Abuse and Neglect.

Bond, H. (1998) 'Need to know.' *Community Care,* 12–18 February, 23.

Brearley, C.P. (1979) 'Understanding risk.' *Social Work Today 10,* 31, 28.

Brearley, C.P. (1982) *Risk in Social Work.* London: Routledge and Kegan Paul.

Burke, P. (1997) 'Risk and supervision: Social work responses to referred user problems.' *British Journal of Social Work 27,* 1, 115–29.

Campbell, J.C. (ed) (1995) *Assessing Dangerousness: Violence by Sexual Offenders, Batterers and Child Abusers.* Thousand Oaks, CA: Sage.

Carson, D. (1994) 'Dangerous people: Through a broader conception of "risk" and "danger" to better decisions.' *Expert Evidence 3,* 2, 51–69.

Carson, D. (1995) 'Calculated risk.' *Community Care,* 26 Oct. – 1 Nov., 26–7.

Carson, D. (1996) 'Risking legal repercussions.' In H. Kemshall and J. Pritchard (eds) *Good Practice in Risk Assessment and Management 1.* London: Jessica Kingsley Publishers.

Carson, D. (1997) 'Good enough risk taking.' *International Review of Psychiatry 9,* 303–8.

Central Council for Education and Training in Social Work (1996) *Assuring Quality in the Diploma in Social Work – 1: Rules and Regulations for the DipSW.* London: CCETSW.

Corby, B. (1996) 'Risk assessment in child protection work.' In H. Kemshall and J. Pritchard (eds) *Good Practice in Risk Assessment and Management 1.* London: Jessica Kingsley Publishers.

Corfield, T. (1994) 'Risk assessment and health and safety management training.' *Modern Management 8,* 5, October, 10–12.

Counsel and Care (1992) *What If They Hurt Themselves.* London: Counsel and Care.

Counsel and Care (1993) *The Right to Take Risks.* London: Counsel and Care.

Crosland, J. (1992) *Risk Taking and Rights: Safety or Restraint?* Leeds: Nursing Development Unit, Seacroft Hospital.

Davis, A. (1996) 'Risk work in mental health.' In H. Kemshall and J. Pritchard (eds) *Good Practice in Risk Assessment and Management 1.* London: Jessica Kingsley Publishers.

Department of Health (1988) *Protecting Children: A Guide for Social Workers Undertaking a Comprehensive Assessment.* London: HMSO.

Douglas, M. (1992) *Risk and Blame: Essays in Cultural Theory.* London: Routledge.

East, J. (1995) 'Risk management in health care.' *British Journal of Health Care Management 1,* 3, 148–52.

English, D.J. and Pecora, P.J. (1994) 'Risk assessment as a practice method in child protective services.' *Child Welfare 73,* 5, 451–73.

Feaviour, P., Peacock, D., Sanderson, H., Bontoft, C. and Wightman, S. (1995) 'Score values.' *Community Care,* 2–8 November, 28–9.

Fowler, A. (1993) 'How to evaluate training.' *Personnel Management Plus 4,* 9, 25–26.

Franklin, J. (ed) (1998) *The Politics of Risk Society.* Cambridge: Polity Press.

Gould, N. and Taylor, I. (eds) (1996) *Reflective Learning for Social Work.* Aldershot: Arena.

Griffiths, R. and Waterston, J. (1996) 'Facts, fantasies and confusion: Risk and substance use.' In H. Kemshall and J. Pritchard (eds) *Good Practice in Risk Assessment and Management 1.* London: Jessica Kingsley Publishers.

Grubin, D. (1997) 'Inferring predictors of use: Sex offenders.' *International Review of Psychiatry 9,* 225–231.

Gunn, J. (1997) 'Maintaining a balanced perspective on risk.' *International Review of Psychiatry 9,* 163–5.

Harris, M. (1997) 'Training trainers in risk assessment.' *British Journal of Psychiatry 170,* (suppl. 32), 35–6.

Harrison, L. (1997) 'Risk assessment in a climate of litigation.' *British Journal of Psychiatry 170,* (suppl. 32), 37–9.

Herring, R. and Thom, B. (1997) 'The right to take risks: Alcohol and older people.' *Social Policy and Administration 31,* 3, 233–46.

Hill, M. and Aldgate, J. (eds) (1996) *Child Welfare Services: Developments in Law, Policy, Practice and Research.* London: Jessica Kingsley Publishers.

Howlett, M. (1997) 'Community care homicide inquiries and risk assessment.' In H. Kemshall and J. Pritchard (eds) *Good Practice in Risk Assessment and Management 2: Protection, Rights and Responsibilities.* London: Jessica Kingsley Publishers.

Inskip, H.M., Harris, E.G. and Barraclough, B. (1998) 'Lifetime risk of suicide for affective disorder, alcoholism and schizophrenia.' *British Journal of Psychiatry 172,* 35–7.

Jackson, W. (1992) *Risk Taking, Safety and Older People.* Selected Bibliography on Ageing. London: Centre for Policy on Ageing.

Kaliski, S.Z. (1997) 'Risk management during the transition from hospital to community care.' *International Review of Psychiatry 9,* 249–56.

Kelly, G. (1996) 'Competence in risk analysis.' In K. O'Hagan (ed) *Competence in Social Work Practice.* London: Jessica Kingsley Publishers.

Kemshall, H. (1996) *Reviewing Risk.* London: Home Office.

Kemshall, H. *et al.* (1997) 'Concepts of risk in relation to organisational structure and functioning within the personal social services and probation.' *Social Policy and Administration 31,* 3, 213–32.

Kennedy, M. and Gill, M. (1997) 'Patient litigation following a homicide –
    implications for the assessment and management of risk.' *International Review of
    Psychiatry 9,* 179–86.

Lash, S. *et al.* (1996) *Risk, Environment and Modernity: Towards a New Ecology.*
    London: Sage.

Lawson, J. (1996) 'A framework of risk assessment and management for older
    people.' In H. Kemshall and J. Pritchard (eds) *Good Practice in Risk Assessment and
    Management 1.* London: Jessica Kingsley Publishers.

Littlechild, R. and Blakeney, J. (1996) 'Risk and older people.' In H. Kemshall and
    J. Pritchard (eds) *Good Practice in Risk Assessment and Management 1.* London:
    Jessica Kingsley Publishers.

Lyon, J. (1997) 'Teenage suicide and self-harm: assessing and managing risk.' In H.
    Kemshall and J. Pritchard (eds) *Good Practice in Risk Assessment and Management 2:
    Protection, rights and Responsibilities.* London: Jessica Kingsley Publishers.

Maggs, J.L., Frome, P.N., Eccles, J.S. and Burber, B.L. (1997) 'Psychosocial
    resources, adolescent risk behaviour and young adult adjustment: Is risk taking
    more dangerous for some than others?' *Journal of Adolescence 20,* 103–19.

Manning, N. (1987) 'What is a social problem?' In M. Loney (ed) *Social Problems
    and Social Welfare.* London: Sage.

Manthorpe, J., Walsh, M., Alaszewski, A. and Harrison, L. (1995) 'Taking a
    chance.' *Community Care,* 19–25 October, 20–1.

Manthorpe, J., Walsh, M., Alaszewski, A. and Harrison, L. (1997) 'Issues of risk
    practice and welfare in learning disability services.' *Disability and Society 12,*
    69–82.

McEwan, S. and Sullivan, J. (1996) 'Sex offender risk assessment.' In H. Kemshall
    and J. Pritchard (eds) *Good Practice in Risk Assessment and Management 1.* London:
    Jessica Kingsley Publishers.

Monahan, J. (1988) 'Risk assessment of violence among the mentally disordered:
    Generating useful knowledge.' *International Journal of Law and Psychiatry 11,*
    249–57.

Murphy, S. (1996) 'Managing the risk.' *Health and Safety at Work 18,* 7, 18–20.

Norman, A. (1980) *Rights and Risk.* London: Centre for Policy on Ageing.

Norman, A. (1988) 'Risk.' In B. Gearing (ed) *Mental Health Problems in Old Age: A
    Reader.* Chichester: Wiley.

North West London Mental Health NHS Trust (1994) *Report of the Independent Panel of Inquiry Examining the Case of Michael Buchanan.* London: North West London Mental Health NHS Trust.

Oakley, P. and Taylor, R. (1994) 'An approach to developing risk-conscious staff.' *Health Service Journal 197,* 5–7.

O'Callaghan, D. and Print, B. (1994) 'Adolescent sexual abusers: Research, assessment and treatment.' In T. Morrison, M. Erooga and R. Beckett (eds) *Sexual Offenders Against Children: Practice, Management and Policy.* London: Routledge.

Oliver, J. and Scott, T. (1996) 'Trouble with training.' *British Journal of Health Care Management 2,* 7, 388–91.

Parton, N. (1996) 'Social work, risk and the "blaming system".' In N. Parton (ed) *Social Theory, Social Change and Social Work.* London: Routledge.

Parton, N. (1998) 'Risk, advanced liberalism and child welfare: The need to rediscover uncertainty and ambiguity.' *British Journal of Social Work 28,* 5–27.

Parton, N., Thorpe, D. and Wattam, C. (1997) *Child Protection: Risk and the Moral Order.* London: Macmillan.

Pearce, I. (1997) 'Has your training been worthwhile?' *Training Officer 33,* 1, 5–7.

Pearce, I.D. (1995) *The Assessment and Evaluation of Training: A Practical Guide.* Hitchin: Technical Communications.

Pilgrim, D. and Rogers, A. (1996) 'Two conceptions of risk in mental health debates.' In T. Heller, J. Reynolds, R. Gomm, R. Muston and S. Pattison (eds) *Mental Health Matters: A Reader.* London: Macmillan.

Plant, M. and Plant, M. (1992) *Risk Takers: Alcohol, Drugs, Sex and Youth.* London: Tavistock/Routledge.

Potts, J. (1995) 'Risk assessment and management: A Home Office perspective.' In J. Crichton (ed) *Psychiatric Patient Violence: Risk and Response.* London: Duckworth.

Prins, H. (1996) 'Risk assessment and management in criminal justice and psychiatry.' *Journal of Forensic Psychiatry 7,* 1, 42–62.

Pritchard, J. (1997) 'Vulnerable people taking risks: Older people and residential care.' In H. Kemshall and J. Pritchard (eds) *Good Practice in Risk Assessment and Management 2: Protection, rights and Responsibilities.* London: Jessica Kingsley Publishers.

Pritchard, S. and Brearley, P. (1982) 'Risk in social work.' In C.P. Brearley (ed) *Risk and Ageing.* London: Routledge and Kegan Paul.

Rae, L. (1986) *How To Measure Training Effectiveness.* Aldershot: Gower.

Rae, L. (1995) 'Practical approaches to evaluation.' *Training Officer 31,* 9, 273–6.

Reed, J. (1997) 'Risk assessment and clinical risk management: The lessons from recent inquiries.' *British Journal of Psychiatry 170,* (suppl. 32), 4–7.

Ritchie, J.H., Dick, D. and Lingham, R. (1994) *The Report of the Inquiry into the Care and Treatment of Christopher Clunis.* London: HMSO.

Rossau, C.D. and Mortensen, P.B. (1997) 'Risk factors for suicide in patients with schizophrenis: Nested case-control study.' *British Journal of Psychiatry 171,* 355–9.

Royal Society (1992) *Risk Analysis, Perception and Management.* London: Royal Society.

Ryan, T. (1996) 'Risk management and people with mental health problems.' In H. Kemshall and J. Pritchard (eds) *Good Practice in Risk Assessment and Management 1.* London: Jessica Kingsley Publishers.

Scott, D. (1998) 'A qualitative study of social work assessment in cases of alleged child abuse.' *British Journal of Social Work 28,* 73–88.

Scottish Law Commission (1996) *Incapable Adults.* Report No. 151, Edinburgh.

Scottish Office (1997a) *Scotland's Children: The Children (Scotland) Act 1995 Regulations and Guidance: Volume 1: Support and Protection for Children and Their Families.* Edinburgh: The Stationery Office.

Scottish Office (1997b) *A Commitment to Protect – Supervising Sex Offenders: Proposals for More Effective Practice.* Edinburgh: The Stationery Office.

Scottish Office (1998) *Risk Assessment: A Supplement to the National Objectives and Standards for Social Work Services in the Criminal Justice System.* Draft Circular, January. Edinburgh: Scottish Office.

Schon, D. (1983) *The Reflective Practitioner.* San Fransisco, California: Jossey Bass.

Secker-Walker, J. (1997) 'Risk management.' *British Journal of Hospital Medicine 58,* 8, 366–7.

Sheppard, M. (1990) *Mental Health – The Role of the Approved Social Worker.* Sheffield: Joint Unit for Social Services Research.

Simon, R.I. (1998) 'Psychiatrists' duties in discharging sicker and potentially violent inpatients in the managed care era.' *Psychiatric Services 49,* 1, 62–7.

Soltys, S.M. (1995) 'Risk management strategies in the provision of mental health services.' *Psychiatric Services 5,* 46, 473–76.

Stanley, N. and Manthorpe, J. (1997) 'Risk assessment: Developing training for professionals in mental health work.' *Social Work and Social Sciences Review 7,1*, 26–38.

Steadman, H.J. (1993) 'From dangerousness to risk assessment: Implications for appropriate research strategies.' In S. Hodgins (ed) *Mental Disorder and Crime.* Newbury Park, CA: Sage.

Stevenson, O. (1996) *Elder Protection in the Community: What Can We Learn from Child Protection?* London: Institute of Gerontology, King's College.

Talbot, C. (1992) 'Evaluation and validation: A mixed approach.' *Journal of European Industrial Training 16*, 5, 26–32.

Taylor, C. and Meux, C. (1997) 'Individual cases: The risk, the challenge.' *International Review of Psychiatry 9*, 289–302.

Tindall, B. (1997) 'People with learning difficulties: Citizenship, personal development and the management of risk.' In H. Kemshall and J. Pritchard (eds) *Good Practice in Risk Assessment and Management 2: Protection, Rights and Responsibilities.* London: Jessica Kingsley Publishers.

Titterton, M. (1994) 'Managing change and innovation in community care.' In M. Titterton (ed) *Caring for People in the Community: the New Welfare.* London: Jessica Kingsley Publishers.

Toye, J. (1992) 'Controlling health risks at work – a challenge for training.' *Transition 92*, 8, 12–13.

Vass, A. (1996) *Social Work Competences.* London: Sage.

Wald, M.S. and Woolverton, M. (1990) 'Risk assessment: The emperor's new clothes?' *Child Welfare 69*, 6, 483–512.

Walton, R. (1978) 'Training for risk taking: Applications in residential care.' *Social Work Service 18*, December, 1–5.

Waterhouse, L. and Carnie, J. (1992) 'Assessing child protection risk.' *British Journal of Social Work 22*, 47–60.

Wynne-Harley, D. (1991) *Living Dangerously: Risk Taking, Safety and Older People.* London: Centre for Policy on Ageing.

The Contributors

Bill Beaumont lectures in social work at the University of Bristol. He was previously a probation officer for 15 years and then General Secretary of the National Association of Probation Officers (1985–92). Previous publications include *Probation Work* (1981) and *Working with Offenders* (1985), co-authored and co-edited with Hilary Walker. Recent work includes an analysis of managerialism in the probation service, research on probation service clients' views, women in secure psychiatric services, black young people in a local youth justice system and an edited collection on progressive practice with offenders (forthcoming).

Peter Burke is a senior lecturer in social work at the University of Hull. His teaching and research interests are child care and protection, childhood disability and the needs of siblings. He is the co-author of *Support for Families* (1996) and is presently co-working on a book on learning disabilities in children.

Brian Caddick is a senior lecturer in the School for Policy Studies at the University of Bristol. His background is in social psychology. His research since the early 1980s has mainly been concerned with the work of the probation service and, in particular, with programmes promoting offender rehabilitation.

Joan Langan worked as a social worker for a number of years before moving into the academic world. She is now a lecturer in community care at the School for Policy Studies, University of Bristol and her major teaching and research interest is mental health. She is currently engaged in a research project with Dr Viv Lindow into risk and mental health with a particular focus on service users.

Geraldine Macdonald is Professor of Social Work and Applied Social Studies at the School for Policy Studies, University of Bristol. She is also Archie Cochrane Research Fellow at Green College, University of Oxford and Visiting Professor at the Centre for Evidence-based Social Services at the University of Exeter. Her research interests include the evaluation of the effects of social interventions, particularly social work and probation; decision making in child protection, and ethical issues in social work research and practice. She has recent publications in each of these areas.

Kenneth Macdonald is a lecturer in applied social studies (sociology) at the University of Oxford, and Fellow of Nuffield College. A former director of the ESRC Data Archive, his current interests lie in the nature of moral discourse, and the perplexities surrounding the interpretation of statistical data.

Phyllida Parsloe is now Emeritus Professor of Social Work at the University of Bristol. She chairs the North Bristol NHS Trust and has a particular interest in evidence-based medicine and social work.

Kay Sargent is a lecturer in social work with children and families at the University of East Anglia, and an independent social worker and consultant. She has been a practitioner and manager in children's services and holds the AAPQ Award. She teaches social work practice with children and families to pre- and post-qualifying students, and has a particular interest in assessment in all areas of work with children and families. She is also currently involved in research with children growing up in long-term foster care.

Olive Stevenson is now Emeritus Professor at the University of Nottingham after a career in social work and social work education. She has held chairs at the Universities of Keele, Liverpool and Nottingham and was a member of the panel for the first enquiry into child abuse, the Maria Colwell enquiry. She has combined an interest in child care with a recognition of the needs of elderly people and has written extensively about social work and social policy for both these groups. Her latest work has continued this dual focus. She has published a book about neglected children and has also been commissioned by the Department of Health to analyse the ways in which knowledge about child abuse may be used in understanding what happens to older people who are abused.

Mike Titterton is an independent trainer who works with statutory agencies, voluntary organisations, service users and informal carers. He has worked for the Scottish Office, the Scottish Health Service and the Universities of Stirling and Glasgow. He has also provided research and consultancy services for the Economic and Social Research Council, the Joseph Rowntree Foundation, the Health Education Board for Scotland, the Scottish Office, the Development Group, Dundee University, Edinburgh University, the Open University and many local authorities, health boards and voluntary agencies. He has recently been working in Eastern Europe with non-governmental organisations and service users.

David Watson began his academic career teaching moral philosophy at the University of Glasgow, combining that with service on Strathclyde Children's Panel in its formative years. Moving to the School for Policy Studies at the University of Bristol, he developed teaching and publications on the borders of philosophy and social policy. He took early retirement in 1998 to extend his parallel career on another borderline, in ethical investment.

Subject Index

Author Index